CAHNERS BOOKS

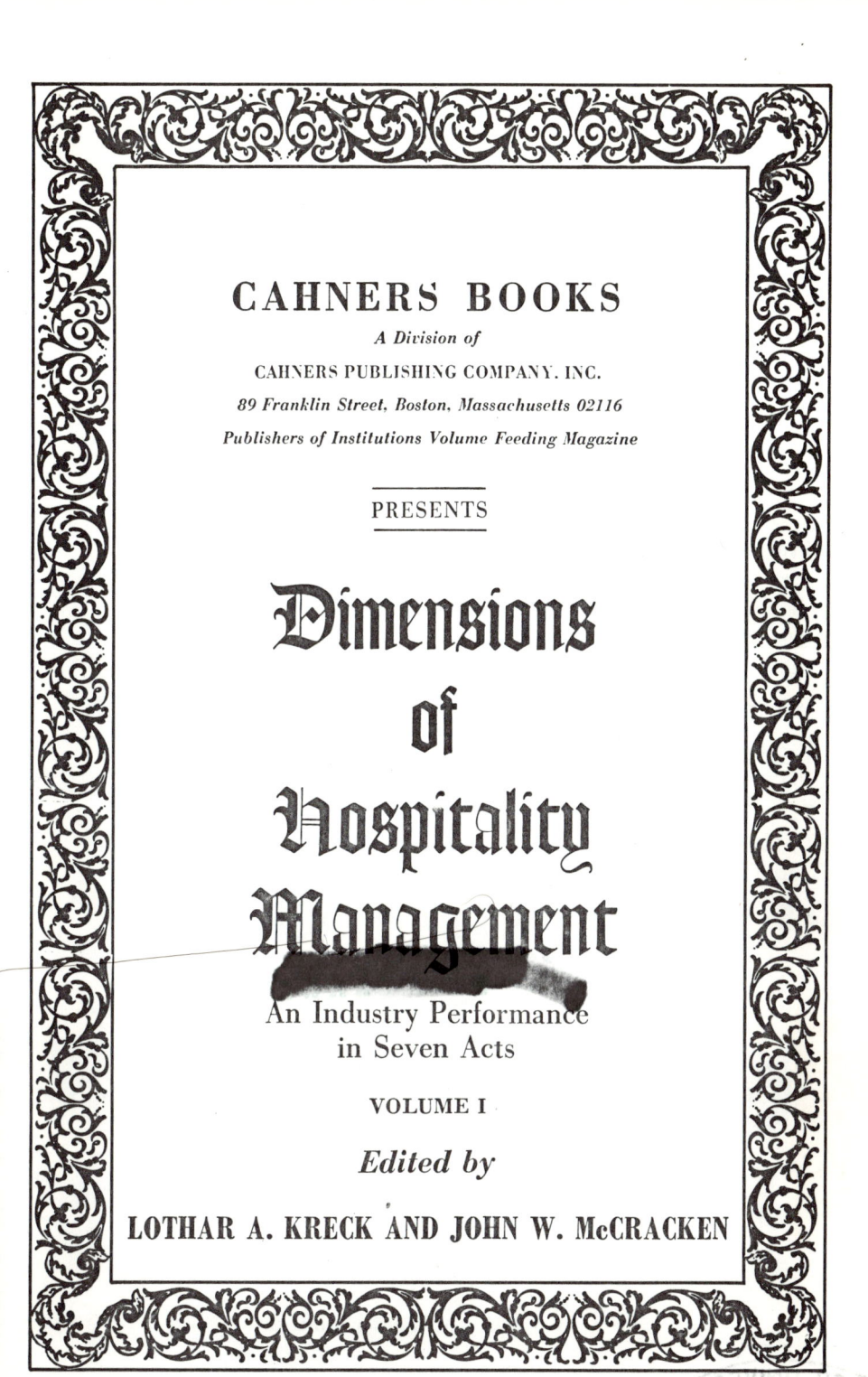

A Division of
CAHNERS PUBLISHING COMPANY, INC.
89 Franklin Street, Boston, Massachusetts 02116
Publishers of Institutions Volume Feeding Magazine

PRESENTS

Dimensions of Hospitality Management

An Industry Performance
in Seven Acts

VOLUME I

Edited by

LOTHAR A. KRECK AND JOHN W. McCRACKEN

Library of Congress Cataloging in Publication Data
Main entry under title:

Dimensions of hospitality management.

    Includes bibliographical references.
    CONTENTS: v. 1. Acts I-III.--v. 2. Acts IV-VIII.
    1. Hotel management. 2. Motel management.
3. Food service management. I. Kreck, Lothar A.
II. McCracken, John W.
TX911.2.D5   658'.91'64794   75-15701
ISBN 0-8436-2086-2

Copyright © 1975 by Cahners Publishing Company, Inc.
All rights reserved. This book or parts of it may not be reproduced in any form without permission of the publisher.

ISBN 0-8436-2086-2 (Set)
ISBN 0-8436-2075-7 (Volume 1)

Printed in the United States of America

Dimensions of Hospitality Management

THE Pl

LOTHAR A. KRECK, ed.

(Chapters in orde

PROLOGUE

A Preface

ACT I

The Producer....CORPORATE ADMINIS-   9
                TRATION

Scene 1: Philosophy—Organization		18
1. Automation and the Guest	Staff	18
2. Hotel Cooperatives—Can Voluntary Hotel Groupings Save the Independents?	J. Kallas	24
3. Grass Roots—Where the Good Times Are	Staff	32
4. Social Priorities and Executive Myopia	M. E. Braun	51
5. Competence: The Cohesive of Future Organizations	R. M. Fulmer, L. W. Rue	56
6. Hotel and Restaurant Management in the Soviet Union	L. A. Kreck	74
7. Slightly Sarcastic		92
Queries		94

ACT II

The Director.....MANAGEMENT   95

Scene 1: Management—Management Outlook		102
1. Hotel Management	J. W. Wood	104
2. Power and the Ambitious Executive	R. N. McMurry	111

AYBILL

JOHN W. McCRACKEN, ed.

(appearance)

3. The Mess in Management Accountability	T. J. Murray	122
4. The New Psychology of Success	Staff	129
5. The Expanding World of Executive Perks	J. C. Perham	140
6. Managing Management Resources Through Corporate Constitutionalism	R. G. Wright	150
Scene 2: Leadership—Motivation		168
1. Delegation: Key to Involvement	M. E. Haynes	170
2. Management Psychology	M. R. Feinberg	175
3. Do You Really Know Your Employees?	W. J. Morgan	182
4. Six Skills Put Motivation Theory Into Action	V. J. Byrne	192
Scene 3: Communication		197
1. Labor-Management Communication	L. A. Kreck	198
2. An Investigation of Some Communication Patterns of Female Subordinates in Hierarchical Organizations	J. C. Athanassiades	211
Queries		230

ACT III

*The Actors....*THE EMPLOYEES   231

Scene 1: Personnel Administration		239
1. Why Hotel Employees Fail to Rise	M. E. Palmer	241
2. Employee Responsibility, A Key Goal for Managers	J. P. Loveland, J. L. Mendleson	243

3. How a Supervisor Wins Employees	R. D. Buchanan	251
4. Labor Supply, Payroll Costs and Changes	T. F. Powers	257
Scene 2: Labor Relations		274
1. Collective Bargaining	B. Werne	275
2. To Join or Not to Join Multi-Employer Bargaining	B. Werne	280
3. Start the Open Shop in St. Louis		287
4. Squelching a Strike		290
5. How Hotel Nova Scotian Survived the Big Strike	Staff	292

Scene 3: Human Engineering		298
1. Operating a Hotel Is a Feat of Human Engineering	E. M. Statler	300
2. Techniques of Industrial Engineering Can Improve Effectiveness of Food Service Operations	B. D. David	306
3. Production Time Standards	K. Ruf, M. E. Matthews	318
4. How to Increase the Efficiency of the Human Body	L. H. Kotschevar	331
5. Help Workers Work Easier	L. H. Kotschevar	336
Queries		345

Foreword

This book serves two of the most urgent needs of our expanding industry. The first is to make it easy for industry members to keep up with new developments in the areas of management and human relations so important in providing progressive organizational environment. The second need this book meets is to provide a catalyst through the presentation of thought-provoking ideas designed to help in achieving the essential goals of improved operating techniques and greater guest satisfaction.

Quite original and appropriate is the choice of a theatre-setting to give the selected material a framework. No matter what efforts have to be expended behind the scenes or on the stage, just as the result must always be a satisfied audience in the theatre, so must it be satisfied guests in the hospitality industry, if we are to succeed in our profession.

This text helps to achieve these goals in a novel and most entertaining way.

> L. P. Himmelman
> Chairman and Chief Executive Officer
> Western International Hotels

Seattle, July, 1975

Prologue

DURING OUR RECENT two weeks' Summer Management Seminars in Seattle, participants concluded that they needed continuing information about the hospitality industry. This information we have now made available in *Dimensions of Hospitality Management.*

Why Continuing Information?

Because of its significant expansion rate, the hospitality industry attracts individuals who lack specific education in the field. These people may have been trained to be school teachers but are now working in restaurants. They certainly feel a need for continuing information.

There are also the busy operators who want to keep up with new developments. There is a smaller group of operators that wants to stay ahead. In addition, there are those who are looking for exposure to and upgrading of technical competency in professional and related areas.

These are some of the areas of concern to such individuals:

1) the formulation, initiation and expansion of the business philosophy;

2) the ability to recognize and successfully integrate leadership, motivation and communication models and styles;

3) knowledge of labor relations practices, operational procedures and guest relations analysis and strategies:

4) information about research tools;

5) related areas such as franchising, convenience foods and aspects of tourism.

It is this spectrum that we have included in our book.

Can it be that the need for such information was created by the change in the character of articles in certain hospitality journals today? The limitations on length faced by today's editors have made it impossible for magazines to produce as comprehensive articles as those published some years ago. However, the need for the kind of information contained in those articles continues to exist.

For the members of our industry who are genuinely interested in more rapid development of the industry, we offer this book as a stimulus. We also hope that becoming informed about the important advancements in the hospitality industry will put the food service, lodging industry in a more favorable position in their eyes.

Who Needs It?

The book is especially designed for the owners and/or operators of establishments of all kinds in the hospitality industry. When we speak of "operators" we include top management as well as middle management. The book is designed also for the large group of students in two- and four-year programs who want careers in the hospitality industry. For them the book will offer insight into areas which they might never have considered relevant to hospitality operations and education.

As pointed out earlier, supervisory trainees with backgrounds that did not include hospitality management will, if exposed to the material in the book, certainly be able to speed up their familiarity with our industry. Finally, the book, when given as a gift to effective non-supervisory or even non-hospitality employees, can be used to provide an incentive for considering the hospitality industry as a possible life occupation. Because of its rapid expansion, our industry is critically short of educated, service-minded people.

Format

Shakespeare's "All the world's a stage . . ." might properly be applied specifically to the hospitality industry. Isn't our industry, perhaps more than any other industry, constantly before the public—the performance of employees noticed at all times? Isn't corporate management, like the producer of a play, making a presentation that is constantly reviewed by society? Isn't the management of a restaurant, like the director of a movie, observed at all times by the guests? Like the moves of actors on the stage, isn't every move our employees in clubs and hospitals make noticed and/or criticized?

Shouldn't every meal period be a perfect performance in every respect? Don't we expect a perfect performance each time we go to a theater? For each performance there should be a stage. As patrons of a restaurant, don't we expect some type of "stage,"—a theme, appropriate dishes, appropriate decorations, appropriate uniforms for the "actors"—not just tables and chairs?

The Audience

Don't we find a gallery, an audience, in every school food service, in every hospital ward, in every motel? Shouldn't the "actor" minutely examine every verbal as well as non-verbal communication of the gallery, notice its reactions to the "performance" and use these as clues for feedback to improve the performance?

To match the supporting cast in a theatrical setting—the playwrights and composers—doesn't the hospitality industry need research, development and tourism to provide its "performance" with the proper foundation?

Doesn't management need to be in constant touch with adjacent areas in order to provide services to which society has a proper right? Being of service to society is what our business is all about. For that reason, society has a right to observe us, to review our performance, to criticize our "acting," as everyone has a right to express his or her likes or dislikes of any theatrical performance.

It is for these reasons that we have chosen the play format for our book, to impress on the members of our industry that we are constantly on stage, in the limelight.

We hope that with the seven "Acts," we have covered all areas that are relevant to our industry. Each "Act" in turn is divided into "scenes," and it is here that we started to encounter a problem: there is practically no end to possible subjects. The result is that we had to eliminate many, including one subject which is very close to us, training. Plans are to prepare subsequent volumes of *Dimensions of Hospitality Management* and to include in them material not covered in the first two. We felt there would be greatest advantage for the reader in covering a few subjects well rather than many subjects superficially.

Criteria for Selection of Articles

There were a number of criteria which we observed while looking for appropriate articles. We felt that the articles should deal with specifics. We are so often provided only with generalities that have little information content, solely because such material will appeal to a larger audience and doesn't play up one segment of the industry over another. Further, articles had to be readable, interesting, never boring. They had to be modestly technical, that is, they had to offer some intellectual challenge.

We paid special attention to the criterion of timeliness: subjects had to be up-to-date. There exists confusion in people's minds between today's date and up-to-date. The fact that written material is not of recent date does not mean that it is out of date. We found up-to-date articles in journals issued 50 or more years ago. One such prime example is *What Is a 'Hotel'?* on p. 7. This was written in 1911. If this is not up-to-date, then we don't know the meaning of the phrase.

Each article had to be thought-provoking and invite one to experiment with the ideas and techniques presented. What difference does it make if we or some of the readers disagree with the ideas of the author, as long as the article stimulates creativity in other readers? We also felt that each article should be no longer than can be read in one sitting, say 30 to 45 minutes.

Our business involves fun and enjoyment so we felt that the book should express these desirable qualities. We included jokes (sometimes these create a serious reaction), funny remarks, odd news bits—several almost 100 years old.

Another criterion for selecting articles was that there be a diversity of authors, diversity in background, practical experience and fields of competency. We have presented the practitioners' and the academicians', as well as the consultants' points of view. We also include the viewpoints of people directly and indirectly connected with our common area of interest: *Serving the public.*

Some articles had been published previously and some were written for this volume by us and by other authors at our request. We will continue to invite writers to send us their works in order to stimulate their ideas and the ideas of our readers. We feel this will help to advance our industry.

Finally, we have tried to incorporate selections dealing with each segment of the industry—from hotels, motels and restaurants to fast food operations, clubs, industrial and institutional food services.

Features

Each "Act" will contain some introductory remarks to delineate the boundaries as we see them and to define certain concepts. Each article will be introduced to direct the reader's attention to the specific area with which the article deals and to point out the significance of the content.

After each "Act," there are a number of "queries" to stimulate constructive thinking, in either a group setting or for each individual, and to tie together the thoughts presented in the articles into the overall theme or area of the "Act." Further, some articles are commented on by us to clarify technical points and/or to provide industry examples.

The reader will find two indices. For ease of reference we have double-indexed the book; first, by subject matter, such as "motivation" and "convenience foods"; second, by industry segment, such as "clubs" and "hospital food service." This will enable a reader whose interest lies in hospital food service, for example, to find quickly those articles which are relevant to hospital food service operations (although the reader might look in vain for the words "hospital food service" in the article he/she was reading).

Note that many of the writings deal with more than one area. For example, the article "Labor-Management Communication" is presented in Act II, Scene 3, "Communication," but could just as well have been presented in Act III, Scene 2, "Labor Relations." This relatedness is only one phenomenon of reality. How can someone segregate "financing" from "club management," or "safety" from "institutional food service"? This would be unreal. Our book is real; it is for real people and for real situations.

LOTHAR A. KRECK   *JOHN W. McCRACKEN*

A good rule to follow in hotel keeping is to provide what will please a majority of the guests, if it can be done profitably.*

---

*The Hotel World, June 10, 1911, p. 15. Reprinted by permission, *Hotel and Motel Management.*

WHAT IS A "HOTEL"

HARRY HESS*

In ancient times, the proprietor of a hotel was not looked upon in the most favorable light. As a consequence, harsh rules of law were made, fixing the liability of innkeepers for loss of property brought into a hotel by a guest. Travel, as we all know, was limited and every visit from home even to an adjoining town was looked upon with some degree of fear.

As commercial conditions changed, travel became greater, and with the increased travel came improved transportation accommodations and improved hotels, until today the modern hotel is the equivalent of the royal palace of the crowned heads of the world. This country has been in a fairly prosperous condition for some years and a class of persons have acquired riches, which enable them to practice deception and secure accommodations at certain hotels or places calling themselves hotels. As the result of this prosperity, many

---

*The Hotel World, January 7, 1911, p. 31, Reprinted with permission, *Hotel and Motel Management.*

persons have acquired sufficient spending money to cause a new class of crime to spring up which is of such magnitude as to now require legislation.

It is a well-known fact that there are many places conducted under the name of "hotel" and similar names which are not, in fact, hotels, but which are establishments conducted on low debased standard as to solicit this trade and thrive by these methods. These alleged hotels which are in truth and in fact "dives," overstep the bounds of decency and not infrequently there stray along into our respectable hotels these people, believing by deception they can take the same liberties.

It is my idea that when one engages in the profession of owner or manager of a hotel, that the person conducting the hotel and the hotel itself should be so strictly morally conducted (as) to cause the proprietor, or manager, thereof to be looked upon by all persons as a standard whereby every leading citizen (would) desire to be guided.

From men like these old Scotia's grandeur springs,
    That makes her loved at home; revered abroad.
Princes and Lords are but the breath of Kings,
    An honest man is the noblest work of God.

I have therefore considered whether punishment for these offenses should be inflicted upon an innkeeper, and I have determined that the act of moral baseness occurring in any hotel through the consent, connivance or omission of duty should be severely punished and not be tolerated under any circumstances. I have considered the advisability and necessity of destroying the right of any person to adopt any name which would indicate that to be a hotel which in truth and in fact is not a hotel, but is conducted along such depraved lines. The demands and necessities for the stamping out of this evil is one of our present greatest necessities.

ACT I

The Producer

CORPORATE ADMINISTRATION

INTRODUCTION

Any discussion of management has to start at the top with the producer, if we are talking about theater, and with the corporate administration, if we are talking about hospitality organization.

The top administrator has as his prime responsibility to guide the affairs of the organization with resources entrusted to him by the owners. Corporate administration is not used here as a legal concept but is considered to be the body of human beings charged with the responsibility of conducting business. In Act I, Scene I, we are going to examine two areas relating to corporate administration: philosophy and organization.

One might ask why we include a "non-business" subject such as "philosophy" in a management book. The answer is simply that the philosophy of any organization is the very basis of that organization.

Before going further into the subject, it seems appropriate to define "philosophy" as it pertains to organizations. In Webster, the concept is defined as "a system of motivating beliefs, concepts, and principles."[1] McGuire explains it as "a set of beliefs which affect their (business colleagues) attitudes and actions."[2]

---

1. *Webster's Third New International Dictionary*, Springfield, Mass.: G. & C. Merriam Company Publishers, 1968.
2. McGuire, J. W., *Business and Society*, New York: McGraw-Hill Book Company, Inc., 1963, p. 53.

DEFINING PHILOSOPHY

A philosophy is the guiding light for any organization; without it there is no guidance, no overall, long-term direction. A business without a philosophy is apt to change directions constantly. Any decision-making, without the help of a philosophy, becomes a major undertaking with a serious threat to the perpetuity of the organization. A philosophy or a set of philosophies does not have to be expressed in written form nor does it have to be lengthy or highly complicated.

Let us look at an example. A husband and his wife decide to open a small sandwich shop with, perhaps, one or two additional employees. In talking the idea over, the husband says to his wife, "We will offer the best sandwiches in the area for a reasonable price." Whether you realize it or not, the husband has just stated his business philosophy.

If we compare the statement to the two definitions, we can see that it is "a system of motivating ... principles" (namely business principles), as well as "a set of beliefs which affect their (future) attitudes and actions." The point could be made that the above philosophy is too broad. This, however, is one of the desirable characteristics of a philosophy: it must be broad enough to cover a multitude of operational situations if it is to be helpful.

As a matter of fact, the philosophy for the above situation could be even more encompassing: "We will open the best sandwich shop in the area," including here not only the quality of the sandwiches but also the contributions of decor, service and location, to mention just a few. A philosophy can seldom be established without regard for society, municipal, state and federal governments or for professional organizations; this constraint has to be expressed in the wording of the philosophy.

A hospital food service might want to provide "wholesome food, surpassing the minimum recommended nutritional daily requirements" or a nationwide corporation might decide "to provide, for a minimum profit, services required by the society." It seems as the size of an organization increases from the Ma-Pa sandwich shop to the corporation, that the complexity of a philosophy and the task of communicating that philosophy to the members of the organization increase in like dimensions.

It is agreed that the sandwich shop has many of the same functions as the corporation—employee relations, marketing, production, etc. However, the complexity and diversity is absent, and thus the sandwich shop might have to develop only a single rather than several sets of philosophies.

Let us look at the above corporate statement and consider a set of philosophies. In employee relations, the philosophy might read "to provide an environment where members of the organization can fulfill their needs, at the same time fulfilling organizational needs." In marketing, we might want "constantly to explore the needs of society and to help in the development of the same." Finally, in manufacturing, we might suggest "to produce goods and services that in no way would cause harm to the environment."

This set of philosophies is definitely not complete; areas such as guest relations, pricing, facilities offered and others are missing. Philosophies belonging to a set have to be coherent. It is impossible to have within the set one philosophy which is pro-society, such as the above dealing with employee relations, and another one, e.g., dealing with manufacturing, anti-society in disregarding the environmental question. This would border on hypocrisy.

POLICIES DERIVED FROM PHILOSOPHY

The question of how this set of unspecific statements becomes operational now arises. There is no doubt in our minds that in order to be operational this set has to be specific. We are suggesting here two more steps of specificity: policies and operational procedures (the latter often contained in an operating manual). A model of the whole process will look like: Fig. 1 on facing page.

Webster defines policy as "a definite course or method of action selected from among alternatives and in the light of given conditions to guide and usually determine present and future decisions." An explanation might be in order here in regard to "given conditions." We can think of at least two conditions, the first being the condition as set forth by the

FIG. 1—MODEL PRESENTING THE SEQUENCE OF "PHILOSOPHY-POLICY-OPERATIONAL PROCEDURE"

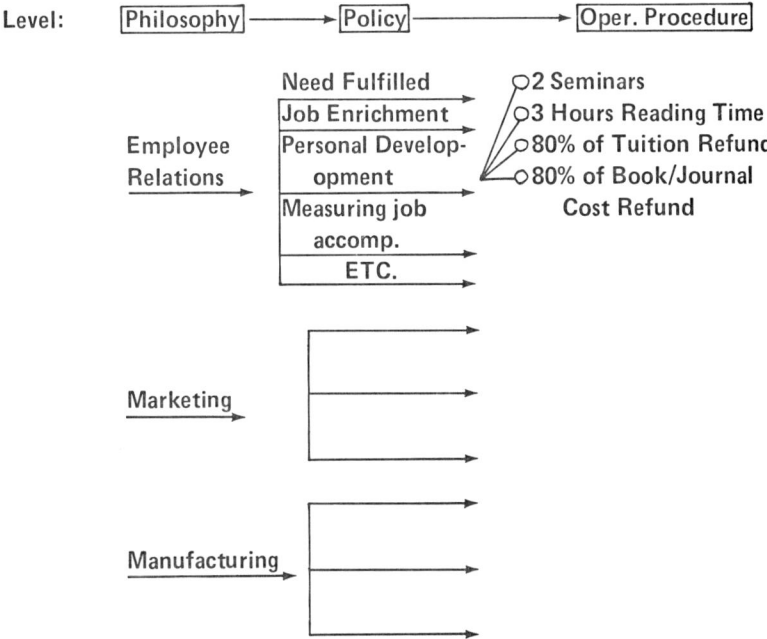

philosophy and the second being the situational context.

Let us take one of the philosophies contained in the preceding set and see how a set of policies can now be developed. In regard to employee relations, the philosophy reads, "to provide an environment where members of the organization can fulfill their needs while at the same time fulfilling organizational needs." The following policies could be developed: "(1) Members' needs should be established and every effort made for fulfillment. (2) An opportunity for job enrichment should be offered. (3) An opportunity for further personal development should be offered. (4) A procedure for objectively measuring job accomplishments should be established. (5) The right to organize and to bargain collectively should be observed. (6) Adequate health care should be provided. (7) Liberal fringe benefits should be granted."

Those are only a few policies pertaining to the philosophy on employee relations. Here it should be made clear that any policy should strictly follow the spirit of the philosophy. We like to use the term "spirit" rather than "word" because of the many varied interpretations of words. While determining philosophies should be the task of the owner(s) of the organization and the top administrative officer, policies should be developed by the top administrative officer and his immediate subordinates (probably vice presidents)[1] after the latter thoroughly understands the philosophy.

One by-product of this process, is that in a situation in which no policy is yet available, the above subordinate can easily suggest one to his superior without lengthy debates. This is exactly what we had in mind when we said earlier that any decision-making process, without the help of a philosophy, becomes a major undertaking with a serious threat to the perpetuity of the organization.

Developing Operational Procedures from Policies

The final step is to develop operational procedures from the policies—a further step toward specificity. Let us consider one policy, i.e., "An opportunity for further personal development should be offered" and try to determine some operational procedures.

1. Each employee should have the chance to participate twice a year in company-sponsored seminars.

2. Supervisors should be given a minimum of three hours per week of company time to read job-related journals.

3. An employee who enrolls on his own time in job-related continuing education courses should be refunded 80 percent of the tuition for two courses per year if a grade of "C" or better has been achieved.

4. The cost of job-related books and/or journals, up to a value of $50 per year, should be refunded at a rate of 80 percent. This is sufficiently detailed to demonstrate the degree of specificity needed on the operational procedure level. It can be noted that numerical standards were used, i.e., two semi-

---

1. This does not rule out consulting lower-level personnel but presupposes an intimate knowledge of the philosophy by such personnel.

nars, three hours. At this level numerical standards are a necessity; there is no room for any philosophical interpretation. Everything is spelled out. Operational procedures will be developed by the vice president in charge of this division together with his subordinates.[1] Here again, the important thing is that the spirit of the philosophy be carried out.

Everything around us—living things, rocks, atoms—is in a particular order; it is organized; so is a play, so is a business organization. There have to be some written or unwritten rules which put diverse activities into a frame of reference in order to prevent unorganized activities or chaos. It is in the spirit of a philosophy that rules for any organization or institution are proposed. These rules are not an end in themselves but provide the basis for achieving an organization's goal and are also part of the set of philosophies.

To achieve predetermined goals, different organizational structures can be used, from "flat" structures where one finds only two or three levels, in use at Sears Roebuck and Company, to "peaked" structures with many levels of supervision. In a single unit hotel, we found five hierarchical levels.[2] One effect of increasing levels of hierarchy is the curtailing of the individual's responsibility which is part of the overall motivational climate of an organization.

Greater Number of Decision Makers

In other words, when we have a "flat" organizational structure, the chance for more individuals to be involved in decision-making processes is greater, simply because the superior has a greater number of subordinates to supervise and consequently, has to spend less time with each. The result is that he is "forced" to have subordinates make decisions on their own, probably within the policy level. This will enhance a subordinate's status and will act as a motivational force. A philosophy dealing with the organizational form will thus have a direct influence on the work environment of the organization.

---

1. "Division" can mean the particular segment, i.e., personnel or a profit center.
2. Kreck, L.A. "Locating Trouble Spots in Organizations," *The Cornell H.R.A. Quarterly*, May, 1973.

What to Look For in Readings

To set the stage for the first "act," we presented a definition of a "hotel." The definition was written more than 60 years ago. It expresses ideas which today we can still applaud. Then two selections dealing with basic philosophic ideas follow: Automation and the Guest discusses the following question: If our industry is part of the service industry, ready to serve guests in hospitality organizations, should service be replaced by vending machines and other "service-saving devices"? The staff of the International Hotel Review leaves no doubt as to the answer.

The next selection forces individual lodging owners to make a decision: whether to lose their operation's individuality and, for economic reasons, become a franchise unit or to stay completely independent and pursue their own ideal or to give up some of their individualism and join a cooperative hotel-motel group.

"Grass Roots—Where the Good Times Are!" is a summary of philosophical statements of operators who run food service and lodging establishments in rural areas, away from big cities. It tells how they provide service and how they deal with the shortcomings of their geographic locations.

The last three selections deal with organizational issues. Although the first two articles do not specifically mention hospitality organizations, there is no doubt that the findings are as valid for our industry as for any other.

"Social Priorities and Executive Myopia" tries to point out the social dimensions immediately ahead of us. These matters must be considered in management's long-range planning in order to avoid past and present shortsightedness (myopia). Some of the social dimensions cited deal with rights of minorities, deceitful practices, public safety, public nuisance and others. The message is clear: organizations should remain or become open systems. Any closed system is doomed to defeat. Open systems observe their surrounding systems and adjust their own policies and actions to make them fit the surroundings—without necessarily undergoing a change in their predetermined goal(s).

In Fulmer's and Rue's "Competence: The Cohesive of

Future Organizations," a number of management experts are asked to look into their crystal balls and predict some of the changes which will take place in the next 15 to 20 years. Will the basis of authority change, and how? Will we see an increase in centralization or decentralization? Will redefining of the functions of administration and management be taking place? Will the role of middle management change? And, finally, will the "pyramid" survive?

The answers to these questions we will not know for sure for 20 years. However, recognizing general trends and adapting to them is what makes organizations survive.

The last article, "Hotel and Restaurant Operation and Management in the Soviet Union," brings us back to some quite concrete issues dealing with actual organizations and their structure, budgets, financial statements and leadership. It is included here to show how similarly or dissimilarly the hospitality industry in other countries, under different economic systems, works.

Scene 1

PHILOSOPHY — ORGANIZATION

AUTOMATION AND THE GUEST*

"Service" and "hospitality" are commonly used to encapsulate the attractions of a hotel to its guest: a "service industry," the "hospitality business," even the word "guest" express an attitude fundamentally at conflict with the notion of providing automatic equipment for hotel residents to look after their own needs. The common feeling in these expressions is pride in personal service and a warmth of human contact.

Advocates of self-service muddy the waters by borrowing such words and phrases for their publicity. The essence of the case for automation is that personal service has less appeal for many guests than the hotel traditionalist believes, or that it is inefficient, uneconomic or, in some situations, impossible.

There is a complacent view shared by many vending equipment salesmen that a boom in their hotel custom is inevitable,

---

International Hotel Review, April-June, 1974, pp. 59, 61, 63. Reprinted with permission.

and that it is not necessary to consider whether hotel users prefer to help themselves. In many instances they will be forced to do so because the hotel industry will not be able to find staff of the right calibre or to pay the sort of wages that will widen the net.

It seems probable that they are right, but there are better arguments. The bias of *International Hotel Review's* researches was towards the interests of readers who are in the hospitality business, who wish to continue to provide for the type of guest who values traditional attitudes and is most likely to be able to pay a premium for them. Such hoteliers will strive to maintain their individual appeal and to improve the standing, job-satisfaction and salaries of staff who serve.

Not surprisingly, hoteliers who fly this flag do not think of personal service and self-service as alternatives to be weighed in the scales of profitability. For them the concept of self-service is so alien that it is practically another business. Francisco Melia, Director General of the Spanish Melia hotel chain, speaking in San Francisco, summed up this attitude in quite a moderate way: "It is advisable, perhaps a necessity, to equip hotels with all the technical advances to ensure an agreeable stay for the client, but I am convinced that the quality hotel industry must fight tooth and nail against the invasion of machines which take the place of man. We do not aspire to convert hotel service into a chain of slot machines, for if we were to do so, we would undermine the essence of an entire industry."

No Dilution of Personal Service

There is no contradiction in this statement. Machinery which simplifies and increases the efficiency of accounting, room management, accommodation booking, or which provides extra service above and beyond established personal service, or which supplies new entertainment facilities, does not dilute personal service. On the contrary, technology of this sort allows staff more time for the guest and relieves them of the tedium of jobs which are no more characteristic of the hotel business than work in a pea-canning factory, and which do not have a vocational appeal much connected with hospitality.

But vending equipment salesmen are not uniquely guilty of complacency. Innumerable hotels pay only lip service to the idea of willing, personal attention to the guest's needs. If efforts in staff education or payment have failed to the degree that members resent their work, or find it demeaning, if the only job satisfactions are those of up-staging clients or specifying why hoped-for services are not available, then it is not surprising if customers welcome the opportunity and relief of providing for themselves.

It is a rare customer who is waited on hand and foot at home. It is not unknown for wealthy men to press their own trousers or pour themselves a drink. Home comforts in the form of labour-saving equipment and having the tools at hand for the job can be sorely missed in a hotel which provides no alternative to dilatory personal service.

Well-planned motels and self-catering hotels have focused a harsh light on the services of more traditional accommodation. When the only choice was between good and bad personal service the challenge was not so great. But now the top-class hotel service must pass the test not just of warmth and willingness to service, but of efficiency.

No doubt there are some guests who value the opportunity to command, who might even relish a test of will with an overbearing headwaiter, who find that the flattery of personal attention is sufficient compensation for delay. But the businessman with work to do, or the wealthy holiday-maker with a family to entertain, is likely to be more pragmatic.

Efficiency or economy are not the only attractions of self-service. Independence and privacy are also to be valued. Mr. Michael McFadyen, general manager of the Sheraton Heathrow hotel at London Airport, which opened this spring, takes charge of a hotel which provides every guest with a Captain Service Centre. These self-service cabinets offer a choice of 12 alcohol and soft drinks, snacks, Continental breakfasts and ice for 24 hours a day. The centre of the unit has a small grill for heating rolls and croissants, and a stainless steel electric jug is provided for heating water to make fresh tea or coffee. Mr. McFadyen expresses the attractions for the guest as follows: "We are trying to give our guests as many home comforts as we can in their own hotel rooms.

We are trying to give them independence and as much convenience as possible, while maintaining the normal hotel room service for breakfast and snacks."

This sounds like the best of both worlds. It educates *all* customers to expect such foods and drinks to be available at any hour, and it should give management of more traditional hotels pause to ask themselves the following questions:

Can personal service in our hotels provide such supplies for guests even at 2 a.m.?

Would the more diffident guests use room service at that hour even if it were available?

Are the rolls delivered for morning breakfast by room service as hot, or is the tea as fresh as those commodities obtained from the self-serve unit?

Do they arrive on time? Would the guest like to have changed his mind about the time he wanted to eat breakfast in his room; if so, was there anything he could do about it?

Is there a woman guest who would like an alcoholic drink at 1 a.m. but prefers not to call attention to the fact?

Would we sell more commodities more profitably if they were constantly on display and constantly available, and if so does this imply that there is a need (that our guests feel) which is not being satisfied?

Does our form of personal service work smoothly because only a small number of guests are determined enough, or convinced enough, to express their every need, are not overawed or discouraged by disdainful or reluctant service, have no objection to tipping, do not feel obliged to tip?

The last question has awesome implications. There may be a silent majority that will change its lodging allegiance altogether, or that will become vocal and demanding thus putting an unexpected strain on personal service resources.

There may be a lesson to be learned from the history of self-service retailing. The success of supermarkets astounded counter-service retailers who attended scrupulously to the whims of shoppers when they reached the counter, but were blissfully unaware of the frustrations of those waiting to be served. Perhaps even their customers were not aware of the disadvantages until they had tasted the efficiency of helping themselves, shopping and choosing, at their own pace.

Self-service units for food and beverages compete directly with traditional services, but there are more and more self-help devices which offer quite new services for which a lack of personal attention will not be apparent. Trouser pressers and shoe cleaning machines are in middle territory, but how many hotels can provide instant shoe cleaning or trouser pressing? More usually there would be a wait involved, and shoe cleaning is commonly an overnight service only, except in exceptional circumstances. But it is quite unexceptional for guests not to carry spares in their luggage, or to get caught in the rain before going out to dinner or an urgent business appointment.

A self-service flower vender is preferable to no flowers at all, and it is the businessman with a tight schedule, on the way to meet a customer and wife, who would value such a service. Computer controlled solariums equipped with automatic massage couches are examples of profitable installations which are luxurious extras, but they are self-service.

Turning from guest satisfaction to economics, it seems an unlikely proposition that self-service food and beverage cabinets in every room, wired into a console which records servicing needs, can pay for themselves. The comestibles need to be specially packaged, and they still have to be taken to the room. Like the guests, the machines need attention, though not at unexpected moments. What is more, these units cannot work on a swings and roundabouts principle like a restaurant or room service department which needs to know only average consumption—every unit must be fully stocked, and it would be expected that wastage would be high, or that some of the foods would soon become so.

We put these points to Mr. John Totten, managing director of Captain International Industries of Europe's British division. His defence is convincing. Captain have more than 25,000 self-service units in operation around the world providing snacks, continental breakfasts, beverages, alcoholic drinks, drink mixers and soft drinks. The appeal to customers is of instant service, in privacy of room, *absence* of personal contact (pause for more thought), no tipping. But Mr. Totten states that Captain "are not sold on the romance of guest satisfaction"; they believe that hoteliers are concerned about below the line profit, and perhaps that says the most significant thing about guest satisfaction. Despite the high capital cost of the equipment it can stand comparison with good investment returns, and the remarkable claim that matters is that 7 percent of the sales value through these machines is accounted for by labour costs. In the case of personal service, 60 percent of the sales value is absorbed by labour.

Evidently there are better arguments for automated service than the one that labour costs will force hotels to adopt it. But at the top end of the business it is essential for guests to feel that self-service offers them something extra in addition to personal service. The machines must look good and have no aura of the staff canteen or factory floor. They must be easy to service and regularly maintained, and prove that they are reliable.

One advantage of personal service is that when things do go wrong there is someone about to make a handsome apology or to absorb and dissipate the anger of frustration. If a machine goes wrong and there is no back-up service, strait-jackets should be to hand. *

---

*This subject of providing service will be taken up once again in a more pragmatic light, in Power's article (Act III, Scene 1) "Labor Supply, Payroll Costs and Changes."

Hotel clerk: "Excuse me, sir, we can not allow you to take those Indian clubs and dumb-bells up to your room."
New guest: "Why, what do your guests do for exercise?"
Hotel clerk: "We have no objection to a limited number of them going to the kitchen before breakfast and pounding the steaks."
America. **

***The Hotel World,* November 30, 1889, p. 9. Reprinted with permission, *Hotel and Motel Management.*

HOTEL COOPERATIVES—CAN VOLUNTARY HOTEL GROUPINGS SAVE THE INDEPENDENTS?*

JEMIMA KALLAS

The decade of confrontation between the chains and the independents is moving into the past as the similarities between the opponents become more apparent than the differences. Traditionally, the traveller has been their only link, the bed-payer who has stood at the centre of a tug-of-war between those who had luxury on offer and those who had unmarketed and often older charms. Since the building of the first chains, however, the wealth of the Western sixties has equipped most hotels with the private baths, central heating, give-away bubblebaths and bedside radio which made chain operations such a get-away dream for the postwar visitors.

Confident of finding creature comforts wherever he stops, the traveller is turning back to the individual hotel.

While the power groups increasingly have to struggle to run expensively so as to operate cheaply, the independent houses which hitherto waived a budget for marketing and promotion in the hope of being left in peace to concentrate on good housekeeping and welcome, are quietly assembling into equally powerful marketing groupings. This is the phenomenon of the cooperative, or *amicale*.

"We are not empire building," stresses Colonel Johnson, head of the federation of the European cooperative Inter Hotels. Co-ops are a self-help movement in which the individual members are freed to run their own show within the phenomenon of the mass power group and its resources.

Bulk promotion and marketing is what brought most cooperatives into existence. "The big groups were getting

---

*International Hotel Review, April-June, 1974, pp. 20-23. Reprinted with permission.

bigger and spending more on marketing. We needed moral support," said A. J. Rothwell, of Britain's 110-hotel Interchange group, which emerged in 1965. Over the last 15 years, hotels with a common market have sought one another out, so as to produce a common brochure of listed names: 22 hotels under the Swedish S Hotels banner; 150 hotels within the European Supranational group (Britain, Denmark, Finland, France, Holland, Italy, Sweden and Switzerland); 1,500 hotels printed in the US Friendship Inns brochure, which shares its 1,200 operations with Inter-Hotels' 300 European members; 40 hotels and 400 restaurants, known as E hotels, which are part of the nationwide Finnish cooperative movement, OTK, that also covers 2,500 shops, 80 department stores and 50 factories.

More to Marketing

At its simplest, such cooperation costs no more than the printers' bill, and the brochure is handed to tourist offices and travel agents to simplify their selections, but marketing generally consists of more than dropping a printed list into an agent's wall rack. S Hotels, a year after being set up, carried out a direct advertising campaign to 5,000 travel agents in Europe; distributed their brochure to most of the big Swedish companies and their travel agents; circulated the brochure to all ex-clients on the 22 hotels' guest lists; covered the Nordic travel market, from bus companies to airlines and car hirers; advertised in the travel press; and they keep brochures everywhere within each of the member hotels. The campaign is in addition to any individual promotion members care to budget for.

The other basic usefulness of a voluntary link is referral bookings, made without commission between members. "Where are you going now?", Inter Hotel receptionists are encouraged to ask a customer as he checks out. "Did you know there is another Inter Hotel in such and such a town?" Switzerland's Inter Hotel branch (13 members) has a Telex in every hotel, to make referrals more reliable. Indeed, possession of a Telex is mandatory to becoming a member.

Groupings generally begin by seeking things in common, and end by imposing more. Indeed, the borderline between the more systematic voluntary groupings, a franchise and a chain could become blurred in the fullness of time. Co-op members are usually chosen because of a similar number of rooms, price range, and stars. Some insist on membership in other bodies: Germany's five MAP hotels, for example, need to belong to the IHA, ASTA, and the HSMA. Over and above such basic details will be a common peculiarity: France's Chateau Hotels (81 members) and Germany's Schlosshotels (43 members) need to be housed in a castle; Germany's Ringhotels (90 members), says their brochure, "all have a personal note and reflect the atmosphere characteristics and cooking of the region." Regionality appears to be the most popular binding point for independent hotels. That, and high standards of service.

Sine Qua Non

Having found the members, the next step is to standardise some of the operations. Luxembourg's seven Congress Hotels, for example, have been able to standardise special rates for conventions in both low and high season. Co-ops establish common policies about what credit cards to accept; tour programmes and cut prices which have to be bowed to; which travel agents receive priority. The groupings have fighting power against abusive commission practices, and many refer obscurely to "special deals" in their favour with American Express and other monopoly credit and tour lords.

Creeping standardisation next affects matters like the group sign, and whether to hang it outside, whether to print it on to the crockery and linen, and how prominently.

Where is the line to be drawn between sharing a badge of individuality, and losing one's image in a group appeal? Colonel Johnson emphasises that, with Inter Hotels in Great Britain, "We don't run this on pressure. We don't discipline our members. We can only cajole them. Those who take the most active part, who go to the meetings, and take advantage of the group purchasing, and who actively practise referrals, those are the ones who do get the most out of membership."

Ultimately, if the members want the work for them done by headquarters, they have to do as they are told. With Inter Hotels GB, which is run on a regional basis, pressures come up from below. The principle of the "cell" still holds good as a method of grouping personalities and problems within a large set-up. Without relentless discussion in small units, groups tend either towards central bureaucracies, or dispersed and sleeping memberships. Most co-ops are formed by the strong spirits who have survived the years of independence in an era of bulk this and mass that, and they have little intention of handing over their individuality. Ringhotels makes individual responsibility quite clear to members before they join: "there will be no complaints to headquarters about falling bookings, inflating costs and personal crises; self-help is more healthy. And there will be no complaints about growing competition either; you are expected to make your own improvements."

There is more incentive towards cooperation when members begin to pool not only the mechanical search for the guest but internal running problems: for example, pooled training of staff, pooled staff benefits and promotion within the group. Or again, mutual help on how to grapple with government regulations that involve substantial changes, such as a new hygiene law or more exacting fire regulations. As labour is getting harder to find, America's Motel Six chain runs a travelling team of maintenance men. There are three maintenance men per each 10 motels for any repair over $200— 84 people in all. The crews consist of an air conditioning and heating specialist, a plumbing and electrical specialist, and a general handyman and carpenter, who visit their motels roughly once every week.

Mutual Help

Germany's ERFA groupings, which are a series of discussion groups set up region by region, meet once a month to mull over how to confront current crises. In calmer times, they crosscheck how members run their hotels, so as to uncover discrepancies on, for example, how many grammes of prawns managers are putting into a prawn cocktail. Maybe the customer does not benefit so much this time, but the discussions do help to bring managers out of their isolation.

Bulk purchasing is a by-product of being a large group, though Bill Richards of Britain's Interchange (87 members) maintains that "independent hoteliers don't need someone to get discounts for them. They can negotiate 10 percent off an item for themselves." A headquarters possibly gives them access, however, to a wider group of manufacturers, with discounts usually ranging from five percent to twenty percent. The arrangement the freer groups make is to negotiate the contract with a large manufacturing group which gives members the facility of making their orders or not, as they please. "Members are not obligated to buy," said Colonel Johnson. "But encouraged." A listing of special purchasing facilities for the year goes out to Inter Hotel GB members. It contains about 70 manufacturers, ranging from floor polish, mustard and kitchen equipment to people like Schweppes, Martini & Rossi and Barclays Bank.

Friendship Inns, at the other extreme, has a central warehouse of obligatory group purchase items in Salt Lake City. At which point, one cries, "where is independence?" Within Europe, a group like Centrelink find freight charges and shipping problems stand in the way of much group purchasing across frontiers.

Empire Builders

The more facilities the co-op offers, the more it needs a formally set-up headquarters, and the more it costs. Some groups work perfectly well with one hotel manager, a part-time typewriter and some headed paper. Supranational, for example, was set up by the British member's assistant managing director, Roderick Fraser of Centre Hotels, in addition to his normal responsibilities, and it has no salaried officers. Most co-ops charge running and promotion costs on a sliding scale, sometimes according to the number of beds in each hotel. The membership fee is supposed to be easily amortised in the referral bookings. Amongst the Interchange hotels, membership depends on turnover and costs between £100 and £1,000. To Bill Richards, the bank of money that accumulates is essential: "One of the failures of consortia has been in not developing capital funding. Interchange now places a percentage of its funds on reserve, but at one time we were living completely from hand to mouth. I would suggest other consortia are all bankrupt in proper terms. If you foreclosed tomorrow there would be no cash."

Finland's E hotels are funded in a radically different way, given that they belong to the nationwide OTK cooperative movement which invests in other fields. Headquarters services are not charged to E hotels, but as the hotels own OTK through their share holdings, they are required to take out shares in proportion to their membership. Any surplus deriving from the commercial activities of OTK is returned to the cooperatives in proportion to their purchases from OTK. Certain chargeable services, such as training, are under consideration. The E Hotels have, incidentally, showed a higher profit ratio than OTK's other investments.

The idea of genius, however, had to come out of America, Land of Opportunity. It took an American to think of setting up a separate company to make a profit out of other people's unoccupied rooms. Membership is free. "Zero cash to get in," the membership letter states. "Zero cash to stay in. Even zero cash to get out."

Ernie Cassill, who conceived the idea of Allstar is a hotelier: its principle is that any member which finds it has 1 1/2 percent of its rooms unbooked offers them free to Allstar. Members' profit is purported to come from food and beverages sale—on the principle that something is better than nothing. Allstar's profit needs no spelling out. The company spent $85,000 on developing the concept lead by directors who budgeted one year in time and money to set it up and it will continue to budget 75 percent of future revenue on advertising. The technique was to pick out the hotels by taking them from the American Automobile Association and Mobil guides, and then publish an Allstar directory. Concessions from petrol and credit card companies go with Allstar membership, which involves only the displaying of a $20 sign. Recruitment began in March 1973 targeted at 200 hotels, but was stated to have reached 300 within five months.

And the appeal to prospective members is one that transcends frontiers: "We recognise that we have to face the challenge of the national chains and their referral systems in some way or another. Hopefully, in a way that will permit us to retain our independence. And a way that makes economic sense."

Linking Cells

What enabled Allstar to start running so quickly was that it could take hold of an existing link-up, and much the same trend is becoming apparent in Europe. All during the 60s, people, businesses and places have gathered, willingly or otherwise, into groupings, and now the structures are being put to new uses: in Britain, Inter Hotels chose to keep to the regional groupings devised by the British Tourist Authority. In Germany, much of the Ringhotel membership is drawn from the 2 to 4-star ERFA discussion groupings. Across frontiers, existing cooperatives have linked marketing and often synchronised their names, so that a group like Interhotels was in a position to woo Friendship Inns with a readymade European network of places. Whether there is a point at which identity can become diluted remains to be seen. What is essential is that the hotels start out knowing what they want to achieve: yesteryear's hotel magazines are full of stories of bravely set up co-ops which flourished for one season, quarrelled and died. S Hotels, on the other hand, proceeded more wisely. "We regarded it as valuable to keep the number of members unchanged at least during the first years in order to stabilise the group and to bring about any form of successful cooperation."

However, even when the strongly independent managers whose personalities jostle within a co-op are not quite sure of a common direction, they have clear minds on one point: no weaklings under *our* banner.

And so, interestingly, the hotel industry is weeding its ranks. Also-rans are pushed out of business not just by economic factors but because they are ignored by the trade itself, which has finally recognised a common identity. "Although we are in competition," the head of a one-town hotel union put it, "we realised we could benefit from the cooperative idea."

A healthy body of hoteliers, clustered into recognised groups, is in a position to exert pressures in areas where the hotel trade has given way in the past. Some may feel that the hotel voice is best expressed by its Associations, but it is one of those misfortunes that once people have elected a body to look after them they stop looking after themselves: their self interest may seem to them to be more clearly represented by the cooperative into which they were chosen to fit. Commenting on the relationship of voluntary bodies with the local hotel association, the head of a five-hotel seaside cooperative in England, J. H. Perry, feels that, "we strengthen their case."

Most cooperatives, so far, prefer not to acknowledge the power of numbers, which they confine to extracting buying concessions, and use as a badge of respectability in negotiating holiday packages with tourist bodies and the transport people. Ringhotels, however, are quite clear about what they expect of themselves: "the aim of our cooperative is to create a strong block of middle-rank hotels which can put its strength to the use of all, both in the economic sector and in the political arena."

If some voluntary groupings do exert protective pressures, the lone hotelier who has chosen total independence is umbrellaed twice over from suffering in silence from shocks to the national system.

When, though, does cooperation become stranglehold?

GRASSROOTS—WHERE THE GOOD TIMES ARE!*

Tourism in the grass roots is growing, growing, grown ...

With the influx of curious sightseers spilling into small rural towns and communities of middle America, many small local restaurants and motels find themselves thrown into the middle of a thriving market. With quick food operations popping up in the most unexpected places, they are gearing up to take advantage of it.

One would think that both commercial and non-commercial food service establishments in these rural communities would be somewhat handicapped professionally by their lack of exposure to so-called big city expertise, conveniences and ideas. But the truth is, the operators in these often overlooked areas are sophisticated, with-it folk running successful —if not downright lucrative—operations. In short, the problems besetting big-time food service entrepreneurs just don't seem to ruffle the men and women who live in Home Town, U.S.A.

That isn't to say they don't have them. They do! And in no less dosage. Food costs, labor, overhead, equipment maintenance are very real flies in the profit ointment. And they do have a few frustrations that large metropolitan and suburban cities don't have to cope with! But the initiative and ingenuity employed by our country cousins make these problems seem less hectic or wearisome.

Down in the Bible Belt, "brown bagging" is the national pastime. Fred "Pal" Barger who owns Skoby's World and Olde West, a dinner-theatre in Kingsport, Tenn., reports that

Institutions/Volume Feeding Magazine, October 1, 1973. Reprinted with permission.

state liquor laws have been a bone of contention for years. Natives in the area have traditionally opposed liquor reform bills. "And the most adamant of them," according to Barger, "will drink up a storm Saturday night, go to church with a hangover on Sunday, and vote against selling liquor in public eating and drinking places on Monday."

"There's no question," Barger avers, "that liquor sales would up volume tremendously, but we do all right as it is. At the theatre, we charge a fixed price for the buffet and show. Our girls keep customers supplied with ice and set-ups, and are well tipped. Customers bring their own booze. At Skoby's, no liquor is sold, but the law permits brown bagging in private dining rooms, so we added a few when we remodeled—just for that reason. These rooms accommodate anywhere from four to a dozen or so people."

Still, despite archaic drinking laws, Barger does a healthy half-million-dollar volume with Skoby's World alone; and his dinner-theatre operation, after costly production, cast and overhead expenses, nets close to $45,000.

The Curse of the Drinking Man

Liquor laws pose a problem for Carl R. Moore, president of Camara Inns, Inc., in Bristol, Tenn. This relatively new chain of five modular unit constructions, priced between moderate and luxury motels, is hitting the local Tri-cities market (Kingsport, Elizabethton, Bristol) currently dominated by Holiday Inns, Ramada and Days Inns of America. "Beer," Moore reports, "can be sold in the restaurants of all Tri-city motels, except in Kingsport. There, the law stipulates you *must* rent a room in order to buy beer. It cannot be sold in the restaurant." Why? He doesn't know. "It's all part of the illogical thinking down here, but as long as it doesn't hurt business, I don't mind."

Moore is certain Camara Inns will out-draw the larger motel chains because his operations are locally owned, operated and managed; and business men and residents tend to prefer "hometown" establishments because they know the owners are neighbors.

For Moore, the modular construction concept is easier and less costly to put up. It takes roughly 45 days to build 60 modular units; stacking them and putting them together as a complete motel takes another 90 days. Average cost per unit is $6,500. According to Moore, the Elizabethton and Petersburg (Va.) Camara Inns are running at a commendable "80 percent and 95 percent capacity, respectively. The others do about 70 percent."

One interesting note: Three of Camara's five managers are female, all locally hired. "Women are more capable at detail work," Moore reasons, "and men appreciate them for this. Ninety-five percent of our patrons are men."

The Younger Generation—Hard-Working Professionals

Idealism and independence are attributes of youth and rarely, if ever, will you find them coupled with professionalism. The exception is a young couple, Tom and Chris Pratt, who own and operate Pratt's Barn, a rustic-looking building in Kingsport, Tenn., guarded by a towering, 32-foot, five-ton statue of an American Indian. Tom Pratt, 23, took over the 80-seat Barn from his father about a year ago. His wife, 20-year-old Chris, daughter of Pal Barger, waits on tables and keeps the kitchen going.

Wanting to be independent, the youthful Pratts saved $10,000, paid cash for their equipment and started from scratch to recoup their investment. Their business acumen has paid off. The Barn averages $7,000 to $8,000 a month during the winter, and $10,000 in the summer.

The determination of the young Pratts becomes obvious when you learn that, despite hard work and long hours, they've continued to pursue their education. They alternate semesters so one is always at the restaurant full-time. Tom received his degree last summer, and Chris will get hers next year.

Youth on the Move ...

Virginia "Jinny" Jenkins owns and operates the Geisha Gardens, a Japanese teahouse, complete with pagoda, rock garden, bridges and dragon carvings on the roof, with the help of her teen-age chef.

Situated on a charming little by-way called Fie Top Road in a bucolic area called Maggie Valley (not too far from Asheville, N.C.), the Gardens require reservations 24 hours in advance for a sumptuous Japanese feast served in the traditional manner from 5:30 to 8:30 p.m. The restaurant, or "Teahouse of the Sacred Bamboo," only holds 40 people. Dinner is cancelled if there are less than eight reservations by 1 p.m. on the day, since all food must be purchased and prepared hours ahead of time.

Hal Jenkins, who conceived, designed and built this obscure bit of enchantment in the heart of the Smokies, died six months ago; and the task of holding the 10-year-old operation together has fallen into Jinny's lap. She relies on John Morris, a 17-year-old student protege of Hal's, who took over the food preparation and cooking chores with the confidence of a seasoned pro at Hal's death. Working part-time to defray school expenses, John learned and absorbed the minute details of Japanese cooking from Jenkins and has pursued the task with a dedication and gusto that is nothing short of remarkable. For Jinny, John and the three college co-eds who work as waitresses have been a godsend, and she has started her own little training session to encourage their interest in her oriental haven.

College Students Research F/S Needs

Appalachian State University, Boone, N.C. (8000 students in a city of 10,000 population), serves 7000 meals a day in five eating areas, says Jairy C. Hunter, student support services director.

Hunter works closely with the Student Welfare Committee named by the Student Government Association. "For more than a year, we've been meeting with the committee quarterly, or more frequently, listening to complaints (sometimes to praise). If they offer a suggestion that is practical and financially possible, we adopt it promptly. If not, we explain in detail why we cannot put it into effect.

"We recently sponsored a trip throughout the state for the Welfare Committee members. They compared our food service and processes with those of other educational institutions. They gave us a very favorable rating and made several suggestions which we adopted for the benefit of all concerned. One was that we invest in a pressure fryer, so customers could have fried chicken whenever they wanted it.

"We did this and the student response has been gratifying."

Nostalgia and Know-How

The original owner of this former truck farm got the idea of opening his property to picnickers on Sunday afternoons, charging a small fee per person. On days when the weather turned foul, he invited visiting picnickers to bring their box luncheons inside.

That was how Maple Shade Farm started. It is now a full-fledged restaurant on Mt. Hawley Road in Dunlap (pop. 200), 10 miles north of Peoria, Ill.

The first owner is long gone, but Le (one "e") Anderson and his wife Milie (one "l") have run the 200-seat operation for 10 years and do a spanking business. That's mainly because the food is good and nightly entertainment and dancing keeps folks coming back.

Anderson, a former Chicago bartender, is an innovative man. He dreamed up a "creme de menthe parfait" in a 10-ounce glass for $1.25 and invented "Milie's Coffee," a combination cafe noir, creme de cacao, shredded chocolate and a cherry. And the country folks love it!

On the food side, there is a beefy 12-ounce sirloin dubbed the B-47 (a pun on "before 7 p.m.") for $2.95. After 7 p.m., the price jumps to $8.00. His menus, printed weekly, are spiced with humorous messages to or about regular customers. He advertises five days a week in the Peoria paper and, occasionally, puts in a "not tonight" ad on Mondays when he closes his operation.

He usually depends on a firm in Decatur to maintain equipment but, he explains, "sometimes you have to wait two weeks before somebody finds his way to (or through) Dunlap. However, there's a guy I buy soap from who knows something about dishwashers and other equipment. He's nearby, so first I give him a call when something goes wrong. It saves time, aggravation . . . and money!"

Tales of a Wayside Inn . . .

Once upon a time, long before the state of Wisconsin was born, there were the lakes. Oconomowoc, Nagawicka, Pewaukee, Pine, La Belle and others.

And long before the peaceful lakes were dotted with outboards, sailboats and catamarans, there was the Red Circle Inn, a lonely way station for itinerant traders, trappers and settlers in the Midwest. The Inn is a by-word in fine dining and trades on good will. For birthday or anniversary parties, owner Wally Ketter supplies the cake if given advance notice. The Inn's famous club cheese, served in the bar, can be purchased by customers or sent in gift packages anywhere across the country.

Indeed, the little town of Nashotah, even though it does not always appear on the map, at least has the distinction of harboring the oldest restaurant in Wisconsin.

Brain Sandwiches, Bell-Ringing, Parties for the Police

What sounds more nostalgic than 'The Old Mill' on New Harmony Road in Kasson, Ind.—where sipping beer and munching brain sandwiches is a venerable tradition? The Mill was among the first eateries in the area to sell beer by the pitcher, and brain sandwiches are a carryover from the 19th-century German immigrants who settled in this part of the country.

Carl and Virginia Wallace bought the mill in 1966. "We have a custom of ringing a bell whenever anyone comes in. It's in the bar area and was once used to call children to school. When we ring it, people think they're being greeted. Actually, it's a signal to the waitresses."

Every anniversary, the Old Mill features a steak dinner at a special low price. At Thanksgiving, the Wallaces sponsor a turkey fry for American Legion members. But their annual party for the State Police probably generates the most good will. According to Wallace: "It's our way of saying 'thank you' to the troopers for the fine job they do. It pays off for us, too, because they recommend the Mill to passing motorists looking for a good place to eat."

There's a Small Hotel

Nestled in a lovely valley offering seclusion to a scattering of rustic hamlets stands Mapleton (population: scanty), site of Boyer's Mapleton Hotel.

Well, not really a hotel. Anymore. The building dates

back to 1924, but the transient traveler through this small rural Wisconsin community is rare now, and it's been 20 years since anyone looked for a night's lodging there, according to current owner Dick Boyer.

The restaurant grosses roughly $125,000 a year catering only to local folk and their families. It seats 80 people plus 28 in the bar where Boyer recently installed an electric dart board. "It takes up no floor space," notes Boyer. "It's noiseless and, most important, it stimulates added bar business. That's why we got it instead of a regular dart game.

"We have very good equipment," Boyer explains, "but we learned a lot about taking care of it. Our dishwasher broke down a few weeks back. It only needed one small gasket to get started again. The particular part wasn't available locally. So, we got our garage mechanic to fashion a kind of makeshift gadget and fixed the machine ourselves. It's washing dishes like crazy! You can always find good mechanics in a farming community. It's a must when, say, your baler or tractor or milking machine breaks down! So we don't have much trouble getting repairs done."

Non-Commercials: Ingenuity By Necessity

As defined by the California Hospital Association (CHA), a "small rural" hospital must:

Be 50 miles, or more than two hours, from the closest medical center in California; Tahoe Forest Hospital, Truckee, Cal., is 95 miles from Sacramento.

Have 99 beds or less; Tahoe has 42.

Employ 10 or fewer full-time doctors, not including specialists; Tahoe has 10.

The total permanent community served must not exceed 20,000; Truckee is about 13,000. And, finally, the hospital must not be situated in an urban or suburban area.

Tahoe Forest is one of about 110 small-town California hospitals which a CHA *ad hoc* committee is studying for possible improvements in several areas, including food preparation and dietary programs. Happily, it has relatively few problems with the latter.

"We have compact, adequate kitchen facilities," reports Janet Franklin, the hospital's dietary supervisor. "Regrettably, we don't have an automatic dishwasher, but we manage well with our manual one. It's operated by the cooks who double as dishwashers. Because of our size, it's more economical—and homier—to use real plates, sturdy silverware and glasses. Naturally, we use disposable items for isolation patients.

"I order bulk canned goods and meats each week from a wholesale operation in Sacramento, and we receive standard milk and bread deliveries three or four times a week.

"We do better financially than some larger hospitals because we have less waste. Leftovers are reusable and excess prepared food can be frozen for later use.

"We have a 30-day supply of canned and frozen foods which could see us through an emergency—for example, bad weather and closed roads. Dry milk could substitute for fresh milk, although we might have to go without fruits and vegetables. Even now, if we run out of lettuce or fruits, we have only to drive down the street to the grocery store and pick some up.

"This is a sparsely populated and quite transient area (popular with skiers and mountain climbers), and we find it hard to keep a stable qualified staff. Most of our girls (four or five a shift) are high school students on work-study programs, although we do have some who stay on for quite awhile. It's not easy to entice trained foodservice or dietary help to an out-of-the-way hospital."

Foodservice as Therapy? Dietitians as Therapists?

Medfield Medical Center, Largo, Fla., a private hospital for the treatment of mental and emotional problems, alcoholism and drug-related disorders, averages 25 to 31 residential patients who are served three meals daily and whatever snacks they want.

"Special dietary needs are common to the types of patients cared for," says Dietary Supervisor Corinne Osborn. "Alcoholics generally require low-protein diets. Drug addicts develop an inordinate sweet tooth while they are being detoxined, so we make cookies, milk shakes and other snacks available to them 24 hours a day. We have a formal snack hour at 8:00 p.m. each evening, and nurses hand out sandwiches, desserts, coffee, sodas and milk shakes which have been prepared in our kitchen."

As part of their therapy, through the patients' unit government which meets weekly to decide who will perform what duties throughout the hospital, patients are assigned as kitchen aides to wash dishes and help clean the kitchen. This puts tremendous responsibility on the dietary department. "We usually have to go get the patients and bring them down to the kitchen for their 'shift'," Corinne Osborne explains. "Tact is important, and patience. Some like to play games with us.

"The difficulty, of course, is to find employees capable of or willing to take on such risky duties. It takes a special type of person to work here. Some dislike being in a place where the doors must be kept locked. Others get depressed working with mentally depressed patients. And those qualified in kitchen skills often aren't good with people. Kitchen personnel are held responsible when serving these patients. They're unstable and must be watched at all times."

Salary is evidently not the problem. "We start kitchen help at $2.00 an hour," Mrs. Osborne continues. "This is competitive with the local pay scale (most places in the area still start at $1.60)."

Corinne Osborne's search for an additional part-time helper has been frustrating. "But I am getting philosophical about it," she signs. "I've been handling the kitchen since the hospital opened almost two years ago. I have grown with the job and am getting accustomed to being a one-man team. If lucky, I'll eventually find some qualified person able to handle the stresses and willing to stay for a long time. If unlucky, I'll simply go on doing it myself."

A "Kind Word" File

At Monmouth, Ill., Community Memorial Hospital, Foodservice Director Paul Cropper is a man of many talents and some ingenuity. One test of his resourcefulness at this seven-year-old, 150-bed hospital is improved "customer relations" with those in the local meals-on-wheels program. Concerned that these people rarely received their meals hot, Cropper repaired a small generator which he found in a scrap heap, hooked it up to a second-hand microwave oven and mounted both on an old, beat-up pickup truck. Between each location, a tray is heated so it can be delivered to the recipient's door piping hot.

Patient satisfaction is extremely high. "We're always getting comments from them. They scribble notes on place mats, menus, napkins, whatever they can find, simply to tell us how much they enjoyed their meals. Many send 'thank you' notes, even though they've never seen our staff because the food made their stay more tolerable. I started a 'Kind Word' file, then began putting the notes on the kitchen's bulletin board. It doubles morale and really cheers up all of the people who work for us."

During National Nurses Week, the kitchen employees bake huge cakes and send them to the nurses on each shift. "The nurses on the 11 p.m. to 7 a.m. shift," Cropper recalled, "made up a 'thank you' card and left it for my staff to find when they came in that morning. This sort of thing creates so much good will. It transfers to the patients, many of whom come down to meet us before they leave."

A Stock Pot, a Charcoal Broiler, 64 Monks on Maintenance

St. Martin's College, Lacey, Wash., in a farming community near Puget Sound, 60 miles south of Seattle, feeds 200 students plus 64 Benedictine monks who staff the school. The task of serving 3,000 to 4,000 meals weekly belongs to Foodservice Manager Don Fagan. Until recently, the equipment used, in many cases, rivaled in age the 75-year-old school. The monks provide their own maintenance crew and, according to Fagan, they must have wrought at least minor miracles in keeping it functioning. However, the incorporation of a boy's high school into the college brought new equipment into the hallowed halls; and Fagan, who is employed by ARA Food Service (Pennsylvania) couldn't be happier about it. He is especially relieved to have a convection oven.

Although there is a large amount of storage and freezer space available, and adequate supplies of bases, concentrates and frozen foods at the college, Don Fagan is looking forward to one acquisition in particular, a stock pot for "home-made" soups, sauces and gravies.

In the summer, St. Martin's opens its facilities to conventions, a practice that helps defray costs during this normally slack season, but also presents problems of its own. For example, a group of 140 people scheduled as guests on the campus last year included a high percentage of vegetarians. Those meals involved extra planning and labor.

As for the students, Fagan offers unlimited seconds and tries to give them a balanced diet with as much variety as humanly possible. He hopes eventually to have a column in the student publication to discuss choices in menus. "I think that's a good way to get their cooperation and ideas."

Absenteeism: a Key to Cost Saving

The University of Georgia, Athens, moved away from contract feeding a decade ago and ran the gamut of all sorts of food plans for several years. "Everything we did made our financial situation worse. We got closer and closer to bankruptcy," reported foodservices head Glen F. Garrett.

"Then, late in 1971, we returned to an improved system of contract feeding. It was our salvation. In the last 12 months, we are over $330,000 better off than we were previously—and comfortably in the black.

"Perhaps even more important, the students who dine at our two cafeterias are delighted with the quality and quantity of what they get. The way it looks now, we will soon be compelled to increase the capacity of these cafeterias; one seats 400, and the other 1000.

"This is quite a contrast with the previous situation, where the campus newspaper was constantly tough on us. They like us now! We are feeding on contract better than 2,000 of our 20,000 students, and the number increases each week. All this in a city of 40,000, and despite the steady rise in labor and food costs.

"We feature a four-week cycle of meals—which means that no range of choices is repeated at any time within that period. Students go back for as many 'seconds' as they can hold. One student didn't believe this. He came back seven times for big helpings of pork chops—and was served each time without comment. (As far as we know, he suffered no permanent ill effects!)

"The reason this plan works so well is that there is no rebate for missed meals. If every student ate every meal, we'd go broke. Instead we take advantage of absenteeism. And if someone wants to make an entire meal on desserts—that certainly is his privilege."

Navajo School Stresses Diet, Institutional Training

Diet is a big item at Intermountain, the U.S.'s largest Navajo off-reservation boarding school, squatting serenely at the foot of the Wasatch Mountains in northern Utah. Here foods are evaluated via a master menu by professional dietitians, and most vegetables and fruits are purchased locally.

Buffalo meat from Yellowstone and other national parks is an occasional menu feature. Some foods are delivered biweekly from the Government Security Administration in Gallup, N. Mex., 500 miles away, while items such as butter, buttermilk and grain are on support contract. A typical day's meal, according to Intermountain's educational specialist Arlie Pittman, "calls for 600 pounds of roast beef, six sacks of potatoes, nine cases of fruits and vegetables, 140 loaves of bread and 1,300 half-pint milk cartons.

"We have enrolled 1100 students—from Navajo reservations in Arizona and New Mexico. They may come back for refills as often as they wish. They come to school hungry and some line up as many as four times."

In addition to the student dining hall, the school operates the Eagle Feather Inn where students learn the science of institutional cooking. Here, on a rotation basis, explains Pittman, "we train 30 students and feed 50. The two-year course comprises 1080 hours of three-hour daily classes. Students are taught to prepare and serve family-style meals. In addition to classwork, they must occasionally demonstrate meal preparation in the auditorium, starting with raw foodstuffs."

Intermountain was built during World War II by the Army and originally operated as a military hospital. It was turned over to the Bureau of Indian Affairs in 1949 and transformed into an educational resource center and boarding school for Navajo youngsters. Facilities include a police training academy and the school offers college preparatory, vocational and technical training as well as rehabilitation programs.

Catering to the Transient Trade

In the 20 years John Lichorwic has owned Dibble's Inn in historic Vernon, N.Y., the restaurant has grown from a single, unimposing dining room to a 900-seat gold mine.

Strategically staked out 12 miles west of Utica and 34 miles east of Syracuse, Dibble's beckons New York State Thruway vagabonds to the ritual of fine dining "en route."

"Our main concern," states Lichorwic, "is finding a better way to keep meat, particularly for banquet affairs." There is a variety of meat holders on the market, he concedes, but "those we've looked at represent too costly an investment for the few times a year we might utilize it. If we could find one that could double in some other capacity as well, that would be ideal."

The Inn has two very large convection ovens which, despite their size couldn't handle the ever-increasing volume of prime rib and turkey orders pouring into the kitchen daily. "But we improvised a little and reinforced the racks. Now we can cook a dozen prime ribs or eight 30-lb. turkeys at one clip."

Dibble's offers a tantalizing drink specialty—fresh fruit daiquiri prepared with whatever fruit is in season (raspberries, strawberries, bananas, apples, pineapples). "It sells for $1.35," reports Lichorwic, "and we go through a lot of rum."

Want the Business? Get the Kids!

One of a chain of eight luncheon/dinner smorgasbord operations in the Midwest is Peoria's Heritage House. Catering strictly to family trade, and perched on the fringes of an interstate highway, it culls the main portion of its business from a 50-mile local radius. Oddly, very little stems from transients, although the Heritage House Country Store with its dollar souvenirs would indicate otherwise.

The Peoria operation features standing rounds of ham and/or beef daily. Weekly specials include Friday seafood and a 1/2-lb. pond-raised channel catfish on Saturdays. Holiday events feature "Breakfast with Santa Claus" or the "Easter Bunny." There is a "treasure chest" of toys, and kids are invited to a grab-bag selection before leaving the restaurant.

Harold Lambert who operates the Peoria establishment knows 50% of his patrons by name and most by sight. Some

35% of the staff consists of part-time college/high school students, many of whom started with the operation when it opened almost six years ago. The youngsters are cheerful, wholesome, hard-working. Most serve a lengthy tenure until they receive diplomas or degrees because the atmosphere is congenial, the staff is compatible, tips are good and the customers are fun.

It's All in the Family

"A family working together makes for good business," says Bob Smith who, with his wife Dorothy, owns and operates Candlewyck, a country inn 17 miles south of Allentown in Pennsylvania Dutch country.

The Smiths, their two sons and their wives, their daughter and her husband all excel at some facet of the operation. Smith himself built the place with his own two hands down to the wiring and plumbing. He serves as the Inn's all-around maintenance man and even mows the 14-acre lawn. Dorothy attends to the books; his daughter is hostess; one son is the bartender; the other, a chef whose Chicken Boissiere (made with a vermouth sauce) and King Crab Delight (a tangy casserole with cheese and eggs) are main attractions.

"Discussions are family affairs," Smith reports. "The ladies talk about problems in the dining room, the boys pow-wow about the bar and kitchen. Dorothy and I are the ones with the money, so we say what can and can't be done. She and my daughter designed the waitress uniforms (a Pennsylvania Dutch outfit).

Smith travels to Philadelphia on the average of once a week to buy cheese and freshly butchered meat. Fresh fruit is difficult to get delivered, and he also purchases that.

The Pennsylvania liquor law states that a liquor license may only be issued in an area that has 15,000 population. The law permits sale of alcohol in a hotel that meets the regulations as to number of rooms, size of rooms, etc. The Smiths circumvented the problem by opening a 12-room motel, the minimum requisite.

The motel building once housed old chicken coops and garages. "Ours is the kind of place where folks don't care whether there's a television in the room," says Smith. "Our guests would rather sit on the porch and look at cows grazing in the fields."

Want Not, Waste Not in the Great Northwest

Wee Willie's on Whiskey Creek Road, near Tillamook, Ore., along the shores of beautiful Netarts Bay! What could be more quaint than this family drive-in run by Myrtle and Willie Williams?

"We keep costs at a minimum," says Myrt, "simply by using common sense. If we have too many raw french fries stocked up, we grind them up for clam chowder base. If banana splits aren't selling, we use the ripe fruit for banana bread. We have practically no waste. Even the biodegradable garbage is used for compost in our garden where we raise our own produce.

"Quality is never sacrificed, though," she went on, "everything is exactly as we'd want for our own family. Most of our menu items are home-made: our onion rings, our fries from fresh potatoes. Our seafoods are breaded just before frying; they're tastier that way. We even make our own hard ice cream because we like real flavor. I make toppings with fresh strawberries and raspberries. All our fruit shakes are made with fresh fruit."

Wee Willie hamburgers are best sellers. "We buy the whole steer and use it all in our burgers. And, of course, our clams and oysters are fresh from local beaches."

The building, volume and menu have all expanded together. "When we opened in 1966, Wee Willie's was indeed 'wee'," Myrt reminisces. "The first site was only 16 ft. by 24 ft. We had planned on take-out lunches with outside picnic tables. But I'd bake a few pies, too, and soon there was a big demand for them. I may bake as many as 30 a day now.

"I even took classes in cake decorating when it proved that many of our customers wanted to celebrate their big days at Wee Willie's," Myrt said. "We serve warm gingerbread, pumpkin bread and brownies."

Showmanship In The Sticks!

A seedy-looking brick structure just spitting distance from the railroad track in Redkey, Ind. (population: 1800, give or take), is really a restaurant called Shambarger's. Opened originally as a French cafe/bakery in 1885 by the grandfather of present owner John Shambarger, the eatery seats about 55 people; does business only three nights a week; charges $18.50 per head (no booze whatsoever); and grosses $75,000 annually. Reservations are a must, and booking a year in advance is not unusual.

The menu is at the owner's discretion, and with a brief intermission between the fifth and sixth courses—dinner—a seven-course epicurean affair lasting about five hours starts promptly at 7 p.m. During the "break," Shambarger invites patrons to tour Redkey. "It'll take about two minutes," he quips.

Shambarger himself is the secret behind this little-known restaurant's success. He is literally a one-man show. Touted by one reviewer as "the clown prince of haute cuisine," the 60-year-old showman's whacky theatrics are exceeded only by his culinary artistry. He does a running commentary and sings and dances as he prepares the food. He even costumes himself in different attire for each course: cheese fondue (a "veddy, veddy" mod outfit); guacamole dip (caballero regalia right down to a "Viva Zapata" moustache); corn fritters (stripped to the waist, sporting denim overalls and colorful bandana).

Shambarger maintains his pace despite a heart attack five years ago that worried him only because it might curb his booming enterprise. "If you like the food," he begs his guests, "don't tell anybody. We're already too busy!" In fact, the man's zest for his work and life is summed up in a memorable remark he made while greeting a group of diners one evening several years ago: "If I should collapse tonight, don't pay any attention. Just go right on having a good time."

Bavaria in Peoria? Jawohl! With Emphasis on Authenticity

King Ludwig II, with his penchant for castle-building, would have found a simpatico rival in James Jumer who has brought a bit of Bavaria to the heart of little ole Peoria.

Jumer's Castle Lodge has 110 rooms—five different types ranging from duplex "loft" rooms to junior suites, some boasting four-poster beds on daises. All rooms, done in blue, gold or red, are named after German provinces or cities. There are no numbers. Floors are dubbed after German "strasses" or streets. The main floor lobby is aptly called the Kurfurstendamm after Berlin's famous drag.

Elevator areas on each floor are gas-lit. Imported German-made oak "surrounds"; carved pillar-like door frames outside various guest rooms on each floor break the "monotony" of the hallways. Jumer's authenticity stretches to a $32,000 Mercedes-Benz limousine which chauffeurs guests to and from the Peoria airport.

A masterpiece of Bavarian design is the small enclosed courtyard, bordered by the restaurant, lodge and cocktail lounge, whose walls are muraled with colorful Alpine-esque scenes. In fact, almost everything in the lodge from the baroque paintings to antique armour and furniture has been imported.

The lodge runs about an 80% occupancy (rooms range from $17 to $40). Nearly 90% of the staff is local, yet back-of-the-house turnover is "terrible. Good chefs for this part of the world are hard to find," says General Manager Clif Hjort, "mainly because few want to live down here. We draw dishwashers, busboys and general waitress/waiter help from Bradley University, but we lose them either because they graduate or because study hours conflict."

Experiment in the Boondocks

A gigantic eating/drinking/entertainment complex (seating 1,000) called Pzazz is the talk of Burlington, Iowa! Population: 30,000.

There isn't one social element that can't be accommodated at Pzazz. The Redrat Saloon with nooky, dark corners and wall-to-wall peanut shells is a beer drinker's paradise; the Tiger Pit features a Las Vegas-style floor show; the plush Starlight Room boasts fine dining in softly lit tranquility; the Luau Room with bamboo ceilings and walls caters to family feeding—with a special addendum: a hot dog/hamburger window for kids who don't cotton to the more exotic smorgasbord fare; Les Artistes, an "upstairs garret" complete with skylight window and gypsy-clad waiters, sells quiche lorraine and fondues.

President of this sprawling dreamland is George Petrow.

"We've got everything under one roof, and there's something here for everyone. We get lots of private parties from nearby colleges, and we commission reps-on-campus for whatever business they send us.

"We plan similar complexes near Denver, Lincoln (Neb.) and Madison (Wisc.). Burlington is kind of a laboratory to see what works in the area and what we may emphasize in another location. For example, gourmet dining may go over well in Denver, but maybe smorgasbord would be more appealing in Lincoln. There's a market for this sort of all-encompassing complex in areas like this.

"We try to be innovative with our menu. We discovered cauliflower is popular around here, so we created deep fried cauliflower hors d'oeuvres. We offer an Early Bird dinner for $2.50. We originally had 52 entrees on our menu, but our three chefs couldn't keep up with the volume. So we scaled it down to the 28 most popular items.

"Our staff consists of young people. We start them in the Country Cafe Coffee Shop or Pzazzitorium (rock music area) first, then move them into the Tiger Pit (for waitresses) or the Starlight Room (for waiters). The labor market is good because we draw from surrounding campuses. If we find a couple of kids showing a genuine interest in the business, we've got nine entirely different commercial foodservice operations to use as training areas. We've got a few on that track right now. When they graduate, they'll stay on full-time and, when we build in Lincoln or Denver, we hope to use them to staff those operations."

Gourmet Dining on a Runway

Small town elegance? A complex of miniature spires and steeples, perched on the fringes of its own private 2400-foot airstrip, separated by a country highway! A virtual museum of stained glass, ceramics and inlaid tile tables in the center of Florida's citrus belt! That about describes Chalet Suzanne in Lake Wales, but . . .

It's gourmet dining—not decor or setting—that is the life root of this restaurant. Baked grapefruit with cinnamon; mint ice served with sizzling steaks; Crepes Suzette a la maison; and savory soups and sauces, prepared in the Chalet's own cannery from closely-guarded family recipes and sold throughout the U.S. and Europe, are just a few of the epicurean lures that delight customers, 15% of whom actually fly in by plane for the experience.

Lunch includes grand extras such as baked grapefruit, Romaine soup, lighter-than-air rolls and apricot flavored Crepes Suzanne; these plus broiled tomato, salad and rum pie come with dinner. The famed soups—14 varieties—are the only ones in the world to receive the Gourmet Society Culinary Merit Award and were among the first terrestrial soups on the moon, courtesy of Apollo 15.

The Chalet, which also rents rooms—30 of them—is operated by Carl Hinshaw, a veteran World War II pilot and now a private plane dealer, his wife Vita and their two children Eric and Tina. Eric handles busboy and kitchen chores. Tina, a college student in home economics, is a hostess and works the salad counter.

New York hotel clerk (to bell-boy): "See what the rumpus is in 620."

Bell-boy (returning): "Col. Bluegrass is mad because there's a pitcher of water in his room."

Clerk: "But that's not to drink. That's to wash in."

Bell-boy: "That's what I told him and he got madder still. He wanted to know if they thought he was a heathen. He said he washed before he started away from home."—*Life.**

The Hotel World, November 30, 1889, p. 9. Reprinted with permission, *Hotel and Motel Management*.

SOCIAL PRIORITIES AND EXECUTIVE MYOPIA*

MARVIN E. BRAUN**

The business executive stands at the center of a network of relationships extending within and without his organization. Internally, he deals with employees and stockholders. Externally, he interacts with customers, creditors, the business-financial community at large, government and the general public. Upon him converge the scrutiny and expectations of these varied groups. While in the long run their objectives may be complementary, they often have divergent or even opposing short term goals. Implicit in the decision and policy-making activities of the executive is the need to structure priorities in terms of whose interests to consider and favor.

Much has been written concerning the legitimate behavior of a business organization in a capitalistic society. We are aware that a firm is primarily an economic institution pursuing goals related to profitability and liquidity. For the most part the business-financial community evaluates management's performance in terms of these criteria. Lapses in financial performance as perceived by stockholders and creditors will usually not be tolerated for more than a few years. As such, executives necessarily and immediately focus on near term financial objectives. By so doing, the welfare of some groups is automatically relegated to residual positions in the line of

---

*Personnel Journal, August 1972, pp. 599-602. Reprinted with permission.
**Marvin E. Braun served in several engineering and administrative positions in industry before entering the academic world. He was a faculty member of Northwestern University's School of Management prior to becoming Assistant Professor. Dr. Braun received his M.S. from the University of Pittsburgh and the Ph.D. from Ohio State University.

priority. One such group has traditionally been the general public. With little if any short run leverage to exert, it could be conveniently ignored by managers in deference to short term economic expediency.

This state of affairs has tended to nurture a breed of executives with a severe case of social near-sightedness. That is, aside from those factors which directly relate to the marketing of a product, executives have tended to exclude the changing values of society from their decision equations. They have resisted recognition of the fact that business in the course of discharging its traditional economic functions impinges on society in a multitude of ways. Accordingly, they could and would not acknowledge their responsibilities implicit in these interactions.

Such myopic conceptualization of the social role of business has in the past been neither particularly unethical, illegal or irrational. Criteria of responsibility and accountability are qualitative and relative. The question of what constitutes proper business conduct is contingent upon the attitudes of society. Public thinking, concerning the obligations of business, can and does change in response to changes in the social, political and economic climate. Historically, such changes have taken place slowly. In the past decade and a half, however, there has been a dramatic acceleration of the rate at which society has been re-specifying the behavioral code of its institutions.

New Areas of Contention

As a result of this phenomenon, a remarkable number of business related issues have rocketed to prominence in the public consciousness. Many have evolved into areas of conflict between society at large and various business interests. This course of events can be attributed to several causes. Foremost is the sudden apprehension of many that physical and social disaster may be the end result of certain entrenched business behavioral patterns. In addition, a general suspicion and intolerance have developed toward the institutions which society had appointed as caretakers of its economic, political and military power. A great deal of emotion is involved in this development.

Let us highlight some areas of contention that were practically unheard of only a score of years ago:

Rights of Minorities. The handwriting has been on the wall since the mid-1950's. Business has awkwardly and unevenly yielded to public (and governmental) pressure. At this very moment, the technical service organization of a major oil company is wringing its hands in trepidation of the recently received directive from headquarters to hire a female engineer.

Deceitful Practices. Truth in lending, deceitful TV advertising, and deceitful packaging practices are just a few of the areas in which public pressure has forced government to impose new stratas of regulation in recent years. Other aspects not directly related to the marketing of a product, such as the ethics (not necessarily the legality) of contributions to political campaigns, have come under greater public scrutiny.

Public Safety. Ralph Nader may go too far at times, but there is no doubt that many industries are extremely vulnerable in this area.

Public Nuisance. In Chicago, a major corporation was on the verge of erecting a skyscraper which would have significantly impaired the television reception of large sections of the metropolitan area. Public outcry and the filing of lawsuits has forced management to "re-study" the problem. One can also cite increased public disapprobation toward high noise levels, advertising signs, the utilization of potential recreational areas and the destruction of old landmarks for commercial purposes.

Price Controls. Violations are widespread by those who do not come under direct surveillance of the Control Board. "Price controls are all right for the next guy."

Ecology. This involves rather awesome economic demands for some sectors of the business community. In spite of a decade of warning, business has continued to invest heavily in the development and promotion of new products and manufacturing methods that violate ecological propriety. Practically every industry is faced with the need for massive investment in new equipment and technology which they are not financially prepared to undertake. There has been an almost total absence of long-term planning in this area. One can perceive a desperate rear guard action on the part of business as it attempts to formulate policies and acquire resources to cope with this dilemma.

Some Recommendations

The rules changed in a comparatively short span of time, with business leadership failing to recognize the new dimensions of its social responsibility. There is little value in dwelling on their previous lack of foresight and insight. The essential question now is how well are managers and their organizations adjusting to the parameters under which they must function? Many members of government, the public and the press seem to feel that it is not happening quickly or efficiently enough. There seems to be widespread belief that, aside from economic and technological reasons, executives are reluctant to give up their myopic view of social interaction.

Since executives are human beings and, therefore, could be expected to identify with the desires of the public at large, one might find their behavior curious. The explanation lies in the fact that individual careers and organizational performance are attuned to the standards upon which the financial community evaluates the economic worth of a firm, i.e., near term profitability and liquidity. It would seem that all parties must come to realize that the business system itself is integrally bound up with the whole of American economy and society. None can prosper in the long run without a vital united society. Near term financial measures must be embellished with longer term criteria.

The present public attitudes will not pass quickly. Our nation's history indicates that areas of conflict between business and the public will eventually be resolved in favor of the public interest. The economic ramifications will be felt by each firm. Operational criteria of profitability and liquidity remain valid and relevant. It is a matter of placing them in a longer term perspective. This general notion needs to be promulgated throughout the business and financial world.

Within each business organization some initial steps should be taken. The following are proposed:
1. Set up strategies for detecting and verifying changes in

social attitudes and then translating this data into tangible long-term plans.
2. Formulate company policies with enough flexibility to accommodate new social truths as they become manifest.
3. Evaluate executive initiative in terms of long-run social-economic realities, as well as near-term financial objectives.
4. Create industry codes and mechanisms which will foster cooperation and permit firms to maintain their competitive positions during periods of adjustment to new social values.
5. As a business reality, engage in public relations to brief the financial community of the long-run economic benefits implicit in socially responsive projects. (How much better off would numerous firms be today if they had seriously undertaken smoke and sewage control efforts ten or even five years ago.)

The Right of Private Property Is at Stake

The basic sanction under which American business operates is the right of private property. This is essentially the right to own and utilize property in the personal interests of individuals or groups. It is the basis of the decentralization of economic and political power in our society. This right of private property, however, is not necessarily inherent in the sense that human nature requires its existence. It so happens that our society believes that the optimum allocation of economic resources can be brought about through its existence. This notion is tentative and subject to erosion.

Due to an inadequate management response to the public will, there is presently a tendency for standards of business conduct to be determined for management rather than by management. This inevitably leads to greater political control and ultimately to the loss of the right of private property. It may not be possible to arrest the ominous direction of our present course of events. If it is to happen, one necessary ingredient is a breed of business executives with social farsightedness.

COMPETENCE: THE COHESIVE OF FUTURE ORGANIZATIONS*

ROBERT M. FULMER**

LESLIE W. RUE***

Charles Kettering once remarked, "I am interested in the future because I plan to spend the rest of my life there." Most people share this general interest in the future. The manager, in particular, knows that his survival is largely dependent upon his predictions and forecasts. Because of the increased pace of change and technological development, managers and key individuals from all institutions in society are progressively becoming more concerned with what will happen in the future.

Traditionally, references to the future cause most businessmen to think about sales predictions, staffing forecasts, and other statistics which measure the performance of their particular company. Furthermore, executives tend to think of

---

*Personnel Journal, April 1973, pp. 264-273. Reprinted with permission.

**Robert M. Fulmer is a past President of the Southern Management Association and a former research associate of the National Industrial Conference Board and the American Management Association. In addition to his teaching responsibilities as Professor of Management, Georgia State University, Atlanta, Dr. Fulmer is a Director of Executive Training & Counsel, Inc. He is the author of *Managing Associations for the 1980's* and many professional publications. Dr. Fulmer holds the MBA from the University of Florida and the Ph.D. from the University of California, Los Angeles.

***Leslie W. Rue has worked as a data processing project officer for the U. S. Army Management Systems Support Agency at the Pentagon, and as an industrial engineer for Delta Airlines. He holds the B.I.E. and M.S.I.E. degrees from Georgia Institute of Technology and is working toward his Ph.D. in Business Administration at Georgia State where he is Instructor in the School of Business Administration.

these statistics as they relate to the present organizational structure. As sales and staffing forecasts increase, managers interpret this as growth and expansion of the present organizational pyramid, with continued application of current concepts of authority, leadership and administration. Such naive faith in the stability of the status quo is a dangerous pitfall for all extrapolists who assume that the future will be like the past and fail to consider the impact of opposing trends or potential discontinuities.

Are premises which assume the continuation of the current rule of authority and organizational structure justified and inconsequential or dangerous naivete on the part of top management?

Management and the New Morality

The so-called "new morality" of modern theology has been accompanied by a challenge to the traditional foundations for moral and managerial decision making.[1] One cannot seriously question the methods for making decisions without first questioning the authority for making them.

Until recent years, there was little question as to the source of a manager's authority.[2] In 1946, Henri Fayol, the French management pioneer, spoke of official authority as being derived from office.[3] Peterson and Plowman described authority in the United States as originating with the will of the people, and slowing down through the constitution, and corporate laws and so on down the line.[4] Ralph Davis described authority as being derived from the right of private property.[5] O'Donnell looks on authority as being ultimately derived

---

1. Robert M. Fulmer and Charles Wellborn, "The New Morality and the New Managers," *Business Horizons*, Vol. 10 (Winter, 1967), p. 98
2. Cyril O'Donnell, "The Source of Managerial Authority," *Political Science Quarterly*, Vol. 67 (1952), p. 573.
3. Henri Fayol, *General and Industrial Management*, (London: Sir Isaac Pitman and Sons, Ltd., 1949), p. 21.
4. Elmore Petersen and E. Grosvenor Plowman, *Business Organization and Management*, rev. ed., (Chicago: Richard D. Irwin, Inc., 1949), p. 62.
5. Ralph C. Davis, *The Fundamentals of Top Management*, (New York: Harper and Brothers, 1951), p. 285.

from the nature of man and being transmitted through the basic social structures of the country.[1] All of these views have contributed to what has become known as the formal or classical theory of authority.

Acceptance Theory

The formal theory of authority was first seriously questioned as early as 1938 by Chester Barnard. Barnard suggested that authority exists by virtue of subordinates granting authority by their willingness to accept orders or directions.[2] He further stated that the subordinate's acceptance of authority is subject to the following requirements: that he understands the order, that he believes it is consistent with the organization's purpose, that it is compatible with his own interests, and that he is mentally and physically able to comply with it. This particular concept was labeled the "acceptance theory" and further promoted by Tannenbaum in 1950.[3] Fulmer and Wellborn have presented evidence to substantiate the evolution from absolute or formal theories of authority toward the acceptance theory.[4] They point out that the once small trickle of rebellion in this country grew into a virtual torrent during the decade of the 1960's. In particular, these authors point to the fields of civil rights, labor negotiations, military involvement, and university administration for examples of the dramatic mushrooming of individuals and groups exercising what had previously been primarily an academic right to challenge formal authority.

Because authority directly affects the scaler chain, the span of control, and the communication channels of the organization, it stands to reason that a shift in the nature of authority will be reflected in organizational structures.

On the surface, we can see no basic differences in the organizational structures described by Fayol, Mooney, and Reiley, and their contemporaries and the organizational

---

1. O'Donnell, *op. cit.*, p. 588.
2. Chester I. Barnard, *The Functions of the Executive*, (Cambridge, Mass.: Harvard University Press, 1938), p. 167.
3. Robert Tannenbaum, "Managerial Decision-Making," *Journal of Business*, Vol. 23 (January, 1950), pp. 23-39.
4 Fulmer and Wellborn, *op. cit.*, pp. 97-104.

structures of today. The organizational charts look the same—both are in the basic shape of a pyramid.

Of course, "organizational structure" and "organizational chart" are not synonymous terms. Organizational structure goes much beyond the organizational chart and includes not only the functions of the organization, but also the human and physical elements of the organization and their interrelationships.

Most organizational charts represent only a part of the total organizational structure. If we examine the current organizational structure, as defined above, and compare it to that of Fayol's era, we can detect subtle but substantial changes. These changes have largely come from the contribution of computer technology and new knowledge of the behavioral sciences.

Although there is no universal agreement on a theory of authority, there has been an obvious shift away from absolute adherence to the hard-line classical approach.

Major Impacts on Authority

Merely observing that changes have occurred with regard to the sources of authority does not provide the clarity of a crystal ball. To make predictions, we must first understand why these changes have occurred. The shifts can be explained partially by applying Maslow's now famous hierarchy of needs.[1] (See Figure 1, p. 60.)

From the days of Frederick W. Taylor in the early 20th century through the Great Depression, formal authority was at its height. The gang boss or manager was never questioned and rarely disobeyed. As the saying goes, "times were hard," and the workman could not afford to lose his job. Welfare programs were nonexistent and the unemployment rate ran as high as 25 percent. Looking at Maslow's hierarchy of needs, it is evident that the great majority of workers at this time were primarily concerned with the physical needs. Putting bread on their tables and clothing on their backs were the primary thoughts of these workers. How can a human

---

1. Abraham Maslow, "A Theory of Human Motivation," *Psychology Review*, Vol. 50 (July, 1943), pp. 370-396.

who is predominantly occupied with the physical needs question the superior whose decision can control the survival of his family?

The period from the end of the depression through the second World War saw the economy recover and unemployment fall. As a result, the physical needs of the majority were fulfilled. However, the war kept the general level of need satisfaction at the "safety and security" level. As opposed to the Viet Nam conflict, the public felt that the second World War threatened the safety of the entire country and its inhabitants. How can a man who genuinely sees the safety of his home and country threatened question the actions of his superiors?

With the close of World War II, the continued growth of the economy, and the increased level of education, a great

FIGURE 1.
Maslow's hierarchy of needs and corresponding periods of dominance.

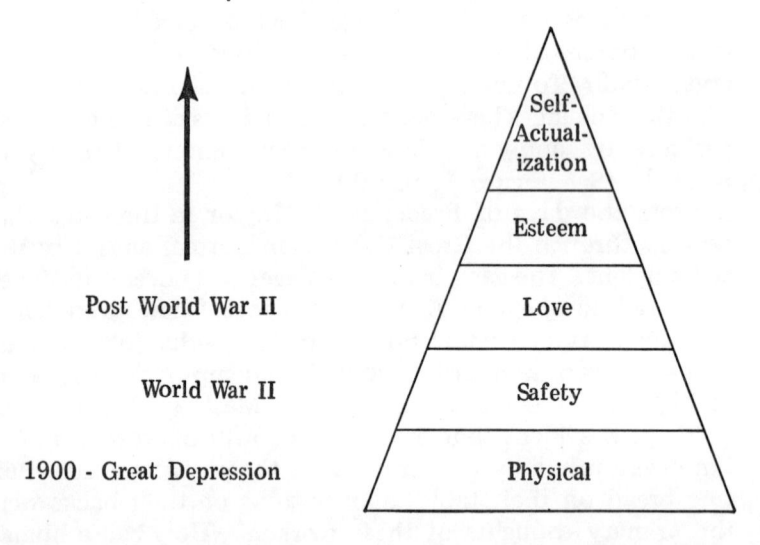

Post World War II

World War II

1900 - Great Depression

Self-Actualization
Esteem
Love
Safety
Physical

Source: Adapted from Abraham Maslow, "A Theory of Human Motivation," *Psychology Review*, Vol. 50, (July, 1943), pp. 370-396.

many workers began to move higher up Maslow's hierarchy. The more the worker became concerned with love, esteem, and self-actualization, the more natural it was for him to question. In this light, the questioning of authority should come as no surprise! The whole idea of the "new morality" is related to this trend. Only after the majority of the people had moved out of the lower levels of need satisfaction did the "new morality" concept appear.

New Morality or Old Immorality?

It is interesting to note that recently the popularity of riots, rebellion, and the new morality has subsided. This phenomenon is readily explained by the recent recession. As the economy began to fade and unemployment began to rise, many people were forced to revert to a lower level on the hierarchy. As a result, the freedom to question was hindered. As the economy recovers, we will undoubtedly see a new surge of unrest.

The phrase "new morality" usually conjures up images of free love, LSD, and student riots. Superficial observers glibly dismiss the entire movement with the comment, "The new morality is merely the old immorality condoned." As a catch-phrase that has struck the public fancy, the term has, not surprisingly, been appropriated by many writers to describe diverse points of view. Lawrence Lipton comes close to expressing the common connotation when he characterizes the new morality as "the erotic revolution." But Ayn Rand refers to capitalism as the new morality, and serious philosophers discuss "the new revolution in ethical theory." Donald Meiklejohn defines the new morality as the achievement of maximum freedom in public and private life, and Joseph Fletcher has subtitled his popular volume on situational ethics "The New Morality."

At the heart of the new morality is the thrust toward uninhibited freedom of expression. Harvey Cox's religious best-seller, *The Secular City*, analyzes the modern temper in terms of man's desire to be free to decide for himself—free from "anything that binds us uncritically to inherited conventions."

The challenge to the traditional foundations for moral decision-making has come as part of the same broad movement which questions the absolute standard of authority in management. No longer can it be assumed that specific and unchanging rules can be established to govern human activities in any area, regardless of their context and environment. Instead, it is reasoned (by the new moralists) that each situation is, in some important sense, unique. While the specific situation must be interpreted in the light of historical experience, general ethical principles, and established moral norms, the peculiar circumstances which provide uniqueness must be squarely faced. There can be no irresponsible hiding behind a legalistic prescription.[1]

Authority, Authority—Who Gets the Authority?

It seems clear that increased education, changing moral perspectives, greater affluence and higher order needs orientation all suggest the likelihood of decreasing dependence on the power of formal authority and legalism. On the other hand, a continued trend toward greater freedom from formal authority leads ultimately to antinomianism and anarchy.[2] Both the morality and mentality of management must be questioned if we assume that freedom and democracy are essential characteristics of tomorrow's organization.

Freedom is always limited. Societies of the past have often passed through four stages of a life cycle: freedom, self-indulgence, social disorder, and tyranny. The American culture moved past the stage of self-indulgence to a serious flirtation with social disorder in the mid and late sixties. Opposition to this trend was evidenced at the ballot box. Additionally, the recent economic recession pulled many dissident citizens—especially the young—back to a more basic concern with physiological and security needs. As the eco-

---

1. This section is adapted from Fulmer and Wellborn, *op. cit.*, p. 98. For additional information and references concerning the "new morality" see *Challenge to Morality*, Charles Wellborn, ed. (Tallahassee, Fla.: Florida State University Press, 1962).
2. Joseph Fletcher, *Situation Ethics*, (Philadelphia: The Westminster Press, 1966), p. 22.

nomy begins to improve, the possibility of a new surge of unrest will increase.

Despite predictions to the contrary, this trend will not continue unchecked until workers, students, and citizens of capitalistic and communistic countries alike dwell in utopian democratic freedom.

There are important countervailing influences. First, there is the impact of deep cultural preferences for order which tend to be evidenced at election times. Secondly, the increasing rapidity of change on all fronts, especially the growing prevalence of temporary project organizations, mitigates against the long-term programs which call for greater democratization. Finally, the computer has also had an impact on authority. From the days of Alfred Sloan until the computer began to make significant contributions to management's information technology, the emphasis was almost entirely on decentralization. This move toward decentralization was motivated by necessity rather than by social issues or moral concerns. The existence of the computer offers the capability, but not necessarily the rationale, for a move to recentralization.

Regardless of the other implications of computerization, this innovation has definitely increased the span of control and the competence of the top management team. Consequently, it is now possible for executives in home offices to be constantly aware of performance in distant operations. The computer gives them the ability to participate in the planning process and to monitor progress made toward the realization of these plans. This additional competence may be a key ingredient in assessing organizational futures.

There is no question that students, workers, soldiers, and government employees have resisted arbitrary imposition of formal authority. But has this been opposition to authority *per se* or has it been opposition to authority which was seen as invalid because it lacked the validity created by competence? "Because I say so" will become increasingly less acceptable as an answer to the eternal question, "Why?" Authority has been historically viewed as the cement that holds organizations together. Tomorrow's management must clearly utilize a better grade of cement if it is to maintain order and progress! The academic argument that competence is a characteristic of leadership rather than a condition of authority has little practical relevance for the once and future manager. Throughout the future, managers who have reached their level of incompetence can expect even greater resistance to their plans, while the competent, well-tempered executive will find technical and moral justification for his proposals.

Competence Brings Results

Actually, the seeds for this changing concept of competence have already begun to bear fruit in many organizations. In companies utilizing a program of product management, extensive, multi-million dollar market strategy proposals are developed by young brand managers, often in their late twenties or early thirties.

While proposals developed by these young men may be approved by three of four successive levels of management, competent proposals (or those perceived as competent because of the reputation for competence enjoyed by the proposal's author) are routinely approved.

In these consumer-product, marketing-oriented firms, top management must rely on its respect for the competence of subordinates because there is simply not enough time to adequately investigate all aspects of all recommendations. In engineering-based, technically-oriented firms, top management is further restricted because it cannot expect to match (or even to always understand) the technical competence of highly specialized subordinates. Thus, the general competence of the individual, rather than the authority of his position or the quality of his work, may be the real source of the practical power he can exert in the organization.

Administration or Management?

In much of the academic literature, the term "administration" is used interchangeably with "management." The different translations of Fayol's classic work very well exemplify this point.[1] Today, however, the terms are beginning to

---
1. The title of Fayol's classic book has been translated as *General and Industrial Management* and as *Industrial and General Administration*.

take on new implications. The administrator can be pictured as performing well-structured, routinized functions. On the other hand, the manager, held in somewhat more awe, is pictured as performing the more mystical functions of planning and controlling.* Analyzing these two positions in terms of Koontz and O'Donnell's five management functions,[1] we see the administrator as performing the organizing, directing, and staffing functions, while the manager is primarily concerned with the planning and controlling functions.

The increasing divergence of the terms administration and management can be attributed to the increased pace of change and the computer. The increased pace of change has forced management to place greater emphasis on the future through the planning function. The expanded size of companies has caused increased concern for control. More sophisticated planning and control have both been made possible through the computer. As a result of these factors, top management has increasingly taken on the planning and controlling functions and pushed the "administrative" function farther down the line.

Focus on the Future

Although there have been many individual expressions of opinion concerning the future of management, there has been a dearth of precise statements concerning the time or probability of potential events affecting the practice of management.

To help in remedying this deficiency, one of the authors recently supervised a project which utilized the Delphi technique to add precision to the major predictions concerning

---

*At this period, both authors, Kreck and McCracken, view administration as the top function in an organization. It is in the corporate head office, with the president and the vice presidents, that policies are established and future actions are planned. It is in the individual hotel, motel, or restaurant of the above corporation where we expect to find management which carries out the directives of the corporation. We do want to underline that management in the individual operation also plans, directs, etc., although on a different level.

1. Harold Koontz and Cyril O'Donnell, *Principles of Management* 4th ed., (New York: McGraw-Hill Book Co., 1968), p. 1.

the future of management and administration.[1] The expert panel was drawn from the Fellows of the Academy of Management—a group of distinguished senior management professors who are recognized as having made significant contributions to the discipline.

This Delphi study is combined with a concise overview of the literature to provide the basis for the authors' view of management's future.

The literature overview is primarily intended to familiarize the reader with some of the conflicting predictions which are prevalent in the field.

Centralized Decentralization?

Many of the arguments and predictions concerning authority in the future deal with the issue of centralization versus decentralization. Furthermore, these arguments are often largely colored by the particular author's perceived impact of automation and the computer on the future.

Leavitt and Whisler, in their now classic article, predict a move toward recentralization in the large firms of the future. They predict

. . . that large industrial organizations will recentralize, that top managers will take on an even larger proportion of the innovating, planning, and other "creative" functions than they have now.[2]

Burch takes a view of the future similar to that of Leavitt and Whisler.

Let's see what's going to happen to executives in the computer age.

---

1. James Earl Morrow, *A Delphi Approach to the Future of Management*, Unpublished Ph.D. Dissertation, Georgia State University, Atlanta, Georgia, 1971. All references to the Delphi Panel are from this source.
2. Harold J. Leavitt and Thomas L. Whisler, "Management in the 1980's," *Harvard Business Review*, Vol. 36 (November-December, 1958), p. 41. In 1970, Whisler published two books. *The Impact of Computers on Organizations*, (New York: Praeger Publishers, 1970) and *Information Technology and Organizational Change*, (Belmont, Calif.: Wadsworth Publishing Co., Inc., 1970) in which he updated his 1958 predictions. His revised predictions are similar but based on a much longer time frame.

> *Among other things "recentralization" will tax top management talents.*[1]

Kosmetsky, writing in retrospect from the year 2000, also predicts a move toward recentralization.

> *As computer applications spread during the 1970's, companies recentralized authority and control.*[2]

Other authors assess the impact of automation and computers from an opposing viewpoint. Dearden states,

> *I seriously doubt that the increasing use of computers and related information technology will affect top management's ability to control divisional operations, and in particular that it will bring about a trend to recentralization.*[3]

In Morrow's study, eight members of the Fellows of the Academy of Management felt that information technology would lead to a greater degree of centralization in management decision-making, while sixteen others expressed the belief that computerization would contribute to greater decentralization. There is obviously no widespread agreement among the writers in the field or among management scholars.

Interpretations Vary

One possible explanation of this disagreement is that the contributors do not interpret the question in the same manner. By this, we mean that a scholar whose major interest lies in the area of control might be (either consciously or unconsciously) predicting the impact of computerization and automation on the control function. The same bias would be natural for the scholar whose main interest revolves around direction or any other function. We can hypothesize that predictions are largely influenced by the prophet's own interests. Working under the assumption of this hypothesis, we attempted to classify the members of the Delphi Panel according to the management functions with which they are most closely aligned. Although the interests of the Panel defied a simple two-factor classification, it does appear that the scho-

---
1. Gilbert Burck, "Management Will Never Be the Same Again," *Fortune*, Vol. 70, (August, 1961), p. 124.
2. George Kozmetsky, "The Reflections of a 21st Century Manager," *The Futurist*, Vol. 3 (June, 1969), p. 74.
3. John Dearden, "Computers: No Impact on Divisional Control," *Harvard Business Review*, Vol. 37 (January-February, 1967), p. 99.

lars specifically aligned with the controlling and planning functions tended to predict a trend toward recentralization, while those aligned with the organizing, staffing, and directing functions tended to predict a move toward increased decentralization. This finding is perfectly consistent with the concept of management versus administration. The functions of top management are becoming more decentralized. The end result would be an organization structure with centralized decentralization! This type of structure would also be consistent with the mood of the new morality in that the decentralized administration would foster flexibility and remove the undesired high level of structure when properly implemented. There should be little objection to competent, centralized control and planning as long as the administrative functions are handled on a decentralized, personal basis.

Deciding Who Decides

Numerous predictions regarding the changing nature of middle management have been made by knowledgeable management authors. They all predict changes of some magnitude or form in the job content of middle managers.

Leavitt and Whisler predict the roles of all management levels will change substantially and particularly the role of middle management.

A radical reorganization of middle-management levels should occur, with certain classes of middle-management jobs moving downward in status and compensation (because they will require less autonomy and skill), while other classes move upward into the top-management group.[1]

Simon forecasts a decline in the relative number of middle-management positions, but concludes that the relative number of over-all management positions will remain unchanged.

We might even conclude that management and other professional activities, taken collectively, may constitute about the same part of the total spectrum of occupations a generation hence as they do now. But there is reason to believe that the kinds of activities that now characterize

---

1. Leavitt and Whisler, *op. cit.*, p. 41.

middle management will be more completely automated than others and hence will come to have a smaller part in the whole management position.[1]

Kozmetsky, speaking of mass-production industries, sees just the opposite effect on middle management.

Job Content Changes

A third of all working people were in these industries by the year 2000, and virtually all could be considered supervisors or middle-managers.[2]

A third viewpoint maintains that the relative position of the various management levels will not change, but that the job content of management jobs will change appreciably. Anshen best personifies this viewpoint.

I think that the primary effect of the evolution will be in the content of managers' jobs rather than in dramatic changes in the skeleton of organization structures.[3]

Concerning the question of middle management, the Delphi panel again failed to reach total agreement. Basically conservative in their opinions, the consensus of the panel was that middle managers will probably remain, but that their decision making will be reduced in some routine situations and expanded in areas where the computer assists them in making more complex decisions. Only four percent predicted that the decision-making role of the middle manager would be virtually eliminated by the year 2000.

Analyzing the Delphi predictions and the literature simultaneously suggests that there may not be as much real disagreement as a cursory analysis might indicate. There is general agreement that middle management job content will change with some of the jobs becoming more routinized and some becoming more demanding. The disagreement comes in deciding what to call middle management! Will we still call

---

1. Herbert A. Simon, "The Corporation: Will It Be Managed by Machine?" *Management of Human Resources,* Pigors, Myers, and Malm (eds.), (New York: McGraw-Hill Book Co., 1964), p. 223.
2. Kozmetsky, *op. cit.,* p. 74.
3. Melvin Anshen, "Organization Structure and the New Decision-Making Technology," *Management: Organization and Planning,* Bowan and Fillerup. (New York: McGraw-Hill Book Co., 1963), p. 34.

down-graded, routinized management functions "middle management? or will we develop a more humble title? And how about the middle management jobs which gain stature because of improved, computer-assisted competence? Do these become top management jobs even if there are the same number of positions above them in the organization? In this light, it seems that the supervisors or middle managers referred to by Kozmetsky are precisely the same managers found on the lower portions of Leavitt and Whisler's predicted organization of the future. In other words, the managers who are between the supervisory and top executive levels in the firms of the future will still be in the middle even though the nature of their work is significantly altered.

Up the Pyramid or Wheel or What?

Will the conventional pyramid predominate or will a new structure evolve in the post-industrial society? Writers making predictions on this subject are predominantly influenced by one of two factors, automation and the computer or the behavioral sciences.

Logically following from their predicted demise of middle-management's role, Leavitt and Whisler envision the future organization chart as a football balanced upon the point of a church bell.

Within the football (the top staff organization) problems of coordination, individual autonomy, group decision making, and so on should arise more intensely than ever. We expect they will be dealt with quite independently of the bell portion of the company, with distinctly different methods of remuneration, control, and communication.[1]

Again referring to the mass-production industries, Kozmetsky adds to his projected growth of middle management the prediction that top management will have increased authority.

The top manager had an enormous amount of authority, compared with the top manager of the 1960's. All lines on the organization chart led to his office.[2]

---

1. Leavitt and Whisler, *op. cit.*, p. 43.
2. Kozmetsky, *op. cit.*, p. 74.

Farmer describes modern, highly advanced firms as approaching an egg-like organizational structure.[1] He also predicts that in highly advanced firms the workers at the bottom have been automated out, thus shifting the structural weight to the middle area. Farmer sees this trend continuing until the structural weight eventually shifts to top levels of management.

The future firm may well resemble some sort of inverted pyramid—no one at the bottom, a few at the middle, and most persons at the top.[2]

Pyramid Out of Touch

Perhaps because of greater influence from the social and behavioral sciences, Bennis predicts the present bureaucratic, pyramidal arrangement is out of touch with contemporary realities.[3]

Meggison, basing his predictions on a changing and more desirable working climate, predicts the pyramid will be replaced by some type of wheel shape.

Organizations will become larger, more interrelated and complex, and will assume different shapes. The organizational relationships will tend to approximate the wheel shape rather than the pyramid.[4]

Seventy-five percent of Morrow's panel predicted that the organizations in the year 2000 would still be in the basic shape of the pyramid.

Twenty percent predicted a shape similar to the football-on-a-bell with the remaining five percent predicting the wheel or inverted-pyramid form.

To date, neither the computer nor social pressure has caused the changes predicted in the late 50's and early 60's.

---

1. Richard D. Farmer, *Management in the Future*, (Belmont, Calif.: Wadsworth Publishing Co., Inc., 1967), p. 80. It is interesting to note that Farmer sees the present highly advanced firms in much the same light as Kozmetsky foresees future mass production industries.
2. *Ibid.*, p. 80.
3. Warren G. Bennis, "Beyond Bureaucracy," *Transaction*, Vol. 2 (July-August, 1965), pp. 31-35.
4. Leon C. Meggison, *Personnel: A Behavioral Approach to Administration*, (Homewood, Ill.: Richard D. Irwin, 1967), p. 663.

In fact, some of the early futurists have already revised their predictions.[1] Just as no other great technological discovery or social movement has completely revolutionized the American system of organization, it now appears that neither the computer nor the new morality will achieve that goal. Change will come as a result of these inputs; but, as in the past, it will not occur overnight. As Harold Koontz has commented, "Some percentages may be eliminated through more sophisticated and better/wiser span of management—maybe five—fifteen but certainly not fifty percent."[2] Contrary to some past predictions, the lower level jobs are not likely to be automated out—not merely because it may be mechanically impossible, but also because it is not consistent with the new morality. These jobs offer the managers in the new morality generation immunity from the politics and interactions of the hierarchical structure which they claim to deplore. Also, the social status of a position is becoming less important as emphasis is being directed to higher order needs.

Throughout this article, attention has been focused on five sets of opposing polarities. Our analysis has led to these conclusions:

1. *Formal authority versus acceptance authority.* Authority is definitely shifting from the hard-line classical approach toward the more liberal acceptance theory. Rather than continuing indefinitely, this evolution will lead to superior-subordinate relationships becoming increasingly dependent on the competence of both parties. This marriage between the concepts of formal and acceptance theories will give birth to a tough-minded breed of authority which recognizes the rights of the governed while exacting responsibility of them. Increased competence will lead to increased confidence which, in turn, leads to order without oppression and authority without autocracy.

2. *Centralization versus decentralization.* The computer is basically neutral concerning the focus of authority. It will

---

1. Warren G. Bennis, "A Funny Thing Happened On the Way to the Future," *American Psychologist*, Vol. 25, (July, 1970), pp. 598-608.
2. Harold Koontz, A response to the Delphi Study reported in Morrow, *op. cit.*, p. 226.

work toward either end depending on the philosophy of its employer. It does, however, help give both top and middle managers the competence to better perform in their respective jobs.

3. *Management versus administration.* The firm of the future will have centralized top management functions (planning and control) and decentralized administrative functions (organizing, staffing, and directing).

4. *Middle management versus top management.* Some of the functions performed by today's middle managers will be routinized, while others will become more demanding. The result will be a redefinition of middle management and greater expectations for managers at all levels. The role of middle management will not be eliminated or significantly reduced. Rather, increasingly competent middle managers will assume more and more administrative authority and ultimately will have greater responsibility for planning decentralized operations. Today's top managers already spend large amounts of time in dealing with the demands of diverse societal institutions. The predicted role of middle managers will free top executives to do an even better job of these external expectations.

5. *The pyramid versus the "new" organizations.* The changing role of middle management, the computer, and the new morality will cause a gradual erosion of the organization pyramid, but probably with all the speed associated with the erosion of the original Egyptian prototypes. In other words, the dominance of the organization pyramid is likely to endure throughout this century and well into the next.

The past continues to serve as a prologue to the future. But just as it has been necessary to "study the past or be doomed to repeat it," it is essential that the manager consider the future or be doomed to destroy it. The future—even more than the past—belongs to those who are prepared for it. The meek may inherit the earth but the competent will control it.

HOTEL AND RESTAURANT MANAGEMENT IN THE SOVIET UNION*

LOTHAR A. KRECK[1]

INTRODUCTION

The information which provided the basis for this article was collected by the author during a two-week stay in Moscow in the summer of 1973. The author is very appreciative of the cooperation he received from most of the managerial personnel of certain hotels and restaurants in Moscow and especially from the Deputy Director for Advanced Courses from Intourist, which is the organization responsible for foreign travel in the USSR.

The collected information comes primarily from visits and interviews which took place in four hotels and their restaurants, a point to be explained later, and also from informal visits to a number of other hotels and restaurants, all in Moscow. Some of the hotels and restaurants visited and studied were of considerable size: 3000 rooms, 1000 rooms, 750 rooms, and 225 rooms, with restaurant seating capacities of 2500 seats (in nine dining rooms), 1575 seats (in five dining rooms), and others.

All of the following statements are based solely on the visited hotels and restaurants; however, there is reason to believe that other hotels and especially restaurants in the

---

1. A grant by Harris, Kerr, Forster and Company, which is gratefully acknowledged, made this study possible.

*Manuscript from which this article is taken appeared as "Hotel and Restaurant Operation and Management in the Soviet Union" in *The Cornell Hotel and Restaurant Administration Quarterly*, Vol. 15, No. 3, November 1974, pp. 71-77. Reprinted with permission.

USSR might operate in similar fashion due to the common economic system.

One peculiarity which came to light early during the stay was the fact that different organizations "own" and operate their own hotels; as an example, the city of Moscow operates 25 hotels. Other operators are the Ministry of Social Affairs, the labor unions, the 15 Soviet republics, Intourist, etc.

Another peculiarity was the fact that, except for Intourist, none of the other organizations operated their food and beverage operation; rather this was done by the Ministry of Trade. Since the Ministry of Trade is responsible for all retail sales, it is also responsible for the retail sales which go on in restaurant operations located within the hotels.

Hotel Organizations

As in the U.S. hotel industry, organizational set-ups vary according to a given situation. In the 1000-room hotel, the organization chart looked as follows:

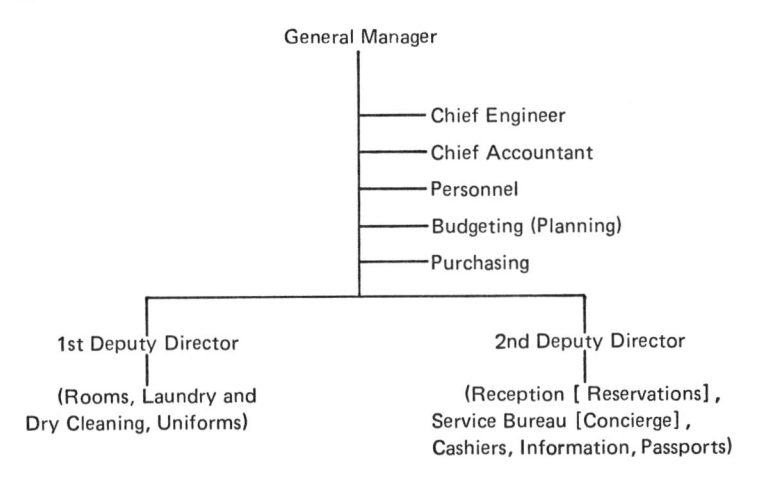

```
                        General Manager
                              |
                              ├── Chief Engineer
                              ├── Chief Accountant
                              ├── Personnel
                              ├── Budgeting (Planning)
                              └── Purchasing
                              |
            ┌─────────────────┴─────────────────┐
    1st Deputy Director                 2nd Deputy Director
            |                                   |
    (Rooms, Laundry and             (Reception [Reservations],
    Dry Cleaning, Uniforms)          Service Bureau [Concierge],
                                     Cashiers, Information, Passports)
```

Since this was one organization where food and beverage was operated by the Ministry of Trade, the food and beverage director's position did not exist in the above organization chart. As a matter of fact no formal ties existed between the two operations. When the author asked what would happen if the general manager were to request that the restaurant director keep the restaurants open one hour later (for any reason), the answer was that nothing would happen. Since the hotels and the restaurants are two different operations, each reporting to different organizations, charges made in the dining room cannot be put on the hotel bill of a guest. In this particular hotel, room service is available only to a sick person. He would call the maid, give her the money for the item and she would go and buy the item in the restaurant and deliver the item personally to the guest.

Budgeting Vital Function

Budgeting or planning, as it is called, is one of the most important functions in any organization in the USSR, including any hotel or restaurant. It is carried out by the "Economic Staff" and requires special schooling. The Budget is prepared yearly and revised every three months. Many negative statements have been made in the literature about "planning," but the author cannot conceive any organization in the USSR or in the U.S. operating without planning (or budgeting, if you wish).

The budget is the responsibility of the Economic Staff. It is discussed and prepared with the help of the general manager and the deputy directors and the final version is sent to the organization which approves or asks for modifications. The latter usually results in another round of talks between the organization and the hotel.

The Economic Staff is also responsible for closing the books and preparing financial statements, while the Accounting Staff usually takes care of only the bookkeeping functions.

While carrying out the traditional functions of housekeeping, including laundry for guests, the housekeeping department also has available a cobbler and a tailor for repairing articles for guests. The receptionist usually takes care only of reservations and distribution of rooms and has little contact with the guest. Considering that the annual occupancy of Moscow's hotels is 96 to 98 percent, this is a hair-raising activity. The Service Bureau performs the traditional function of the concierge which means it sells tickets for theaters, trains, tours, changes money, etc.

All of the Service Bureau's personnel, as many as 36 in one large hotel, speak at least one foreign language rather well.

Corporate Administration 77

Also operating in the service bureaus are Intourist, which takes care of all arrangements for foreign visitors, and Aeroflot, the national airline.

The cashiers, using some USSR, German-and Swedish (Sweda)-made bookkeeping machines and/or cash registers, collect the guest bills.

No guest can leave the hotel with his suitcase unless he has some kind of a statement from the cashier. All doors are guarded by what seemed to be retired men.

The next question to ask would be, what happens to the room keys? A number of floor supervisors are seated on each floor and they report to the Deputy Director for rooms (executive housekeeper), and also control the room keys. Especially in large hotels, it is the floor supervisor (or better, 3 to 4 supervisors) who come in close contact with the guest. As is the case in some European countries, the passport is collected from the arriving visitor and kept under the supervision of the 2nd Deputy Director. At departure time it is handed back to the guest.

The next organization chart is different in character because food and beverage is operated by the hotel.

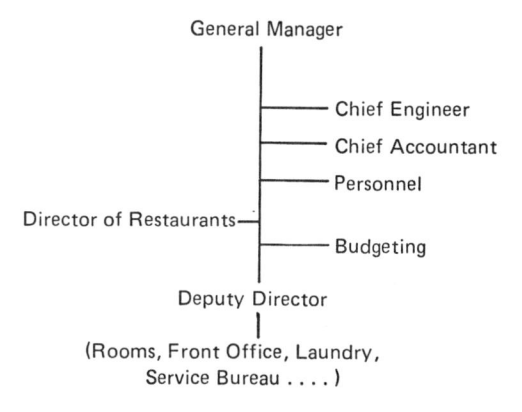

```
                    General Manager
                         |
                         |────── Chief Engineer
                         |────── Chief Accountant
                         |────── Personnel
   Director of Restaurants─|
                         |────── Budgeting
                         |
                    Deputy Director
                         |
          (Rooms, Front Office, Laundry,
              Service Bureau ....)
```

Only one Deputy Director is present in this 750-room hotel. Since the General Manager was on vacation during the author's visit, the Deputy Director was in charge of the operation.

Although nobody seemed to be overworked (from deputy director down to waiters), and only a few secretaries with their typewriters were evident in most of the organizations visited, business seemed to be going on and jobs getting done.

The last organization chart is different, again, because the hotel has been undergoing renovations for quite some time and these were planned to continue in the future. It is organized as follows:

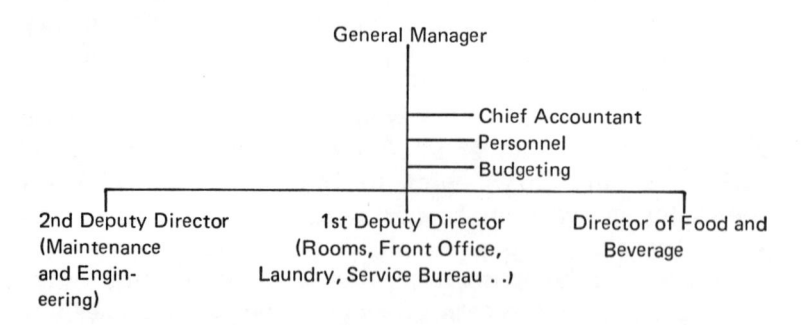

```
                        General Manager
                              |
                              |── Chief Accountant
                              |── Personnel
                              |── Budgeting
        ┌─────────────────────┼─────────────────────┐
   2nd Deputy Director    1st Deputy Director    Director of Food and
   (Maintenance          (Rooms, Front Office,      Beverage
   and Engin-            Laundry, Service Bureau..)
   eering)
```

In summarizing, it can be said that the General Manager controls directly all auxiliary functions, such as bookkeeping, personnel, budgeting, etc. As far as the rest of the main functions are concerned, it depends entirely on the type and size of the operation.

This situation is probably also true of most hotel operations in the United States.

Departmental Organization

(I) ROOMS

The organization chart of the 1000-room hotel looks like this:

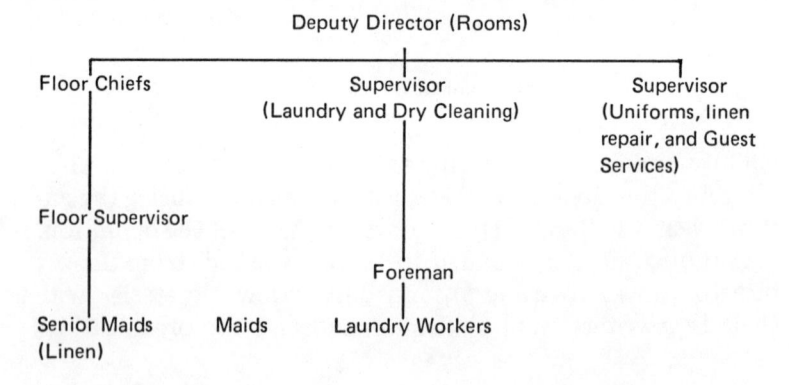

```
                    Deputy Director (Rooms)
                              |
     ┌────────────────────────┼────────────────────────┐
Floor Chiefs              Supervisor                Supervisor
     |                (Laundry and Dry Cleaning)   (Uniforms, linen
     |                         |                    repair, and Guest
     |                         |                    Services)
Floor Supervisor               |
     |                      Foreman
     |                         |
Senior Maids     Maids     Laundry Workers
(Linen)
```

In this hotel, on the average, for each two floors there is a floor chief; a total of ten.[1] Strategically located on each floor are four floor supervisors, who, as pointed out before, are responsible for the maids and the keys, and also for the proper guest count in that they compare guest records which are passed on to the reception desk.

The floor supervisors work a 24-hour shift, and then they are off for two days. No one works more than 40 hours a week. Two senior maids on each floor are responsible for linen: collection, counting, and exchanging. For every 78 rooms, there are 30 maids available. This number covers days off, vacation and no-shows. A maid is required to clean eight rooms per shift, but normally she cleans five to six and does some other cleaning, such as the lobby, etc.

Since the rooms are not more elaborate than their U. S. counterparts, this ratio of maids to rooms to be cleaned seems low. There is also one houseman per floor who looks after the wood floors. However, in another hotel a higher ratio was in existence, due to shortage of personnel.

Shortage of Maids

The writer learned that maids very often take off during the summer to go to the countryside to enjoy themselves and then return in the fall. This is possible because many of the maids are above 55 years of age, the legal retirement age,[2] and during the summer they live on the pension they receive.[3] As in U. S. hotels, supervisors complain about the shortage and the quality of the available maids.

What is different is the act of "supervision." Questioning a floor supervisor as to whether she had personally inspected any of her rooms during the last two weeks, we received a negative answer. This apparent lack of supervision was noted in other parts of the hotel as well. However, and this puzzled the author, for the most part the operation survives. Nor is it implied here, "barely survives."

---

1. The hotel has almost thirty floors, but as the hotel rises, the number of rooms on each floor decreases.
2. For men, the retirement age is sixty years.
3. The wages earned, when they work as maids, are complimentary income and have no bearing on the pension.

Asking a deputy director of a large hotel how many memos she received from the General Manager, she replied that she gets about one or two per week. It seems that a loose (not necessarily permissive) type of supervision exists from the top down to the floor supervisors. This type of supervision had no adverse effect on the quality of the work. The room which the author used for two weeks was always clean. One could counter-argue that maids have only up to eight rooms to clean. This is a valid argument. One general impression was, as pointed out earlier, that nobody seemed overworked and/or in a rush, including maids and waiters.

(II) FOOD AND BEVERAGE

As may be remembered, the hotel with the 1000 rooms had the food and beverage operation separated from the hotel operation.

The food and beverage operation consisted of a restaurant (5 rooms) with 825 seats and a cafe (somewhat limited menu) with 750 seats. In addition, a culinary shop was included which required 20 employees.

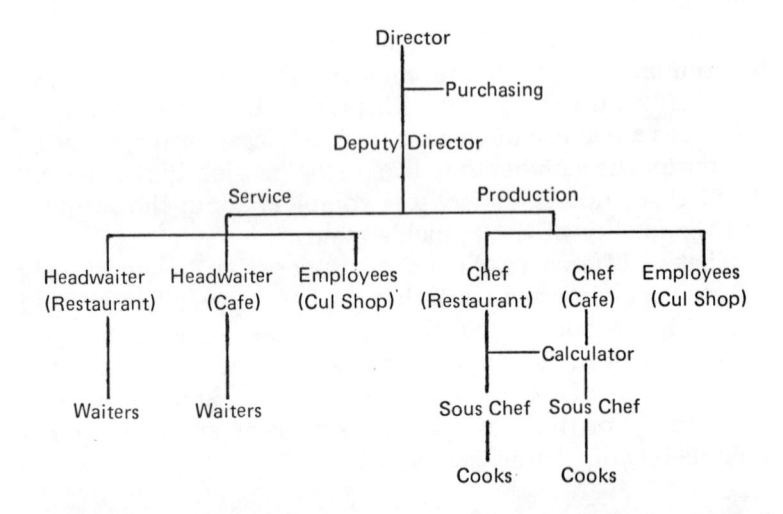

```
                         Director
                            ├──Purchasing
                      Deputy Director
           ┌────────────────┴────────────────┐
         Service                         Production
    ┌──────┼──────┐                 ┌────────┼────────┐
Headwaiter Headwaiter Employees   Chef      Chef   Employees
(Restaurant) (Cafe)  (Cul Shop)  (Restaurant)(Cafe) (Cul Shop)
     │         │                    ├──Calculator
     │         │                    │         │
  Waiters   Waiters              Sous Chef  Sous Chef
                                    │         │
                                  Cooks     Cooks
```

The restaurant required 12 headwaiters and 168 waiters and waitresses who worked a 12-hour shift every second day and handled about 10 seats each.

The kitchen was staffed by four sous chefs and 70 cooks; personnel in each category worked 9 hours per day,[1] 40 hours per week. The cafe employed 80 waiters and waitresses (the number of headwaiters was not ascertained), two sous chefs and 45 cooks.

A skilled waiter or waitress was expected (the norm) to sell 120 rubles worth of merchandise during a 12-hour shift.[2] It should be noted that the service personnel received a fix salary from 70 to 85 rubles per month, depending on their skills, plus 5 percent from the sales. This should make it important for them to try to sell and to provide efficient service in order to increase the turnover. However, this was not the case. The service was extremely slow, the personnel uninterested, not friendly[3] and supervision nonexistent, or differently expressed, existing, but totally ineffective.

When the author mentioned this negative facet of the USSR hospitality industry, to an official of Intourist, he advanced a plausible explanation for some of the above points. He said that traditionally the citizens would frequent a restaurant only for very special reasons: weddings, meeting friends, etc. Therefore, it made no difference how long it took for a waiter to present a menu or to bring something to eat and drink to the table. Changes in the demands on the USSR hospitality industry have occurred faster than changes in attitude among the service personnel.

The kitchen is departmentalized into the following: soups, hors d'oeuvres and desserts, roasts, bread, tea and coffee, china, and dishwashing. The china station is somewhat peculiar. The clean china goes from the dishwasher to the china station (behind the counter) where an employee is stationed to pass out the individual dishes to each waiter, e.g., if the waiter has four main dishes to pick up he goes to the station and asks for four warm, empty plates.

---

1. Including meals.
2. With the price structure the way it is, this would mean providing service for 35 to 40 patrons during a 12-hour shift.
3. This is contrary to what the author had to say several years ago about the subject. See L. A. Kreck, "Moscow Airport Food Service," *The Cornell Quarterly*, Vol. 7, No. 4, February, 1967.

The sales control system follows the traditional European system closely. The waiter takes an order, goes to the cash register where he has a key for himself, rings up the amount for each item, receives a coupon with the amount printed on it and with the coupon "buys" the food from the kitchen. When the guest leaves, the waiter makes out the bill, collects and keeps the money until he checks out at which time his key at the register is read and the total amount collected from the waiter. This system has many loopholes.

Prices Set in Kitchen

An interesting point is presented by the position of a calculator in the kitchen under the chef. Price setting in a socialistic economy is, of course, different from that of a market economy. The author had already reported on that facet in his previously mentioned article (1967). More information is now available and will be brought out under the next heading "Financial Information." It is, in any case, the calculator who, with the help of the chef, sets the price to be used on today's menu. All menus are then hand signed by the director of the restaurant and the calculator.

A somewhat different organization chart is available from the hotels which operate their own food and beverage operation. This operation had 600 seats (plus 250 for banquets) and provided room service from 7 a.m. to 12 p.m. The kitchen was open from 8 a.m. to 3 a.m. The chart below reflects these considerations.

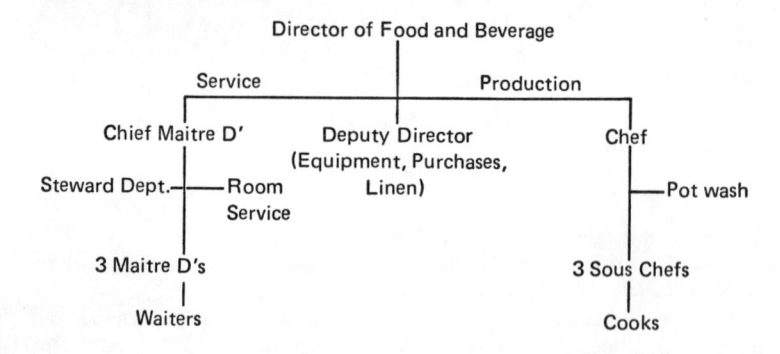

```
                    Director of Food and Beverage
                                 |
            Service                           Production
              |                                   |
   Chief Maitre D'      Deputy Director          Chef
                        (Equipment, Purchases,
   Steward Dept.——Room         Linen)            ——Pot wash
                  Service
              |                                   |
         3 Maitre D's                        3 Sous Chefs
              |                                   |
           Waiters                              Cooks
```

Finally, there is the 3000-room hotel which posed a somewhat new problem. It contained nine restaurants with 2500 seats, 20 snack bars, and a number of public bars. The total number of employees in food and beverage added up to 2500.

Here is the organization chart for this operation.

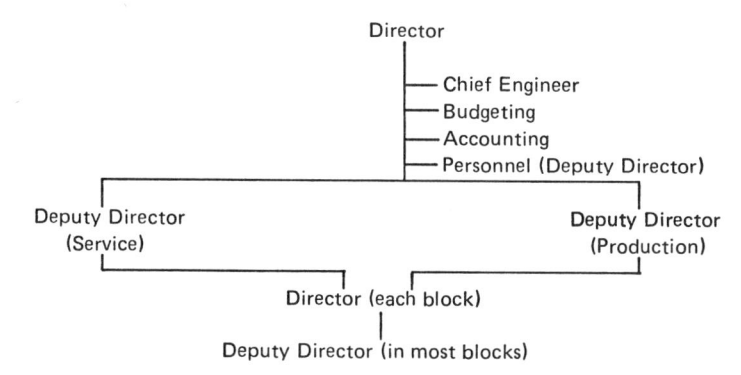

```
                          Director
                             ├── Chief Engineer
                             ├── Budgeting
                             ├── Accounting
                             └── Personnel (Deputy Director)
         ┌───────────────────┴───────────────────┐
   Deputy Director                          Deputy Director
     (Service)                                (Production)
         └───────────────────┬───────────────────┘
                    Director (each block)
                             │
                   Deputy Director (in most blocks)
```

Since the hotel occupied a large city square, each block or side of the square had its own Food and Beverage staff,[1] consisting of 500 to 600 employees each. Included in the staff were five executive chefs for the nine kitchens, senior maitre d's in some blocks, orchestras, etc. It is, without doubt, one of the largest food and beverage operations in the world.

In this particular operation each morning the maitre d's were involved with the chef in the planning of the menu. This is done because the maitre d' knows his customers and, therefore, knows what they have demanded and what they like to be served. This did not necessarily turn out as planned. Often items were listed on the menu, with prices, but were not available.[2] As this writer learned, room service was available in two blocks and in the presidential tower for 18 hours each day but no special room service menu was in use.

---

1. It also contained separate front offices, etc.
2. Items which were not priced on the printed menu were not available anyway.

Financial Information

(I) HOTEL OPERATION

The author could not ascertain whether or not a formula was used for pricing rooms. However, he did find out something equally interesting. In at least one large hotel, the prices for a room for USSR citizens differed from those charged tourists, e.g., a single room with television cost 3.40 rubles for the USSR tourists and 12.40 rubles for foreigners; doubles cost 5.00 rubles and 13.00 rubles respectively. A suite was 8.53 rubles and 18.00 rubles; and a luxury suite (up to 8 rooms) was 15.00 rubles and 240.00 rubles.

There is a simple explanation for this. Private USSR tourists (and they exist) simply cannot pay the prices which are charged foreigners, e.g., a general manager of a hotel earns 300 rubles per month, a doctor in a hospital only 250 rubles. It goes without saying that foreign guests, with hard currency, are welcomed because of the higher prices they pay. They make a direct contribution to the profit of a hotel which, in most cases, goes directly to the employees of the hotel in the form of premiums.

Check-out time was 12:00 noon. If one wanted to stay over, say three hours, one had to pay for another half day, or 12 hours. However, the next guest occupying the same room was then only charged from 12:00 midnight because the previous guest had paid up to that time.

From the numerous discussions, income statements were constructed. (See pages 85 and 86.)

The low norm for the maids (8 rooms), of course, shows up in a rather high labor cost of 36 percent and 25 percent respectively as compared with 16.1 percent for U. S. hotel operations.[1]

"Amortization" includes depreciation and charges for rent. The 1000-room hotel was 15 years old and had an original cost of 23+ million rubles. It can be assumed that the hotel is written off over a 30 to 40 year period. Amortization in the amount of 1.06 million rubles is directly transferred to

---

1. Harris, Kerr, Forster and Company, *Trends in the Hotel-Motel Business,* 1973.

INCOME STATEMENT (1 YEAR)
(1000 Rooms)

	Ruble (Mill.)	
SALES (ROOMS ONLY)	4.4	100%
EXPENSES		
Labor	.890	36%
Maintenance ⎫		
Utilities ⎬	.600	14%
Supplies ⎪		
Laundry ⎭		
Amortization	1.06	24%
TOTAL	2.496	74%
PROFIT	1.904	26%

the organization which "owns" the hotel. The profit of 1.904 million rubles stays with the hotel and is distributed among all the employees by the general manager in the form of premiums (based on the basic salary), financial aid, special contributions and loans. The author was told that the premiums would amount to 25 percent to 30 percent of the basic salary.

No ruble figures, only percentages, were available from the hotel, which operated food and beverage as well.

No Ratios Available

The ratio of room to food and beverage sales was also not available. However, in a third hotel, operating its own food and beverage department, the ratio was 1:3 (room to food and beverage) which is almost a complete reversal of U. S. hotel operations (54.7:28.2).[1] The reason for the particular ratio of this 225-room and 825-seat food and beverage operation in the USSR, is the high utilization of the restaurant facilities by guests other than houseguests. There are almost always waiting lines in front of the better restaurants, including those of the hotels.

---

1. Harris, Kerr, Forster and Company.

INCOME STATEMENT
(700 Rooms)

SALES (ROOMS)	100%
EXPENSES	
Labor	25%
Maintenance }	
Utilities }	16%
Supplies }	
Laundry }	
Amortization	20%
TOTAL	61%
DEPARTMENT PROFIT	39%
	100%
SALES (FOOD AND BEVERAGE)	100%
EXPENSES	
Labor	20%
Cost of Food and Beverage	65%
Amortization	5%
TOTAL	90%
DEPARTMENT PROFIT	10%
	100%

Summary

Summarizing, it can be said that the income statements (excluding food and beverage operation, which will be discussed later) show a relatively high cost of labor (due to low productivity), despite low wages (80 to 90 rubles for a young floor supervisor) and a relatively high portion of profit, probably due to the elevated prices charged to foreign tourists.[1]

---

[1]. The 1000-room hotel had a permanent contingent of 500 beds set aside for Intourist guests and the 700-room hotel had all beds assigned to Intourist.

(II) FOOD AND BEVERAGE OPERATION

Menu pricing in the USSR had been investigated earlier and discussed in an article by this author (1967). It will only be touched on here and new information added.

The basis for pricing is a standardized recipe for each dish. First, all ingredients are listed in grams. The raw material cost (or cost of food sold per dish) is computed and forms the next step toward the final price. Assuming that the cost of food that makes up a dish is 83 kopecks (.83 rubles) a certain percentage, depending upon the actual amount of labor involved as determined and prescribed by the Ministry of Trade, is added. It amounts to 70 percent to 75 percent for fish dishes, 60 percent to 65 percent for meat dishes, and 30 percent for dishes not covered under the above, e.g., soups, eggs, etc.

If the previously mentioned dish is a meat dish, a minimum of 60 percent or 49.8 kopecks, depending on the type of meat dish, will be added. The menu price for this dish for today's menu is 1.33 rubles. Prices are not rounded off. If the cost of food sold for the dish changes tomorrow, a new price is calculated and typed into a new set of menus for the day. This is also done for beverages. All restaurants can add only the following percentages to their retail prices (there are, of course, no wholesale prices): 10 percent for beer, 25 percent for brandy, which is called Cognac (illegally), 35 percent for wines, and 50 percent for vodka. This is one reason for a rather startling food and beverage financial picture to be discussed shortly.

The author observed two bar operations, one without any effective control, and the second with a reasonable control. In the first case, the barmaid would fill the order using a measuring glass, collect the money and put it into a drawer. She did not use any tickets nor did she ring up any item. There was no cash register available anyway.

In the second case, three copies for the daily stock were made out by the barman, listing purchase price and potential sales value for each item. For each sale a ticket was made out and rung up by the barman on a cash register. Although this system still leaves many loopholes,[1] such as under-ringing,

---
1. This system is still widely used in the U. S.

INCOME STATEMENT
(3 Months)

	Rubles	
Budgeted Food and Beverage Sales	1,964,000	100%
Actual Food and Beverage Sales	2,000,000	
Cost of Food and Beverage Sold	1,420,000	71%
Total Food and Beverage Gross Profit	580,000	29%
DEPARTMENTAL EXPENSES*		
Wages	276,000	13.8%
Utilities; cleaning and laundry	32,000	1.6%
Transport (Food and Beverage items)	65,000	3.3%
Rent	30,000	1.5%
Replacement for linen, uniforms, china, glass and silver	42,200	2.1%
Repairs	15,400	.7%
Refrigeration maintenance	2,100	.1%
Training	13,800	.7%
Advertising	3,700	.2%
Containers (Tara)	3,800	.2%
Spoiled Food	3,700	.2%
Other	36,300	2.0%
TOTAL EXPENSES	524,000	26.2%
NET PROFIT	56,000	2.8%

*Some items are adjusted to fit net profit.

under-pouring, bunching, etc., it was definitely superior to the first example. The general manager of this particular hotel struck the author as especially knowledgeable, considering the fact that this professional had absolutely no contact with the Western world where many new ideas originate.

The most detailed food and beverage statement on the facing page comes from a restaurant operated within a hotel with 825 guests, a cafe of 750 seats, and a culinary shop.

This statement reveals two peculiarities: an extremely high cost for food and beverages sold and an extremely low labor cost. One reason for the high cost of food and beverages is the relatively small amount added to arrive at the sales price, e.g., up to only 75 percent, for labor cost, in case of a fish dish, or as little as 10 percent for beer, apparently without taking any of the other expenses into consideration.

The second reason is the high cost of raw material, especially meats. One kilo (1000 grams) of rather poor quality pork belly sold for 2.80 rubles; one kilo imported turkey, with bones, 3.80 rubles. During his frequent visits to butcher shops, the author never saw quality cuts of meat, such as fillets, rounds, etc. The prices for such cuts can only be imagined.

A third reason for the high cost of food and beverages sold is the relatively low menu prices. The author found prices to be rather low for U. S. tourists, but definitely in line with the earning power of the local population. While room rates were adjusted upwards, this was apparently not possible for restaurant prices.

In another operation, the statement showed that the cost of food sold was 69 percent; the cost of beverages sold 21 percent and combined costs were 60 to 62 percent.[1]

Labor cost is low, despite low productivity, because wages are low, e.g., a waiter or waitress starts with 70 rubles per month, with a tariff of 85 rubles (plus 5 percent of his sales) as mentioned earlier. A chef earns 205 rubles, a cook 150 to 170 rubles and a headwaiter 200 rubles. It was reported to

---

1. Cost of food and beverages sold must be more or less similar throughout the industry because of the same percentages added. Differences occur only through the sales mix.

the writer that a "super" chef may go as high as 350 rubles which is 50 rubles more than the general manager's salary.

The Income Statement lists 13,800 rubles for training. A portion of this amount is spent for foreign language lessons, especially for the service personnel.

Everyone is encouraged to participate. Perhaps one day this will be the case in the U. S.

Another interesting item is "Spoiled Food." The author has long advocated[1] that the restaurant industry face up to the fact that, like any other industry, it has spoilage. Daily spoilage should be recorded and treated in the income statement like any other expense.

A final expense is advertising. This includes the printing of menus and also the cost of items which are used in connection with foreign guests, e.g., brochures which are used abroad.

In discussing the statement, the restaurant official expressed his disappointment about the small amount of sales achieved beyond the budgeted amount, or "The Plan," and also the low profit.

As was pointed out before, the profit stays with the restaurant and is distributed among the employees (including management).

In order to increase sales, and over-fulfill "The Plan," constant competitions are held between certain groups of service personnel. One restaurant employs 45 waiters who work one day and 45 waitresses who work the next day. These groups are in competition with each other. The author was told that almost always the waitresses win and, therefore, receive higher premiums. Sales progress throughout a time period is carefully charted daily; percentages of plan fulfillment are noted and conspicuously displayed in color. The writer thinks that if there were effective supervision in the dining rooms, "The Plan" could be considerably over-fulfilled. Many times he observed potential guests leaving because of empty tables not cleaned yet, tables with fake reservations and especially lack of attention for the seated guests. This lack of attention unnecessarily prolonged

---

1. See L. A. Kreck, "Menu Pricing—A Reflection of Total Cost," *Cooking for Profit*, November, 1965.

the time of the meal and, therefore, the table was not available for new guests in a reasonable period of time.

Summarizing the food and beverage operations, it can be said that the most noticeable feature is the very high cost of food and beverages sold due to the low percentage added to arrive at the sales price. The second feature deals with labor which shows a very low labor cost percentage. This is not due to high productivity but to the relatively low wages paid.

Summary

This was a most interesting and enjoyable study, not only because little is known about the subject but because of the friendly cooperation the writer received from the USSR's professionals.

The writer found some aspects similar to the U. S. hospitality services industry, such as the organizational structure of hotels and restaurants, and some aspects dissimilar, such as ownership of hotels and restaurants, type of leadership (and control), and especially the financial statements.

However, anywhere he went he found professionals who cared about the organization entrusted to them and tried to do as good a job as their U. S. counterparts.

Customer (finishing his hash)—Check, waiter.
Waiter (who forgot what the order was)—What did you have, sir?
Customer—I haven't the slightest idea.
New York Sun. *

**The Hotel World*, November 30, 1889, p. 9. Reprinted with permission *Hotel and Motel Management*.

SLIGHTLY SARCASTIC—
NOT ENTIRELY NEW BUT NOVEL "HOTEL RULES"*

The late proprietor of the Queen's Hotel, Salisbury, Rhodesia, Mr. Geo. Harthing, who died last November, compiled a quite unique notice-card, which was posted up in each guest's room. The top part of the card is taken up by the following witty piece of sarcasm arranged in three columns:

1. As an introduction to this hotel, you are invited to scan the following paragraphs in connection therewith.

2. On arrival, every guest is expected to express his view of the situation and design of the hotel. Should these not prove satisfactory, the building will be at once demolished and re-erected on the Causeway side, or near the Makabusi in any or every style of architecture.

3. Corner or front rooms are provided for every visitor. Turkish, needle, and mud baths; hot, cold, lukewarm and iced water; laundry, Marconi apparatus, telephone, fire escapes, acetylene gas, bar, English daily and weekly papers, the morning *Glory*, piano, tame clergyman, and all other modern conveniences in every room.

4. Special accommodation is provided for pets such as elephants, hippos, crocs, or lions, but dogs, including those of high birth and doubtful parentage, must be kept in the bedrooms, which, for this purpose, are furnished with a special line in white counterpanes. For verification of this rule visitors should apply personally to the housekeeper.

5. As the ladies of this country are specially trained to enjoy bad language, ribald songs, step-dances, and shouting

---

The Hotel World, March 25, 1911. p. 17. Reprinted by permission of *Hotel and Motel Management*.

at all times, male visitors arriving home between midnight and the milk are requested to make as much noise and curse as flowery as they possibly can.

6. Every guest will have the best seat at the table, and meals will be served every minute if required, irrespective of the fact that our chef has just a few more besides your individual self to provide for.

7. Waiters of every color and nationality are kept in stock. Each one is furnished, with a bouquet and dress suit (sometimes), and has his hair nicely parted down the middle. These waiters have been carefully selected to please everybody, and can lead in prayer, shake for drinks, play draw poker, and answer questions in Hebrew, Greek, Latin, Scotch, or any other polite language without turning a hair.

8. English, French, German, Chinese, Dutch, Irish, Kaffir, and Esperanto dictionaries are furnished to every visitor, so that he may write out any bill of fare he fancies, and to assist him in entirely disregarding the hotel menu.

9. A liberal supply of illustrated papers and periodicals is provided in the reading room. It is, however, a mistake to suppose that these are for general use, and visitors are therefore urgently requested to immediately remove to their own rooms *as many as they can carry*. When finished with, such papers should be buried, to avoid the danger of anyone else seeing them.

10. Valuables should on no account be locked up, but should be thrown anywhere, or, for preference, placed outside the door with the boots. Locks are fixed on the doors solely for ornamental purposes. Should anything be missing, in spite of this, visitors are asked to remember that the proprietor must get a living somehow. He enjoys being called a thief, and is open to be searched whenever required.

11. The proprietor will be highly pleased to hear that some other hotel is the best in town, and special attention will always be paid to the gentleman who can hold forth as to how hotels are run in such small towns as London, Paris, New York, or the latest Atlantic liner. You will also fail to consider his feelings—and in fact, he will take it as a special affront—if, on leaving the hotel, you fail to dispute your account, call him a swindler—(he likes the truth sometimes)—his house a barn, table vile, liquors murderous, and to state that you (the

guest) were never so imposed upon in all your life, will never stop here again, and intend *to warn ALL* your friends.

12. Only one funeral in the last twelve years— the guest called in a doctor instead of trying our choice brand of antiquary. Result: Doctor departed—so did the guest.

In the lower part of the card there is, on the left, a really fine poem on "Fortitude"; on the right is an ingenious burlesque jingle on "Solitude," and in the middle a small picture of the low-lying building, with the time at which the meals are taken, and so forth.
—*London Caterer.*

QUERIES

1. Suppose attorney Harry Hess, the author of "What Is a 'Hotel'?" has just hired you as the general manager of his planned hotel. He has told you about his philosophy, the way he sees a hotel, and now asks you to develop necessary policies on the subject of "community relations." What would you suggest to him?

2. Present arguments for and against automation in the service industry by using as examples: (1) a hotel like the Brown Palace Hotel in Denver, Colorado and (2) the Holiday Inn in Star City, N. W.*

3. Clearly distinguish between lodging franchises, referral groups and voluntary groups. Where does Allstar fit into the group of classifications?

4. Choose several hospitality corporations and determine their organizational structure.

5. How can you in the future become the formal authority in a food service company? Prepare a detailed plan of action from graduation to 10 years after graduation.

6. Go back in history and find social systems which did not survive. Were they closed or open systems?

---
*N. W. = No Where

ACT II

The Director

MANAGEMENT

INTRODUCTION

The director of a play is an interpretive artist. He takes the drama created by the playwright, combines it with the talent of his actors, the skill of his technicians and the assets of the stage to develop an audio and visual experience for the audience. He must have the ability not only to recognize and utilize the superior qualities of these factors but must be able also to identify their shortcomings and take all necessary steps to overcome them.

The manager of an organization must perform functions similar to that of the director. First, he must interpret the philosophy of the corporate administration so that the resulting production is consistent with its goals and objectives. If, for example, the corporation seeks to maximize short run profits, then the manager must combine all of the components of the operation in a way that will assure that all efforts are directed toward achieving that goal. However, if the corporation changes direction and places top priority on the achievement of operational longevity, then the manager must have the flexibility and expertise to restructure the factors in a way that will assure the attainment of the new goal. Generally these managerial requirements can only be satisfied by individuals who possess a variety of diverse talents, as well as an inexhaustible supply of energy and an insatiable desire for personal success and achievement.

The scenes of Act II deal primarily with some of the talents that are required for successful managerial functioning. We *emphasize the word "some" because it would be impossible for any book, regardless of its size, to adequately examine all of the skills needed by the manager of today's hospitality operation. One minute the manager may find himself submerged in a supervisory problem that developed during the previous night's "graveyard" shift and then the next minute find himself creating a more efficient quality control system.*

This diversity of tasks calls for a variety of skills as well as an ability to shift quickly from one situation to another. Many of the situations encountered require only the application of basic managerial principles; however, a large amount of the manager's time is spent with problems which call for expertise in a specific discipline. For example, the manager in dealing with the "graveyard" problem must not only utilize his leadership skills but must also examine the principles of communication to determine whether a breakdown in that area is the underlying cause.

Act II looks at three areas within the following framework: Management and the Outlook for Management; Leadership and Motivation; and it concludes with an examination of Communication.

Management can be defined either as a group of people or as a process. When referring to a group of people, the word describes those individuals who are responsible for coordinating the available resources and directing them toward the achievement of the predetermined goals and objectives. In the most limited sense of the word, only those individuals who occupy the highest rungs of the organizational ladder are referred to as management.

However, we now find that many theorists and practitioners are advocating the idea that all of the individuals within an operation are managers with respect to their specific areas. The dishwasher can be taught to manage the operation and maintenance of his machine, while the waiters and waitresses can be directed to manage their stations as well as the presentation and serving of the meal.

When management is spoken of as a process, it describes the various techniques and tools that are utilized by management personnel to bring about the desired goals. The process is often broken down into the four basic functions of management. These functions are: Planning, Organizing, Directing, and Controlling.

PLANNING is the function that is concerned with preparing for the future. Effective planning requires that maximum effort be expended in an attempt to project reliable forecasts of the future. The forecasts require an assessment of such factors as: potential changes in product demand, possible economic fluctuations, supply trends of both labor and raw material and the probable actions and reactions of the competition.

If members of management refuse to forecast the future, then they are operating under the assumption that the conditions of tomorrow will be identical to those that exist today. Such an attitude can only spell disaster. When the probable future has been outlined in detail, management then can go about the task of developing plans which will permit the operation to stay one step ahead of the changing conditions.

ORGANIZING is the function that is utilized to put plans into action. It involves the development of an organizational structure, the establishment of a procedure for implementing the plans and the coordination of the factors and support facilities needed to activate the procedure. If this function of management is not undertaken, the result will be chaos and confusion. Everyone will be going in different directions. Corporate objectives will be delayed, if not permanently lost, and the effects on employee morale and discipline may prevent adequate recovery in the future.

DIRECTING has the responsibility of putting into action the organization that was established in the previous function, which in turn was determined by the planning phase. In reality, these first three functions are difficult to separate as they often are occurring simultaneously due to the nature of management as a process. If this function is ignored, then "the best laid plans of mice and men" will be worthless. The energies and time that went into the planning and organizing phases might as well have been conserved, for without proper directing, they are valueless by themselves.

CONTROLLING is the management function that recognizes that man is not infallible, especially when he is involved in predicting the future. Basically, controlling is concerned with comparing "what is" with "what should have been."

The first three management functions are the determinants of "what should have been" and the reality of the situation is the indicator of "what is." If a variance occurs between the two, then it is the responsibility of the control function to take corrective actions. These actions can take the form of plan alterations, organizational restructuring, changes in directional techniques or any other adjustment that is capable of reducing the gap between reality and the way things should be.

There are many principles of management implied in each of these functions and a partial task of the initial scene in this Act is to isolate some of the more important ones. In addition, Scene 1 examines the future for management, both on an economy-wide basis and on the hospitality industry level.

What does the future hold for management personnel? What changes in techniques will have strong repercussions on managerial functions? How will the role of the manager change in the face of a rapidly changing society? What can hospitality managers expect in the form of compensation, ten years from now and twenty years down the road? These are just some of the types of questions that are confronted within the confines of the first scene.

Leadership, which is examined in the second scene of this Act, is a concept that defies an exact definition. We can quantify the results of effective leadership just as we can list the attributes that good leaders have seemed to possess. But when we attempt to identify why an individual is an especially competent leader or how he/she became one, we begin to run into a multitude of problems.

One method of attempting to obtain a grasp of the concept is to examine case histories of effective leaders and then isolate those personal and managerial traits which are found to be common among them.

Previous studies have found such personal traits as: intelligence; willingness to accept responsibility; open-mindedness; emotional stability; people-handling skills; and an ability to *communicate as being essential to the effective leader. In addition, managerial traits such as: a capacity to analyze problems; an appreciation of human problems; an understanding of the complex nature of today's organizations; and a sense of social responsibility have been isolated and labeled as being vitally important to the productive leader.*

The second portion of Scene 2 deals with another abstract area containing many of the same conceptual difficulties encountered in the discussion of leadership. Motivation and the effective use of motivational tools are based on the capability of management to recognize human needs.

People are ever-needing creatures. As soon as one need is satisfied, another appears and will remain until it too has been alleviated. This process remains with us throughout our lives as we continually progress from one need level to the next.

The capable manager is able to determine the various need levels of his employees and then attempt to find satisfactions for their needs in the jobs that they perform. The manager who assumes that all of his employees are operating on the identical need plane will undoubtedly be confronted with numerous personnel problems. These can range from reductions in productivity to actual conspiracies and to sabotage.

Motives are the forces behind the behavior that the individual directs toward the satisfaction of his needs. When the manager is confronted with a particular behavior pattern that seems foreign to the individual who displays it, he should attempt to determine what the motives are behind the behavior and, ultimately, try to discover the need that has undoubtedly been blocked. Too often, management attempts to treat the symptom, through disciplinary action, rather than cure the problem by providing a need-satisfying atmosphere.

The final scene of Act II discusses communications in general, and more specifically how they can be utilized effectively within the framework of the basic managerial functions. Communicating can be simply defined as the process whereby ideas are relayed from one individual to another individual or group of individuals for the primary purpose of achieving a desired result.

A given communication can be termed successful only if

the desired action takes place at the time and in the manner envisioned by the transmitter of the message. Feedback is the mechanism that is utilized by the sender of the communication to determine, before it is too late, whether the message is being received, understood and accepted. Feedback can take a verbal form such as, "Yes, I see what you mean," or it can be presented in a nonverbal form, such as a nod of the head or a violent shaking of a fist in the air.

In addition to understanding of the basic communications models, an effective manager must be aware of the various barriers to effective communications, especially as they exist in his own operation. The individual with whom you are attempting to communicate may very well have a background quite dissimilar from your own and thus his interpretation of the message will be based on a different frame of reference.

Communications can also suffer from such barriers as poor physical conditions (e.g., excessive noise levels), differences in attitudes and status levels. The importance of effective communications to the overall success of an operation cannot be over-emphasized, and it is management who is responsible for seeing that the proper communications network is established and maintained.

We want to re-emphasize the point that Act II does not purport to contain discussions of all the vital management tools. On the contrary, its function is only to highlight a few of the important areas for the purpose of illustrating the depth of knowledge that is needed and to stimulate the reader to delve into those other areas which, unfortunately, had to be ignored in Act II.

Scene 1

MANAGEMENT— MANAGEMENT OUTLOOK

The opening selection entitled "Hotel Management" first appeared in 1922. Although it rambles from topic to topic (i.e., from efficiency engineers to unionization and from cost accounting to noise elimination), its major point is worth restating today. Basically, the article is saying that although the use of sophisticated management techniques is vital to the growth of the industry, practical solutions to many problems should not be overlooked just because they appear to be so simple.

McMurry's article takes a controversial stand and claims that the only way that a manager who lacks equity in the business can survive is through the attainment of power. His Machiavellian position is founded on the belief that power, gained through the cultivation of appropriate alliances, will assure the development of the necessary authority relationships.

"The Mess in Management Accountability" examines the

large, fast-growing firm and determines that there is a great need for the development of management accountability programs which will help determine which people are responsible for what functions. Only when this is accomplished can the firm hope to eliminate waste and prepare for future growth.

The final portion of the scene is concerned with the manager as a person. "The New Psychology of Success" seeks to find out what motivates management personnel in the hospitality industry. The results obtained will undoubtedly catch many companies by surprise. Perham's article is much more specific as it focuses on the fringe benefits that are just beginning to emerge but which promise to predominate in the near future.

The scene concludes with an article by Roger G. Wright entitled "Managing Management Resources Through Corporate Constitutionalism," which advocates the development of a corporate constitution for those individuals not protected by a contract. The philosophy behind his somewhat radical position is partially revealed in the following quote. "Nonsensical demands for conformity, according to someone's set of norms, will continue until we recognize that major enterprises need people with diverse patterns of thought and behavior, and until we give explicit franchise to individuality through written policies."

HOTEL MANAGEMENT[*][1]

J. W. WOOD

The reason for management in any business is to obtain a certain desired result. In a hotel that desired result is usually financial success. Occasionally it is to give prestige or more business to a railroad or a real estate development, but generally you will be classed as a good or a poor manager according to your ability to make money.

The real manager of a hotel, regardless of who may hold the title, is the person who controls and carries out the policy made by the proprietor or the manager himself. There are managers who manage in the name only; look into the business of their hotels and you often find that a chief clerk manages one part, the steward another. The financial part of each department may be brought into a profit and loss statement by the auditor and still there may be no management of the hotel as a whole. The place may be successful but it could be more successful if it had real management.

No one can define exactly what the manager's duties are; the real manager must find many of them as he goes along, and they will vary from day to day and month to month. An applicant for a hotel management was asked by a director: "What would you consider your duties here, Mr. B.?" "I would consider that I had bought this business, that it had cost me every cent, now how shall I make it pay?" was Mr. B.'s answer. Hire the best heads of departments you can,

---

The Hotel World, May 27, 1922, pp. 7-9. Reprinted with permission of *Hotel and Motel Management*.

[1] For reasons of historical validity, the language utilized, and the discrimination implied were not omitted. Neither is condoned by the authors but we felt that they provide a good indication of some of the changes that have occurred in our society since 1922.

but best for you does not always mean the highest priced.

You might know a fine steward, but your business might not warrant the salary you would have to pay him. A chef cheap at $400 a month for one hotel would be dear at $200 in many others.

Do not let organization frighten you and do not regard it as something pertaining only to large places. If you have two employees, you have an organization; it may be better than many of five hundred. It may be fair or it may be absolute zero. A fixed scale of wages in a business as variable and complex as a hotel should be avoided.

Among any six waiters, dishwashers, housemen, maids, bellmen or clerks there are invariably one or two worth twenty to thirty per cent more to you than any of the others, although supposed to do exactly the same work. By rewarding those who show real loyalty, love of the work and results, you will keep a permanent hold on them and thus build up a splendid organization. Rewards may be promotion, increased wages or occasional presents, according to which is most pleasing to the particular employee. It is sad but true that the greater number of your rank and file of employees have little permanent interest in your business, particularly those working for tips. They reason thusly: "If this place don't make a go, I will get a job somewhere else and most likely it will be a better one." They are usually quite optimistic of their future and pessimistic of the present.

Monthly prizes for the best rank and file employees are worth while. Where both white and colored were employed we gave a blue ribbon and five dollars and a red ribbon with five dollars to the best colored employee. This ribbon was worn until the next month's prizes were given out.

Try to keep every employee busy so you can pay him a good salary. Often this can be done by combining jobs. I have seen three men each drawing $75 a month where with a little thought and planning by the manager the work could all be combined into two jobs and filled by two men at $100 each, the house saving $25 or 11 per cent, and also obtaining more satisfactory and more satisfied employees.

Do not let two employees work together on two one-man jobs. A custom of many housekeepers of having a chambermaid and a cleaning girl in the same room at the same time is wrong. If one is through first, she wastes her time waiting for the other, to say nothing of loss of time to each one by the unnecessary conversation between them. On the other hand, it is even worse to have one person on a two-man job. He will do it poorly, inefficiently or something may be broken. A houseman carrying a long ladder alone and pushing doors open with the end of it, scratching and damaging them, is often seen. No place is so small that there is not someone who could give him a hand for a few minutes.

If there is any business in the world that can least afford to be thoroughly unionized with one man to open a door and another to shut it, it is the hotel business. Its complex weaving of little jobs with big jobs requires even those holding the best positions to do many little things not always approved by labor unions.

Eliminate noises. You will be surprised after you start at how many can be lessened. Does a door squeak? The maid reports it to the housekeeper, who has housemen put a drop or two of oil in the hinges, that's all that is necessary in nine out of ten squeaks. Does the butcher make a lot of noise using the cleaver on the meat block? Just tack a piece of a discarded inside tube on each foot of the block. A lot of loud, cheerful "Good mornings" between housekeeper, maids, and others in the halls may be good psychology but is quite disturbing to guests, also the constant trying of doors to see if the guest is out. Tell your night clerk you want every noise inside or outside of your hotel stopped, if possible, by him at once, or an effort made to stop it. At least a report can be made of it and you can next day take steps to avoid a repetition.

Nothing exasperates a guest more than to be told, when he asks a question, "I don't know, I just came on watch," particularly if the question pertains to some previous inquiry or request. This can be avoided by the clerk keeping a "Memoranda Sheet" in front of him and noting on it things to be done and the steps taken toward that end. For instance:

"Transfer 206 to a $2.50 room soon as possible," signed by Clerk A.

"Have taxi for 110 here at 4 a.m.," signed by Clerk B and

followed in the next column by "Called Green Co. at 11 p.m. by Clerk C."

"Send out laundry for 126," Clerk A. "Gone," Clerk B. Then the guest's further questions:

"When am I going to get that room?"

"Was my taxi called?" "Did my laundry go?" can be answered at once by whoever is on watch.

Too great a value cannot be put upon the accounting, but it must be accounting that tells you what you ought to know. Close attention should be paid to the cost accounting and the inside bookkeeping in general. I have seen great stress put upon checking and re-checking dealers' bills for errors and no figures made to find out the ratio of the cost of the raw food to the dining room receipts or the per dollar cost. The saving from the exhaustive checking of the bills did not average $5 a month, while the actual waste from not finding the per dollar cost was over $100 a month.

In every good hotel management there must be a plentiful supply of judgment. If three things ought to be done today and only one can be done, do the most important one first, but don't confine important to liking; the thing you may like to do best may not be the most important. A captain of industry has been quoted as saying, "If I could obtain a man of perfect judgment, he could be a physical cripple. We could bring him to work every morning and take him home every night. He need have no previous knowledge of our business, but I could pay him an enormous salary to sit at a desk and use that perfect judgment on our daily problems."

Consider carefully and see if you cannot afford a man, woman, boy or girl in your establishment with no regular job, a sort of a home-made efficiency engineer. He can look for wasted energy, broken machines or more often machines and utensils giving indifferent service; he can help employees to obtain better results from a machine; he can use every endeavor to decrease breakage of all kinds, and possibly save his salary in this one item. He can count useless steps, he can check up closely on butter one day and on potatoes another; he can become a valuable unit in your organization.

I once found a place where ten or twenty dishes had been broken every lunch hour for three months. This was caused by the elevator stopping six inches short of the floor level. When the busboy pushed his loaded wagon onto the elevator, crash went the dishes! You must say, "Why didn't the steward or the manager notice this?" Of course, it should have been discovered, but this was a very busy place at the lunch hour; the steward was overseeing the kitchen, the chef was giving a hand all over the kitchen and the manager was in the front. Our home-made efficiency man would have saved all that breakage.

The management of a hotel should enter into the spirit of local celebrations and be a part of it, but do not be misled into contributing lavishly and beyond the amount that any other business does because you may sell a few extra rooms or meals. At a famous resort I saw a beautiful colorful spectacle: ten thousand people were looking at a pageant depicting the history of the locality; the flags of many nations waved in the sunshine, and the great hotel facing it all had neglected to put up any flags. Those empty flagstaffs stuck up stiff and straight seeming to coldly say, "This hotel does not want anything to do with that celebration." The simple hoisting of a few flags would have been better than a $200 contribution.

In a certain city it is the custom for real estate development companies to take the prospective purchasers on a free auto ride to the property and serve a complimentary picnic luncheon to them at noon. The second or the third cup of free coffee is poured with more gracious hospitality than the same people receive at their hotels when they ask the waiter to pour a second cup of coffee from the pot for which they are paying. Why? Because the hotel management has not put across the idea that these patrons are to be treated as real guests. These prospects may not buy real estate and may never be seen again by the promoters, yet they are treated more hospitably than by the hotels which hope to receive the continued patronage of the same people.

Listen to suggestions from guests but do not always follow them. The late Henry Weaver used to say, "Let everybody think you are going to spend a million dollars on improvements—but don't do it!" Remember, you have two ears and one brain, one ear to receive, a brain to separate the wheat and another ear to let out the chaff. Think over the suggestions made by your patrons and generally you find nine out of ten are for the spending of your money on what most pleases the suggester. Is it not the man who always eats in a hurry who suggests that your portions are a little small? Isn't it the artistic young lady who suggests your spending five dollars or more every day for flowers?

The manager having many things upon which to be posted must himself use efficiency methods as well as require the same for his subordinates. A proper arrangement of his desk will aid him greatly. On the flat top of your desk have a folder called "Today"; this is divided into indexed leaves marked as you wish, for instance, Steward, Housekeeper, Engineers, etc., keeping separate the letters, circulars, notations, etc., which you wish to give to or take up with the various department heads. Have another similar one in the upper left hand drawer marked "Holdover." If any paper is not to be taken up today but possibly tomorrow, put it in the corresponding leaf of the "holdover" folder.

In the lower right-hand drawer have an indexed file numbered 1 to 31, one for each day of the month. If any paper does not need your attention again until the 20th, put it in the 20th compartment. It is often desirable to put the copy of a letter you write today in the file under date of three or four days ahead when a reply may be expected. The reply received, both letters may be sent to the permanent file or put farther ahead if the matter is not yet completed.

In the upper left-hand drawer have an alphabetical 3 by 5 card index with plenty of cheap blank cards. Any data that comes to you incidentally pertaining to your coal, ice or water consumption, breakage, etc., may be noted on one of these cards and placed in its proper letter. Up-to-date data on other hotels may also be filed for comparison. Later, if these notes seem worth while, they may be transcribed on the typewriter and proper space left for subsequent information or summaries.

It is surprising how much real information regarding any one thing pertaining to your hotel may be condensed on a 3 by 5 card. In the same drawer have a different colored set of 3 by 5 guides in which to file the cards of salesmen, according to the article handled. You may have no interest in rubber mats today but tomorrow you may be in the market. Sometimes it is well to file one card under the firm's name as well as one under the article sold.

Write orders to department heads on a pad with carbon; put the copy on file, check them over once or more a day and insist upon the thing being done, started or a satisfactory reason given for no action. Don't try to do everything personally; when anything you have been doing becomes routine, pass it on to someone else. An establishment in which the manager's time is worth $2,500 or more a year—I said worth—can afford at least $900 a year for a combination secretary-stenographer. He or she can be easily trained into becoming the manager's right hand.

The basic law handed down from Mt. Sinai through the first lawyer, the great Moses, and later summarized by the Great Teacher into "Do unto others as you would they should do unto you" should be rigidly applied to your hotel. In no other business is it needed more; in no other will it be more appreciated; in no other will it bring better results in the long run. Charging all that the traffic will bear, profiteering, giving inferior accommodations, serving poor food may and frequently does pay well for a long time, but the man adopting that policy must frequently change his location.

In the Old Book is another saying wonderfully applicable to your hotel. It is: "Whatsoever thy hand findeth to do, do it with all thy might." Look carefully at this sentence for a few minutes. "Whatsoever"—is there anything in your hotel not included in that "Whatsoever"?

"Thy hand"—which takes in the hands of all your helpers.

"Findeth"—you do not find unless you look, if you look there will always be something found "to do" and those two little words "do it," which followed or neglected often mean success or failure.

"With all thy might"—"might," a great word comprehending brain and brawn, money, power, ability, and carefully note it says "thy might," not his or hers or that elusive theirs, but the might belonging to and controlled by you—Y—O—U.

POWER AND THE AMBITIOUS EXECUTIVE*

ROBERT N. McMURRY

The methods of holding top-management power in a company strike many people as devious and Machiavellian. They involve calculated alliances, compromises, and "deals"—and often they fly in the face of practices advocated by experts on organizational behavior. From the standpoint of the beleaguered and harassed executive, however, there may be no substitute for them—if he wants to survive at the top.

Mr. McMurry has been writing for *Harvard Business Review* since 1952, when an article he wrote on "The Executive Neurosis" caused a minor sensation in the management community. Executive recruiting, labor relations; management communications, value conflicts, and other matters have been the subjects of his articles since then. The article in this issue is inspired by material in a book manuscript he has recently completed. It will be published by Amacom (the publishing subsidiary of the American Management Association) in 1974 under the title, *The Maverick Executive*. The author heads up The McMurry Company, a firm of management psychologists and personnel consultants in Chicago.

The most important and unyielding necessity of organizational life is not better communications, human relations, or employee participation, but power. I define *power* as the capacity to modify the conduct of other employees in a desired manner, together with the capacity to avoid having one's own behavior modified in undesired ways by other employees. Executives must have power because, unfortunately, many employees resent discipline; to these employees, work is something to be avoided. In their value systems, "happiness" is the ultimate goal. For the organization to be made productive, such persons must be subjected to discipline.

---

*Harvard Business Review, November-December, 1973, pp. 140-145. Reprinted with permission. © 1973 by the President and Fellows of Harvard College; all rights reserved.

Without power there can be no authority; without authority, there can be no discipline; without discipline, there can be difficulty in maintaining order, system, and productivity.

An executive without power is, therefore, all too often a figurehead—or worse, headless. The higher an executive is in his management hierarchy, the greater his need for power. This is because power tends to weaken as it is disseminated downward.

Gaining and Keeping Power

If the executive owns the business, that fact may ensure his power. If he does not, and sometimes even when he does, his power must be acquired and held by means which are essentially political. Of critical importance, since most of his power is derived or delegated, his power must be dependable. Nothing is more devastating to an executive than to lose support and backing in moments of crisis. It is for this reason that the development of continuing power is the most immediate and nagging concern of many professional managers.

How can chief executives and other managers who possess little or no equity in a business consolidate enough power to protect their jobs and enforce their dictates when necessary? The eight recommendations which follow are the fruit of 30 years of observation of a great number of executives managing a variety of enterprises.

A number of these conclusions conflict with the findings of other writers. The most that can be said in defense of my recommendations is that they did not spring from an ivory tower. They are based on strategies and tactics employed by demonstrably successful executives who lacked financial control of their enterprises. The executives were working pragmatists. Their prime criterion of a desirable course of action was: Will it work? While the strategies presented here are not infallible, they have proven their worth more often than not in the hard and competitive world of business.

1. The executive should take all the steps he can to ensure that he is personally compatible with superiors.

In the case of the chief executive, this means compatibility with the owners and/or their representatives, such as bankers, lawyers, and family members; in the case of other managers, senior executives and owners are the key groups. The point is that though a manager may have all the skills, experience, and personal attributes his position requires, if his values and goals are not reasonably consonant with those of the persons who hold power and he is not acceptable to them personally, his tenure will probably be brief.

To protect against subsequent disillusionment and conflict, the prospective manager should, before he joins the company, endeavor to become acquainted with his prospective superior or superiors informally. This could be done at dinner with them, on the golf course, or on a trip. At such a meeting he can learn his superior's values, standards, prejudices, and expectations. If any significant evidence of incompatibility emerges, he should call off negotiations—incompatibility tends to worsen rather than improve with continued contact.

If at all possible, the manager's wife should meet the superior, also under informal conditions, since compatibility with her can play an important part in the new man's acceptance. Likewise, if it can be arranged for the manager's wife to meet the chief's wife, early in the course of negotiations, that should be done. Compatibility between these two can be very advantageous; incompatibility can be fatal.

2. Whether he comes to the company from outside or is being promoted from within, the executive should obtain an employment contract.

While many owners and senior executives protest that they never make such agreements and that it is against their policy to do so, the prospective manager must insist that every policy is subject to change and that he will not accept the position without one. A failure to win out at this most critical juncture can be fatal to him. The reason is not so much that failure strips him of any vestige of job security and power but that it indicates to those in command that he is somewhat docile and submissive and probably can be pushed about at their whim.

This is particularly true where the executive's primary assignment is to salvage and rehabilitate a sick or failing operation or to initiate and pioneer a new and radically different field of activity that no one in the business knows much about. The compensation may be alluring, the status attractively elevated, and the challenge exciting. But the risks have to be great. If worse comes to worst and the executive is removed, he will have a tidy sum to carry him over the six months or longer that he needs to find a new job.

3. On taking a major assignment, the executive should obtain from his superiors a clear, concise, and unambiguous statement in writing of his duties, responsibilities, reporting relationships, and scope of authority.

Such a document is absolutely essential if the manager is not later to make the humiliating and frustrating discovery that the parameters of his job have been changed, often with no notice to him. He may have been led to believe at the outset that he had certain responsibilities and commensurate authority to carry them out. Later he may learn that he has no such authority and that some of the people who were to report to him in effect do not do so. He may discover that figuratively he has been castrated; all of his authority has been taken from him, leaving him powerless. If, when he protests, he cannot substantiate his charges with a written commitment, he is likely to be told, "You have misunderstood our original agreement."

4. The executive should take exceptional care to find subordinates who combine technical competence with reliability, dependability and loyalty.

As many a top executive has learned to his sorrow, he is constantly vulnerable to sabotage by his underlings. This is especially the case where he comes in from outside and "does not know where the bodies are buried." It is for this reason that he should be so careful in the choice of his immediate subordinates.

In theory, each superior, regardless of his level in the management hierarchy, should have a strong, competent number-two man who is ready and willing to step into his place should he be promoted, retire, leave the company, or for any reason be unable to continue to function. Some executives do just this. But in practice the policy can be hazardous, at least in terms of the senior man's job security.

An aggressive, ambitious, upwardly mobile number-two man is dangerous to any chief, weak or strong. For one thing, the number-two man is often very difficult to control. He has his own personal array of goals and objectives which may or may not be consistent with those of his superior and/ or the company.

Since he is usually inner-directed and a man of strong convictions, it is often difficult to divert him from the course which he has set for himself and which he sincerely believes to be best for him (and secondarily for the company). The risk is considerably lessened if the chief has only one strong subordinate, for then it is easier to watch and constrain him.

Moreover, since the strong subordinate tends to be an individualist, he is more apt to find himself in conflict with his peers. He has a compulsive need to achieve *his* goals regardless of the needs or expectations of the others or of the welfare of the enterprise as a whole. Not only may his influence be seriously divisive, but he tends to fragment the enterprise, to induce a centrifugal effect in it. This is why such businesses as advertising and consulting are so notoriously prone to fragmentation; they attract too many entrepreneurs.

Strong, decisive, qualified men are rarely willing to remain for more than a brief time in a secondary role. Their impatience is accentuated if, for any reason, they do not respect their superior or feel frustrated in their careers.

Sometimes they conclude that their greatest opportunity lies not in seeking advancement by moving to another company but by undermining and eventually supplanting their present superior.

In consequence, the politically astute top executive seeks subordinates who not only have the requisite technical skills, but who are also to some degree passive, dependent, and submissive. Their "loyalty" is often a euphemism for docility. They tend to be security-conscious and prone to form a dependent relationship with their chief. If the chief has held his position for many years, this building of a submissive group has usually taken place slowly by a process of trial and error. But when he comes in from outside or takes over as the result of a merger, he is often prone (and is usually well advised) to bring his own associates with him or to give preferment to men whom he knows and has worked with previously.

5. A useful defensive tactic for the executive is to select a compliant board of directors.

Of course, the chief executive is the one most immediately concerned with this ploy, but second- and third-level managers, too, may have a vital interest in this matter. In recent years, changes in directors' responsibilities have made it somewhat more difficult to stack the board in the old-fashioned sense. But its membership and operation can still be influenced in a significant way.

Inside directors tend usually to be more malleable than outside directors. Few will be courageous enough to cross swords with the chief executive. While board members by law are the stockholders' representatives and thus are the holders of ultimate power in the business, in practice this is often little more than a polite fiction. In many instances they have largely abdicated their management or even corporate supervisory responsibilities.

Sometimes the directors are too busy to interfere in operations. And not infrequently they have little equity in the business and, hence, are disinterested in it. Sometimes they have been chosen principally because they are "big names" who add status and respectability to the company but can devote little time to its affairs. Much as some observers and authorities dislike such tendencies, they are the realities. The top-management group that knows how to use and exploit power will make sure that it, too, enjoys the blessings of a compliant board.

6. In business, as in diplomacy, the most important stratagem of power is for the executive to establish alliances.

The more alliances the executive can build, the better. He can establish several kinds of relationships:

With his superiors—He can make personal contact with and sell himself to the owner of the business or, where the ownership is widely diversified, to the more influential stockholders. One chief executive I know has luncheon once each month with the widow of the founder of his company. As long as she is convinced that he is a "wonderful man," he has both power and tenure.

Where banks, insurance companies, or mutual funds have a controlling voice in the company, the executive can seek to ingratiate himself with their key executives. If certain of his directors are unusually dominant, he does everything he can to win their favor and support. This does not necessarily mean that he is obsequious and sycophantic in his relationships with them. On the contrary, he may regularly stand up to them and confront them directly.

The key to success in a relationship of this nature is the ascertainment of the other person's expectations. If the man or woman whose support he hopes to win likes tigers, he is a tiger; if the person prefers a mouse, he restrains his more aggressive impulses. Above all, he studies each person's prejudices and values and is careful never to offend them.

With his peers—The adroit manager also builds allegiances with others at his own level. While these people may not be direct sources of power to him, they can often be valuable as supplementary means of support and intelligence. Included among his contacts should be prominent industry figures. Since government intervention in business is increasing daily, acquaintance with senators, congressmen, and major department heads in government can also be helpful. (The owners of a company doing business with the Defense Department will think twice before sacking an executive who is on intimate terms with the Secretary or his deputy.)

One good means of ensuring support from peers is to identify common goals and objectives toward which all can strive. An even more powerful step is to find a common enemy—an antibusiness government official, let us say, or a hostile labor leader. Often influential rivals for power or even disgruntled subordinates can be neutralized by being taken into groups having common goals or enemies.

With subordinates—I have already mentioned the importance of selecting dependent subordinates in whose selfish interest it is to support their chief. Such persons may also be useful as sources of internal intelligence. The information they provide is not always completely accurate or reliable, but it can be cross-checked against data from a variety of other sources.

7. The executive should recognize the power of the purse.

He knows that the best control he can exercise over his subordinates is fiscal. Hence he seeks as quickly as possible to position himself where he approves all budgets. Nothing is as effective in coping with a recalcitrant staff as the power to cut off financial support for their projects. On the other hand, nothing so often promotes gratitude and cooperation as fiscal support of subordinates' favorite projects.

8. The executive should understand the critical importance of clear and credible channels of communication upward from all levels of his personnel and downward from him to them.

Without such channels the executive is an isolate who does not know what is transpiring in his enterprise. His commands will be heard only partially by his subordinates; they will be infrequently understood and rarely acted on. He should recognize that many of his staff have strong motives to keep the truth from him and to block or distort his downward communications.[1]

To overcome deficiencies of communication, the executive must learn not to depend too much on his hierarchy of assistants (many of whom are not communication centers at all, but barriers to it). Where possible, he will address his people directly, conducting periodic "State of the Company" reports to them and encouraging direct feedback from them by soliciting anonymous questions and expressions of dissatisfaction. He must supplement his formal channels of upward and downward communication by all available means, such as work councils, opinion polls, interviews with natural leaders, and community surveys.

---

1. For a fuller explanation of this point, see my article "Clear Communications for Chief Executives," *Harvard Business Review*, March-April, 1965, p. 131.

Personal Style

The place of a chief or other top executive in a business in which he has little or no equity is somewhat analogous to that of a diplomat working in an unfriendly, if not openly hostile, country. He may have much overt status and prestige, but he has little real power. He needs to accomplish certain goals, but he has little true leverage to apply to those people whom he seeks to influence. In view of this, he sometimes finds it necessary to use indirect, oblique, Machiavellian stratagems to gain his ends.

Observation of many politically astute executives in action indicates that most of them utilize supplementary ploys in coping with and influencing owners, associates, employees, and other groups.

They know that an executive-politician must:

Use caution in taking counsel—He may take the views of others into account, but he knows the decisions must be his. Advice is useful, but unless its limits are recognized, it can easily become pressure.

Avoid too close superior-subordinate relationships—While he must be friendly with his subordinates, he is never intimate with them. His personal feelings must never be a basis for action concerning them. His door may be "open"—but not too far.

Maintain maneuverability—He never commits himself completely and irrevocably. If conditions change, he can gracefully adapt himself to the altered circumstances and change course without loss of face.

Use passive resistance when necessary—When under pressure to take action which he regards as inadvisable, he can stall. To resist such demands openly is likely to precipitate a crisis. Therefore he initiates action, but in such a manner that the undesired program suffers from endless delays and ultimately dies on the vine.

Not hesitate to be ruthless when expedient—No one really expects the boss to be a "nice guy" at all times. If he is, he will be considered to be a softy or a patsy and no longer deserving of respect. (A surprisingly large segment of the population has a strong need to be submissive. Hence these people are more comfortable under a ruthless superior. This can be clearly seen in the rank and file of many labor organizations.)

Limit what is to be communicated—Many things should not be revealed. For instance, bad news may create costly anxieties or uncertainties among the troops; again, premature announcements of staff changes may give rise to schisms in the organizations.

Recognize that there are seldom any secrets in an organization—He must be aware that anything revealed "in confidence" will probably be the property of everyone in the establishment the next morning.

Learn never to place too much dependence on a subordinate unless it is clearly to the latter's personal advantage to be loyal—although some people are compulsively conscientious, most are not. Most give lip service to the company or the boss, but when the crunch comes, their loyalty is exclusively to themselves and their interests.

Be willing to compromise on small matters—He does this in order to obtain power for further movement. Nothing is more often fatal to executive power than stubbornness in small matters.

Be skilled in self-dramatization and be a persuasive personal salesman—He is essentially an actor, capable of influencing his audiences emotionally as well as rationally. He first ascertains his audience's wants and values. He then proceeds to confirm them, thus absolutely ensuring his hearer's acceptance of his message.

Radiate self-confidence—He must give the impression that he knows what he is doing, and is completely in command of the situation, even though he may not be sure at all.

Give outward evidence of status, power, and material success—Most people measure a leader by the degree of pomp and circumstance with which he surrounds himself. (This is why the king lives in a palace and the Pope in the Vatican.) Too much modesty and democracy in his way of life may easily be mistaken for a lack of power and influence. For example, most subordinates take vicarious pride in being able to say, "That's my boss who lives in the mansion on the hill and drives a Rolls Royce."

Avoid bureaucratic rigidity in interpreting company rules—To win and hold the allegiance of his subordinates, an executive must be willing to "bend the rules" from time to time and make exceptions, even when they are not wholly justified.

Remember to give praise as well as censure—Frequently, because he is under pressure from his superiors, he takes out his frustrations on his subordinates by criticizing them, sometimes unreasonably. He must remember that, if their loyalty is to be won and held, they merit equal amounts of praise and reassurance.

Be open-minded and receptive to opinions which differ from his—If he makes people feel that anyone who disagrees with him is, ipso facto, wrong, his power will suffer.

Listening to dissent is the principal means by which he can experience corrective contact with reality and receive warning that the course he is following will lead to trouble. Also, openness to disagreement helps him to use his power fairly—or, more accurately, use it in a manner that will be perceived as fair by subordinates.

Conclusion

The position of a top executive who has little or no equity in the business is often a perilous one, with little inherent security. If things go well, his tenure is usually ensured; if they go badly, all too often he is made the scapegoat. Since many of the factors that affect his performance are beyond his control, he is constantly subject to the threat of disaster. His only hope for survival under these conditions is to gain and retain power by tactics that are in a large measure political and means that are, in part at least, Machiavellian.

Such strategies are not always noble and high-minded. But neither are they naive. From the selfish standpoint of the beleaguered and harassed executive, they have one primary merit: they enhance his chances of survival.

THE MESS IN MANAGEMENT ACCOUNTABILITY*

THOMAS J. MURRAY

Irvine Robbins, the chairman of Baskin-Robbins, seemed to have it made. As Americans in droves took to the fancy concoctions served up by its increasingly familiar pink-and-brown ice cream parlors, Baskin-Robbins' sales and earnings nearly tripled in just four years.

But inside the company, Irv Robbins was having problems. Baskin-Robbins was suffering from growing pains. "The problem was," says Robbins today, "that the conventional system of delegating authority and responsibility just wasn't working. Various departments were each going their own way, with little or no regard for one another. We had failed," he admits, "to clearly identify responsibilities and the relationships between our managers and departments, so that almost literally the right hand often didn't know what the left hand was doing."

Robbins' predicament is by no means uncommon. The mess in management accountability, a full-fledged problem today, has been brewing since the booming 1960s. In that rapid growth period, many companies scattered management responsibilities far and wide but failed to set up proper lines of authority or accountability for carrying them out; they confused the roles to be played by executives with a combination of inadequate job descriptions, poorly defined working relationships between managers and fuzzy links among departments and divisions. The price top management is paying today for this lackadaisical executive accounting is bad decisions, communications foul-ups and conflicts between

---
*Reprinted by special permission from *Dun's*, Dec. 1973, pp. 117-119. Copyright, December, 1973, Dun & Bradstreet Publications Corporation.

managers. "To put it simply," says Warren Schmitt, professor of management at UCLA, "many companies are finding they really aren't sure who is responsible to whom for what."

But a few of them, at least, are trying to find out. Companies ranging from giants such as Weyerhaeuser, Union Carbide and Lorillard to smaller ones like Non-Linear Systems, Baskin-Robbins, Sage Administration Corp. and A&W International have instituted new management accountability programs to tighten up their loosely knit methods of reckoning responsibilities and objectives. Some of the programs have already shown results.

Coming Apart at the Seams?

Take the one at Baskin-Robbins. When the company started growing rapidly, various responsibilities were assigned to different departments in what seemed to be a logical manner. Then suddenly, conflicts began to erupt among executives. "Individually," says Robbins, "the problems were not of major importance. But taken together, they added up to a serious situation." In fact, as one company executive sums it up, "The company was in danger of coming apart at the seams."

One example: A squabble among several departments over the point-of-sale display signs that are distributed throughout the firm's more than 1200 franchised stores. The operational support department had had the sole responsibility for creating the signs—a major item in the company's marketing program—for several years. But then the legal department began to insist that it had to clear the signs for legal purposes. And then the operations department claimed it should have primary responsibility, since it placed the signs in all the outlets and had firsthand knowledge of store operators' needs. The result: Bad feelings among fellow executives that soon escalated into virtual warfare. When the conflicts and rivalries finally began to get out of control, Robbins called in a consultant, Robert Melcher, who had devised a system for managing accountability, to see what could be done.

Melcher's first step was an in-depth, individual interrogation of each of Baskin-Robbins' top-level executives, including

Robbins, to identify every task each man felt responsible for. Once the tasks were identified, they were lined up vertically on a written, linear chart: then across the top of the chart were written the positions of every executive.

Each executive was given a copy of the chart and asked to indicate under his title what kind of responsibility he believed he held for each listed function. To designate the kind of responsibility, an alphabet code ranging from A to G was used: A stood for general responsibility, B and C for operating or specific responsibilities; D, E and F for "must be consulted," "may be consulted," or "must be notified"; and G for "must approve."

When all the individual charts had been consolidated into one master form, all the executives were gathered together to confront the results. "It was almost a comedy," says Robbins. "Some jobs, we discovered, were claimed as a primary responsibility by three or four men. Others were claimed by no one, so that we suddenly realized some tasks were not being done by anyone. For instance, the maintenance of our corporate headquarters: Somehow or other the job got done, but none of us took any responsibility for it."

During the confrontation, the tensions, conflicts and petty jealousies festering just below the surface broke out almost immediately. "It was hard to believe how many there were," Robbins admits. "We found guys harboring grudges of all kinds. Some felt their neighbors were goofing off on the job whether they were or weren't. Others believed their fellow managers were covering up for subordinates' errors—and sometimes they were."

Aggravating as these revelations were, Robbins knew it was a breakthrough when they finally broke out into the open. Indeed, to Robbins the real plus of the accountability process lies in the participation of all managers and their confrontation with each other. "The value of surfacing conflicts is that once they have been identified they can be dealt with," he points out. "That didn't happen right away, but over the course of a dozen or so meetings we were able to thrash out and resolve most of them."

With responsibilities, roles and relationships now clearly

identified, he says, Baskin-Robbins has been able to pinpoint priorities for every manager as well as show how every department should interface with every other. Besides that, there is less of a tendency for departments to jealously guard prerogatives. For example, after years of being responsible for selecting franchisees to operate its outlets, the franchising department yielded its power to Operations. It was not an easy transfer, admits Robbins, but by using the accountability process to show that it has to live with the franchisees after they have been chosen, Operations proved its right without the usual rancor of the past.

To guard against regression, Baskin-Robbins' managers repeat the confrontation process every few months. "This way," says Robbins, "we can make sure that any changes in roles or relationships are followed by necessary modifications in operating plans." Also, it might be said, it serves to re-invigorate Robbins' own enthusiasm for the accountability technique. For as he admits, "If it doesn't have the enthusiastic backing of the top man, it's a dead duck. But if he's behind it all the way, others in the company will give it a chance."

That point is being borne out hundreds of miles away from Baskin-Robbins at the huge Weyerhaeuser Co.

It all started a few years ago, when Weyerhaeuser top management discovered there was a bitter squabble going on at corporate headquarters. The planning and manufacturing departments were fighting over which one controlled the product mix in the company's big particleboard division.

After trying unsuccessfully to resolve the jurisdictional battle by conventional means, management realized that it did not have a working mechanism in-house to cope with such a situation. So, says Donald Swartz, a senior consultant in the company, it was decided to try an accountability exercise (much like the one used at Baskin-Robbins). Starting with the senior vice-president in charge of the operation, all tasks throughout the division were charted, cross-referenced to identify kinds of responsibilities, and put together for a confrontation of managers to resolve their differences.

The first payoff was just coming in, says Swartz, when

President George Weyerhaeuser decided to accelerate the decentralization of the entire corporation into eleven major geographic regions. During the reorganization, the accountability process was tried out in two other areas of the company, and now, says Swartz, Weyerhaeuser will attempt to apply it company-wide under the new corporate structure. First, a model linking headquarters with one region will be built. If that works, the model will then be adapted to cover all the regions.

While Weyerhaeuser considers the merits of accountability for an already restructured organization, President Edwin S. Weber of the $309-million rootbeer franchiser A&W International has found it helpful as he tries to overhaul his company's obsolete franchise system. Unlike the tightly controlled franchise operations of McDonald's and Kentucky Fried Chicken—which dictate everything from decor to the kind of buns used—A&W has had to work with hundreds of franchise contracts bought many years ago for a pittance and requiring little more of a franchisee than an obligation to buy A&W root-beer concentrates.

In his efforts to convert hundreds of these aged operations to a modern base, Weber sensed early on that some potentially big internal stresses and strains were brewing. For one, the assignment of responsibility at headquarters for monitoring construction at the franchise units was too widely diffused to be effective; for another, poorly defined job descriptions coupled with a high turnover among managers was making it difficult for new employees to figure out exactly what they were responsible for. To top things off, Weber himself was not always sure which of his executives should take on certain assignments. "I was often giving projects to the wrong people," he admits ruefully. "So when they goofed, whom could I blame?"

At the beginning of this year, Weber decided to act. He began in a low-key way—informal meetings, individual briefings—to put across to his executives the idea that individual responsibilities needed to be blended more tightly with company objectives. Then in late summer he took his fifteen top executives away for a week-long retreat. There the executives were put through the accountability process. As at

Baskin-Robbins, a lot of animosities emerged, but Weber believes that by resolving the controversial issues among his executives and defining their jobs, a major step has been taken in the reorganization of the company. "It was a laborious process," he says, "but any fast growing or fast changing company is headed for disaster if it doesn't build a thorough system for defining the jobs of its managers and how they interact."

The Price of Permissiveness

Some companies, of course, have deliberately chosen to avoid definitions of this kind. Spurred on by the theories of behavioral scientists such as the late Abraham Maslow and Harvard's Chris Argyris, various corporate experiments have been tried in recent years to free employees, including executives, from tightly defined job limits. But the harsh realities of the recent recession raised some strong second thoughts about free-form management techniques even among the most ardent followers.

One is Non-Linear Systems, Inc., the tiny San Diego electronics firm that attracted widespread attention during the 1960s for its pioneering efforts in participative management. In pushing the theory, Non-Linear President Andrew F. Kay allowed employees to organize their own work units and gave departments enormous autonomy, even to the point of keeping their own financial records.

After several years of spectacular growth, however, the company's much-admired experiment fell apart in the sudden aerospace slump of 1970. When sales started plummeting, Kay now admits, he realized that he had lost touch with day-to-day operations. Unfortunately, line managers had also lost touch with what they were supposed to be doing and had little idea of how they were progressing. In the accounting department, for example, a free hand had led to sheer incompetency. "I used to poke holes in the balance sheets they sent me," he says. "Errors were frequent, but I figured that I could make them more competent just by holding meetings with them." Besides that, poor controls in the materials department led to a huge buildup of inventory in 1970, an expensive mistake for the company as the recession hit.

While still a firm believer in the participative management approach, Kay is now convinced that he has to develop more accountability among his managers—and better control over them. He has already set up financial controls over department budgets, and although he will not detail the further steps he plans to take, he states flatly that during the year ahead he will be working on more definitive operating methods, a sharp departure from the highly informal structure of the recent past.

But while some companies are trying to do something about it, poor accountability remains a headache for most of industry. And in the view of many management men, it is likely to get worse. The most vulnerable companies, they say, are not only those experiencing fast change but those so big they have formalized every step of their operations. "When you formalize everything," says UCLA's Warren Schmitt, "too many things slip through the cracks."

The aims of Irv Baskin and George Weyerhaeuser, then, may be the most practical. By shooting for some flexible but comprehensive system of management accountability, they may at least find that fewer problems slip through. And it goes without saying that the major beneficiary of a good management accountability system is the chief executive himself.

THE NEW PSYCHOLOGY OF SUCCESS*

*Today's Executives look for
more than cash at the end
of their rainbow; put family
happiness, job security first*

The American dollar has undergone a stunning devaluation in the minds of men. Suddenly, money doesn't talk so persuasively.

In foodservice, its power has been checked by the heftiest salaries the industry has ever known. Just look at the salaries and fringe benefits listed on page 137. At last, middle management is reaping its financial due.

If money doesn't talk, what does? Fringe benefits, for one thing. But a host of other personal considerations, from job satisfaction to family happiness, have assumed unusual importance now that foodservice executives can afford to think about them.

"Sure, I look at the money they're offering," admits one Midwest restaurant supervisor, "but a company has to make me an offer as a person, not just as a payroll number."

The organizations that understand this—that offer personal instead of simply financial rewards—will capture the top executive talent of today and tomorrow.

*Explanations for mid-career
switches have new focus*

Marion Hicks had worked 17 scattered accounts as a Houston supervisor for Canteen Corp. Three years ago, at age 32,

---

*Institutions/VF Magazine, November 15, 1973, pp. 37-44. Reprinted with permission.

he left Canteen to become foodservice director at Rice University. "One of the reasons for the mid-career switch," he recollects, "was the more stable working hours. I've now got more time to spend with my family. It's a great life."

In Salt Lake City, School Foodservice Director Irene Griffith says, "I don't make very much in this position. But I'm satisfied and I've learned to live on what I make. More important to me is my family and the nights, holidays and weekends I can spend with them."

Marriott's regional marketing man Jim McAlister spends nearly 75% of his working time away from the office—and away from home. It's hard on his wife, but as the daughter of a hotel manager herself, she understands the business. McAlister believes she has become more self-sufficient, while his family has become more interested in his work. "My family understands. I come home and tell them what's happening, and they're involved. If I didn't enjoy myself, they'd know it and home life would just deteriorate."

District of Columbia School Foodservice Director Jim Stewart says, "It doesn't matter how much I love my job, I also love my family and want to be with them. I've got to forget this place when I leave the office, or I won't do a good job when I come in the next day."

A family man with four children, Barney Blashill counts his home life as important as his career as foodservice director of Levy's department store in Tucson. "Real success comes from accomplishing what you set out to accomplish, both on the job and at home. I say 'at home' because if you have a family, that should be as important as your career."

Financial security is only one consideration for John Dixon, 34-year-old general manager of the Burlingame (Calif.) Hyatt House. "Of course I want to be compensated adequately for my contribution, but my moves have not been based entirely on compensation. They have been based on challenge and opportunity, both of which contribute to my marketability."

D. Michael Jeans, catering director for 10 years and food and beverage man for the past three years at Chicago's Pick Congress Hotel, recollects, "At the time I joined Pick, there was motivation salary-wise. I had two sons in college at the same time, and, therefore, money was a consideration. But, today, it wouldn't be the prime concern. A factor, yes, but hardly a major one. And for young people to reach the top jobs today, they need exposure in more than one corporation. That explains the turnover in middle management."

Mike Leven, Dunfey's outspoken marketing director, has only one financial objective: "I want to make enough over the next 15 to 18 years to have what you'd call 'go to hell' money—a reserve fund so that at age 50 or 55 I don't have to get knocked around or kicked out."

One well-placed Marriott executive appreciates company benefits: a retirement plan; $150,000 life insurance policy; annual performance review; and the famous Marriott profit-sharing plan which will bring him nearly $1 million in cash and stocks at retirement. "Bonuses and pensions and such just make things easier," he admits. "Not in the job itself but in the periphery. I simply don't have to worry about certain things. I'd hate to have to work the way I do and also worry about personal matters."

Comments a hotel chain exec: "People get to levels where they're so concerned about job security that they don't want anybody down the line to shake it. I don't give a crap about job security. When the day comes that I'm too afraid to let a guy down the line make waves, then it's time to get out."

Hunger for accomplishment and
a chance to determine one's destiny
mark the search for the "right" job

Ed Cohen, district manager for Western Pancake House, has been in foodservice for 15 years—most of it in his own restaurant. "Running your own place can become a hassle," he explains, "so I came to Western Pancake for the challenge and opportunity here." Cohen is in charge of 11 Western operations in the Columbus, Ohio, area—all open 24 hours. "I practically work those hours myself, seven days a week. You have to be crazy to be in this business, and you have to like work. I admit to both. If money alone were motivating me, I'd look for a job with less hours and more money. But after 15 years in the business, I never felt that I'd really accomplished anything. Now I look back on what I've done here and say, 'Hey, I did this or I did that!' "

"I'd like to walk out of any job, or out of this industry for that matter, with the feeling that I left something behind," says 35-year-old Mike Leven, marketing director at Dunfey Family Corp. "I like to see people progressing. I want people to say they're better for having worked with me. I'd like to leave my mark. I want companies and people to feel that I was a positive influence—that I touched their lives a little bit. Two weeks ago, I had the toughest business day of my entire career. One of my salesmen had a drinking problem, and I had to get him to commit himself to a detoxification program. He went, took the cure, and now he's back on the way. He called me yesterday and said, 'The doctor said you saved my life.' To me, that's success."

District of Columbia Public Schools Foodservice Director James Stewart made his move from college feeding to school lunch "because the field seemed broader in magnitude and scope. I went from 20,000 meals per day to 70,000. But I also went into what had been primarily a woman's area. Eight or nine years ago, young guys just weren't into school foodservice. Now more men are getting into it—even those without a formal education. Money is certainly a motivating factor, but it's the wide open opportunities in this field that attract both men and women. Besides, I find it a real challenge, even a lot of fun, to fight government restrictions, red tape and regulations even though you can't beat the bureaucracy. If you're not locking horns with USDA, then you're off fighting community ignorance of nutrition. I honestly don't know of anything that could offer the challenge of what I'm doing right now."

"As corny as it sounds," says Jim McAlister, regional director of marketing for Marriott Hotels, "it all boils down to fun." Married, with four children, McAlister "lives" in Alexandria, Va. But the demands of his work keep him on the road three weeks out of every four. At one point, he spent a solid year commuting from Washington to New York to work on Marriott's Essex House (he raised its occupancy 15%). "There's no way I could keep up that pace or be out for a week opening the Los Angeles Marriott, go home for a day to two, and then fly out again to Camelback if I'm not having fun."

"One of the things I like about this job," reports D. Michael Jeans, food and beverage director at Chicago's Pick Congress Hotel, "is the constant challenge of food and labor costs. Another is the challenge of attracting people to our industry. Teaching people what I know is one of the most satisfying things about my job. If I find some youngster with the right attitude and he has adaptability, then I'm anxious for him to succeed, to learn more and more. Motivating people is the key to success." A testament to his methods came unsolicited from a young Irish waitress doing double duty one hectic Monday in the hotel's Tipperary Inn. Harried by the luncheon crowds, she shyly apologized for the delay in service, whereupon Jeans assured her he appreciated her efforts on behalf of all the patrons. Reassured, she beamed to his luncheon guests, "There aren't many bosses who, on a day like this, will take the time to pick up your ego, dust it off a little, and gently lay it down when you need it."

Opportunity is viewed as the chance to expand personal and professional horizons

John Dixon had been working for three years as director of sales coordination at Sheraton headquarters when he asked to transfer into operations. Sheraton had no immediate vacancy. Meanwhile, Hyatt Corp. did, so he joined them. "It was a matter of timing," the Burlingame (Calif.) Hyatt general manager says. "I wanted more responsibility, and Sheraton said 'not at this time.' Hyatt came along and said 'we need you right now.' Hyatt was a young, aggressive, innovative company that attracted me immediately. I am a high-risk, high-reward type of individual. I work very hard and avidly seek out greater responsibility and challenge. Hyatt gives me what I want. It's a dynamic environment, compatible with my lifestyle and rhythm of existence."

An incompatible exception expressed by a former Stouffer's executive: "My superiors at Stouffer's made it difficult for me to function, leaving me the choice of outlasting them or finding another job. I left because I had a different business philosophy than my boss. We were friends and drinking buddies, but we couldn't reconcile business differences."

Comments a hotel research expert: "The most successful companies allow individual differences. If you don't take time to treat people individually, people won't perform well consistently. My frustrations constantly come from second-guessing from the top. There's a total lack of understanding by people up the line, so I spend more time educating than doing. People at the top got there during a different era. They're so far above it, they don't have their ears to the ground. If they want me to be their ears, they've got to listen."

Formerly with Sky Chefs, Barney Blashill prefers the working environment at Levy's department store in Tucson (owned by Federated Dept. Stores, St. Louis). As Levy's foodservice director, he feels: "At Federated, we don't have the extensive support that Sky Chefs offers. We're really on our own. Developing the facility, advertising, promotion—it's 99% up to the foodservice director. But the environment here is better for me because things aren't as controlled as at Sky Chefs. They were more 'manualized,' complete with specification books. I like the opportunity to express myself that I have here."

"The ideal job," believes Jim McAlister of Marriott, "is one in which you're encouraged to take sensible risks to make an idea work. Sure, if you blow it you'll hear about it. But unless you make the wrong move consistently, your job doesn't hang on one decision. And if you do pull it off, the company recognizes that and praises you."

"The greatest fulfillment I've had on this job," says Los Angeles Hyatt Manager George Harbaugh, "was the chance to hand-pick my own team. Some hotel companies run by the book. At Hyatt, if the manager is good, he runs his own property."

Thirteen years ago, D. Michael Jeans left another hotel to become catering manager at the Pick Congress. "What I liked about the Pick then, and what I still like about it, is the freedom to express my own individuality. The Pick lets me create something and then gives me the freedom to produce it."

Ben Moore, Hardee's v.p.-operations, enjoys the excitement of fast growth at the quick service chain's headquarters. "If you don't like growth," he warns, "you won't like it here."

*Success isn't measured by the size
of the paycheck but by how big
the man feels who has earned it*

Four years ago, up-and-coming Barney Blashill traded his comfortable five-figure salary, generous benefits package and a heck of a lot of responsibility at Sky Chefs for what he'd been seeking all along: a place to sink roots. Faced with his fourth major move in almost as many years, he says, "We decided we wanted to remain in Tucson instead of continually moving around the country. We wanted a permanent home." He left Sky Chefs in 1969 to join Levy's department store as foodservice director. Been there ever since.

"I could make a helluva lot more money selling life insurance," states Mike Leven, young marketing director for Dunfey Family Corp. "But I think this industry has to change, and I'd like to be a part of the group that makes it happen. I am, by nature, a change agent. As such, I don't look at the financial things. But I do look for pats on the back. Everybody wants to feel important. I'm no status seeker, but I do seek recognition for my degree of competence."

Hardee's Vice President of Operations Ben Moore declares, "If somebody said to me, 'Ben, I'll give you $1 million a year to sit in this room and paint the walls over and over,' I wouldn't do it. Money merely serves a dual purpose: it permits enjoyment of life's comforts and it gives recognition for achievement. Though monetary gains are still used as a measure of success, over the long haul that's not going to be enough for an individual."

It's not enough for Harvey Schilling. A North Dakota native, he was installed last month as the new foodservice director of the 17 public schools in Bismarck. At age 33, Schilling has his BA and MA; until recently, he was actively pursuing his PhD. But no longer. "The college degree used to be the all-in-all. That emphasis has changed," he believes. "Now it's strictly performance. Performance will get me where I'm going, not paper. Of course, money is important to some extent. Everybody needs so much to live on. But more important are personal feelings and getting to know who you are. Money won't buy that."

Now general manager of the Los Angeles Hyatt, George

Harbaugh recalls: "I used to travel a good deal when I was in sales. About five years ago, Hyatt offered me the position of director of sales with a beautiful pay hike. I turned it down because of the amount of travel it meant."

One restaurant chain regional manager believes: "As long as I have a certain latitude in which to do my job, I'll be satisfied. And I know that if I continue to prove myself and do the job well, I'll reap financial rewards. But, more important, I'll start feeling that I'm doing something worthwhile and deriving a good feeling from it."

Jim McAlister, a regional marketing man for Marriott, says: "I once had an offer that would have increased my pay by 40%. It was a small hotel company with leisure holdings. But they wouldn't back me up with a willingness to give me a team that could solve their problems. "I didn't take the job. If you're not doing something you enjoy, all the money and bonuses and profit-sharing can't make it worthwhile."

"Westy" Westover, recently retired foodservice director of the 92 public schools in Clark County, Nev., adds: "A man doesn't have to go to the top where the money is. He's successful just being happy and busy."

Jackie Hackbart, consulting dietitian at Park Sutter Convalescent Hospital in Sacramento, Calif., agrees: "It's fine to be up there, but sometimes you can't do the best job from the top."

"I guess I just wanted to see if I could handle a multiple unit operation all by myself," explains Margaret Benton, foodservice director for Denver public schools, who came to her present position from Tulsa, Okla., in 1971. "I like to get directly involved," continues the Denver Bronco football fan.

"Back in Tulsa, I used to run the boiler rooms better than any man. Here, I like to run the dishmachines. But what really makes it great is watching some red-haired, freckled-faced boy about to eat the lunch I've helped prepare. Or receiving a letter of thanks from a school manager whose kitchen now sports a new steam kettle. That kind of satisfaction no amount of money can buy.

For an idea of what jobs in five key markets are going for, Roth Young Personnel provides the following benchmarks.

The fringe benefit package for each market is not typical; they were chosen from returns of our *1973 Executive Status* survey to illustrate what some organizations are offering to keep pace with the rising demands of today's labor market.

RESTAURANT

Unit Manager	$12-20M
Executive Chef	12-25M
Multi-Unit Gen. Mgr.	20-25M
Reg./Dist. Manager	15-20M
Div. Manager	15-20M
Dir. Layout & Design	20-25M
Dir. Adv. & P.R.	20-25M
Dir. Purchasing	15-25M
Dir. Real Estate	20-25M
Dir. Mkt./Res.	20-25M
Executive V.P.	20-30M
President	30-40M

Restaurant Fringe

Holly's offers its average employee $3,000 in fringe benefits, including income protection, long-term disability and major medical insurance, educational reimbursement, seven paid holidays (including birthdays) and stock options for executives. In 1974, profit-sharing started for everybody right down to hourly employees.

SCHOOL

Unit Manager	$12-14M
Dietitian	11-13M
Supervisory Diet.	12-14M
F&B Director	12M
General Manager	15-20M
Bus. Mgr./Admin.	15-20M
Reg./Dist. Manager	18-22M
Div. Manager	25-30M
Dir. Purchasing	12-15M
Dir. Oper./FS Dir.	15-20M

School Fringe

Anyone working for the Buffalo Board of Education from a unit manager on up receives medical and hospitalization insurance, a maximum of $20,000 life insurance, approximately 10 paid holidays, sick leave of 10 days a year accumulative to 180 days, plus the New York State Retirement Plan for all Civil Service employees. The total package averages $3,800 per employee or 26% to 28% of salary.

FRANCHISE (FAST FOOD)

Unit Manager	$12-15+M
General Manager	25+M
Reg./Dist. Manager	15-20+M
Div. Manager	15-20+M
Dir. Layout & Design	15-20M
Dir. Adv. & P.R.	15-20M
Dir. Purchasing	14-16M
Dir. Real Estate	20-25M
Dir. Mkt./Res.	20-25M
Executive V.P.	25+M
President	25+M

Franchise Fringe

In addition to seven holidays, hospital and term life insurance and a company car for general managers, George Webb Corp. offers division managers 25 shares for four years at book value, pays 100% of the retirement pension for all employees, and shares 10% of the yearly net with unit managers on up.

COLLEGE/UNIVERSITY

Unit Manager	$12-14M
Dietitian	11-13M
Supervisory Diet.	12-14M
F&B Director	12M
General Manager	15-20M
Bus. Mgr./Admin.	15-20M
Reg./Dist. Manager	18-22M
Div. Manager	25-30M
Dir. Purchasing	12-15M
Dir. Oper./FS Dir.	15-20M

College Fringe

Michigan State University provides $20,000 family hospitalization insurance, a retirement plan to which the university contributes 6% of salary, plus nine days of school-year holidays, paid sick leaves and paid vacations. The total package adds an average of $3,000 to salaries.

DIVERSIFIED MANAGEMENT

General Manager	$18-25M
Bus. Mgr./Admin.	20-30M

Dir. Layout & Design 20-25M
Dir. Adv. & P.R. 20-25M
Dir. Purchasing 15-25M
Dir. Real Estate 20-25M
Dir. Mkt./Res. 20-30M

Diversified Fringe

At CVI Service Group, Inc., all employees down to assistant managers receive insurance for which the company contributes an average of $120, while supervisors on up receive a company car plus Blue Cross and Blue Shield coverage.

The definition of success may be shifting away from straight cash considerations, but it hasn't yet reached the stage where anyone would take a job that underpays them. The question being asked, however, is "How much can I get out of this job as a person?"

THE EXPANDING WORLD OF EXECUTIVE PERKS—
FROM SUPER-MEDICAL PLANS TO
SOCIAL-SERVICE SABBATICALS*

JOHN C. PERHAM

With a squeal of brakes, John Smith's car careened up to the hospital door. Jumping out, the distraught executive carried his son into the emergency room. There a team of doctors sprang into action to treat the several injuries the youngster had sustained when a car smashed into his bicycle. A frantic half hour later, his bleeding brought under control, the boy seemed to be in reasonably good shape.

So, by that time, was his much-relieved father. The crisis over, Smith, a vice-president of one of the nation's major corporations, flashed the medical credit card he always carried with him. A nurse jotted down his name, policy number and a few other details, and off went Smith, assured that all the bills for his son's emergency and follow-up care would be sent directly to an insurance company—without a penny of cost to Smith.

A futuristic dream? Not at all. Credit-card medical care is a reality right now for key executives of one large Midwestern company. Each of its top men carries a card that guarantees direct insurance-company payments of all amounts due hospitals, doctors, dentists, psychiatrists or anyone else who treats a member of his family.

Nor is that company unique in lavishing special medical care on its top executives. Declares Pearl Meyer, vice-president of research for management consultants Handy Associates: "Probably one in every five of the 500 biggest corporations in the nation now has some kind of super-medical plan

---

*Reprinted by special permission from *Dun's*, Sept. 1973, pp. 65-67 and 147-148. Copyright, Sept. 1973, Dun and Bradstreet Publications Corporation.

for a handful of those executives who are at the very top."

Executive Compensation

As this growing coverage suggests, executive compensation is getting ever more diverse and complex as companies struggle to come up with more imaginative ways to attract topflight executives. As one consultant puts it: "New executive perquisites will continue to come into being as long as Congress keeps tightening up the tax laws."

And, he might have added, as long as the Internal Revenue Service and the accountants keep coming up with new interpretations and rulings of their own—and the stock market continues to flounder. So the list of perks keeps getting longer, and the choices—for company and executive alike—keep getting harder. Even the consultants turn prayerfully to their computers to keep track of all the possibilities and to rate one perk against another.

An executive's fringes now, for example, may include anything from social-service sabbaticals to above-contract payments for long-term disability, from furnishings for his office at home to the opportunity to buy used company cars at a discount. Actually, the compensation laundry list is as long as the ingenuity of man. On the other hand, it is not made up of separate but equal parts. In the warning words of George H. Foote, director and compensation specialist at McKinsey & Co.: "Not everything on it will stand up in the wash."

So the company that wants to keep exceptional executives must choose its lures carefully. On pages 147 to 149, *Dun's* has adapted a list of perks compiled by compensation consultants Hewitt Associates.

In its original form, it listed more than 150 items, including benefits available to all employees. *Dun's* list, limited to executive-type fringes, still offers some eighty possibilities, and does not purport to be all-inclusive.

The Changing Scene

As the whole field mushrooms, individual perks are constantly rising or falling in favor. Toppled from its former throne, for example, is the onetime king of them all: the stock option. Some companies today could not give one away. As one consultant quips: "What they should offer now is a stock option that the holder could sell short."

Moving up sharply, in contrast, are those medical benefits. The thorough physical examination most companies provide their top men is alone worth a lot more in dollars than it used to be. But much more important is that many companies, as noted, are quietly—not to say secretly—installing a special plan for a few executives. The company either reimburses these men for every dollar of personal medical expense for themselves and their families, including even nursing home care, or arranges to have bills paid directly by the insurer, as in Smith's case, thus saving the executives from having to make any outlay. Says one vice president who enjoys the latter benefit: "It's one of the best perks I've ever had."

What's more, for the employer, the coverage is not even especially costly. Explains one corporate compensation director: "Once you have everybody in the company bundled into a fairly generous medical-surgical policy, the extra cost for each of the few executives given the 100% coverage is probably no more than $1,000 a year."

The super-medical plan, then, looks like one of the most popular benefits of tomorrow. Says Donald Simpson, compensation expert for Philadelphia's Hay Associates: "The companies that have a really comprehensive medical plan for their top executives are very much pleased with it. Given today's high cost for medical care, I think this whole area is going to explode before long."

Another perk that is gaining new popularity is an old-timer: restricted stock. This, of course, is stock that the executive cannot dispose of until after a specified period (anywhere from two to 25 years), when the restrictions the company has put on it expire. To offset that disadvantage, companies often make such shares available to the executive at less than market price. Xerox Corp., for one, some years ago sold many of its executives restricted stock at half the market price—and then loaned them the money with which to buy it. Use of this perk, as compared to any kind of option, has the advantage that right from the start the executive gets physical possession of his shares, and begins receiving dividends on them.

THE TOP FIFTEEN

The perks executives want most vary enormously, depending on a man's age, temperament, family circumstances, life-style—even the city he lives in. Still, there is a select group of perks that are used to attract the U.S.' most talented executives, and offered by the companies that are most adept at holding such talent. The company that gets more than its share of outstanding executives, then, generally will be providing a high percentage of these most-wanted fringes:
1) Financial counseling
2) Tax assistance
3) Legal assistance
4) Company automobile
5) Chauffeur
6) First-class plane travel
7) Club memberships
8) Liberal expense accounts
9) Personal use of business credit cards
10) Special loans at low interest
11) Home entertainment allowance
12) Travel to conventions, etc., for wives
13) Thorough physical examinations
14) Medical reimbursement plan
15) Early retirement—at the executive's choice

But restricted stock was thought to have been done in by some of the 1969 tax changes that served to devalue so many stock options. Not so, says Howard Meadors, a compensation specialist for Hewitt Associates. "Restricted stock," says Meadors, "even now enables a company to reward a man handsomely for outstanding performance."

But how? Take the case of an $80,000-a-year man whose company wants to give him an extra $20,000 in recognition of a job superbly done—but they both want to defer payment, so he will not have to pay any tax on the money now. Here they run into a problem that is still not widely recognized. As most executives are well aware, the highest tax rate that can now be levied on earned income is 50%. What many of them do not realize, however, is that unearned income—the kind that comes from interest, dividends or rent, for example—may still be taxed at anywhere up to 70%. So may any income that is deferred—with the single exception of restricted stock, which qualifies for the more generous earned-income tax.

The difference can be considerable. If the company gives our $80,000 executive a lump sum cash payment of $20,000, to be paid in retirement, the tax on that $20,000, when he gets it, could come to $14,000, or 70%. But if he takes it instead in restricted stock, and holds the stock for as little as two or three years (if the company will be so generous), then his tax on the same $20,000 is figured at the earned rate, a maximum of $10,000. Total tax savings: $4,000.

Of key importance to a growing number of executives is financial counseling covering all their personal affairs, a benefit that has come from nowhere in two short years ("Financial Counseling: Now It's the Top Perk," *Dun's*, July, 1973). Counseling has already proved a major plus for many a company eager to woo an exceptional executive away from a rival—and there is no question it will loom still larger as a perk in the months to come.

Meanwhile, some benefits go on year after year, unspectacular but highly prized. Take that traditional symbol of executivedom, the use of a company car. "When executives begin clamoring for company cars," observes McKinsey's Foote sardonically, "you can be pretty sure the corporation has no major compensation problems. They are just looking for another candle to put on the compensation cake." For that matter, a few companies—Armstrong Cork, 3M and Bethlehem Steel come to mind—sternly oppose company cars as an inexcusable extravagance.

Nonetheless, survey after survey shows that this perk ranks high, sometimes highest of all, with executives—in tandem with that simplest of executive fringes, a reserved space in the company parking lot. Some corporations get even more mileage from their cars by selling them eventually to their executives at bargain prices. The company car, then, as simple as it may seem, should not be underrated as an executive motivator. "Like most perks," observes Hewitt's Meadors, "it offers a combination of personal prestige and dollar savings."

Those savings will vary, of course, depending, among other things, on where the executive lives and works. In the Midwest, for example, a man can save perhaps $1,800 a year by using a company car instead of his own—particularly if his company is generous about how he accounts for its use, as between private and corporate purposes. In the Greater New York area, compensation specialists peg the company car as a benefit worth upwards of $2,500 a year.

Vacations and Expense Accounts

Another ageless benefit that is taking on new life (believe it or not) is the vacation. Time was when a lot of men at the top grimly refused to take their two or three weeks off every year, in the belief they were indispensable (or perhaps the nagging suspicion that they were not). Today those same men, watching long-service employees at the lowest corporate level going off happily for a month or so, feel that they have been needlessly losing out on a good thing. So suddenly awakened top executives are starting to take all the time off that the company allows. Some have even discovered a new perk: extra vacation.

For that matter, there is more than just tired humor in that old standby of corporate life, the expense account. It still is a mark of one-upmanship if a man can flaunt more of the long green, or its equivalent, in credit cards, than his colleagues. And what separates the men from the boys in this department? A select few have virtually unlimited amounts at their disposal, for entertainment at home or elsewhere. But they are the exception.

Home entertainment is a special kind of perk, because an executive who does it on his company's behalf usually accounts for what he spends directly to the IRS, not to the company. But this sort of thing is out of bounds for most executives. Says Hay's Simpson: "It is only the very top guys who are allowed the luxury of entertaining customers and others for dinner at home. Most companies prefer to have all their other executives take guests out to dinner, where there is tangible substantiation of everything that is spent. In home entertaining, there are often lingering questions."

As for expenses outside the home, companies vary greatly in what they will allow. Says one consultant: "The companies that are liberal with expense accounts make it a practice not to question anything. Others have very specific guidelines about what they will or will not allow. They have hard and fast rules, for instance, as to who travels first class and who must go tourist. And they are just as rigid about where a man stays when he travels. Some companies expect him to stay at the swankiest hotel in every town. Others insist on a Holiday Inn."

Interestingly, expense-account mores differ not only from company to company but from industry to industry. Declares Simpson: "In industrial companies, the lowest man on the totem pole always picks up the check, so someone higher up can okay it. In non-industrial companies, especially insurance firms, the game is played just the opposite way. There the top man pays the chit, because nobody ever questions his judgment."

Always important, but more or less static on the perk list right now, are club memberships. Many companies that have joined the recent exodus to the suburbs would like now to make greater use of country clubs in particular, if only because they are so convenient. But, says Simpson: "Clubs are not gaining further because the revenuers are cracking down in that area. They are refusing to allow a deduction unless a man uses his membership more than half the time for business. To avoid endless haggling with IRS, many executives now use one club exclusively for business and another strictly for personal recreation and relaxation."

And what is ahead for executive perks? Amid such rapid shifts, it is almost impossible to say. But aside from the increasingly popular fringes already mentioned, several consultants think the next big surge will come in a perk that already has spread fairly widely in the past few years: early retirement.

"Early retirement," declares Peter Friedes, a Hewitt partner, "is increasingly important to many executives. They are greatly concerned about getting a full pension without having to wait until they are 65. What they really want is a choice between continuing to work and retiring in relative comfort. Above all, they want that choice to be their own, not the company's. And that trend can only gain momentum in the months ahead."

Unless, that is, the other executive perks simply get too good to leave.

The Executive Laundry List

No executive today fully realizes how many perquisites may go into his compensation package—not, at least, until he sits down and adds them up. While it is unlikely that any one executive gets all of them, the following list gives some idea of how many perks and extra-compensation benefits—both current and deferred—are now being used to supplement the executive salary.

RESERVED COMPENSATION

Capital Accumulation

Deferred salary plan
Deferred bonus
Savings plan
Deferred profit-sharing
Stock bonus plan
Stock purchase plan
Restricted stock bonus plan
Share unit plan
Stock appreciation rights
Restricted stock plan
Stock option plan
Phantom stock
Incentive growth fund

Financial Protection

Pension
Deferred profit-sharing
Savings plan
Retirement gratuity
Long-term sick pay
Sickness or accident insurance
Long-term disability benefit
Personal accident insurance
Accidental death, dismemberment insurance

Severance pay
Group life insurance
Split-dollar life insurance
Survivors' benefits
Hospital-surgical-medical insurance
Dental and eye-care insurance
Health-maintenance organization fees
Home health care
Nursing-home care

INDIRECT PAY

Services

Moving and relocation costs
Placement fees
Business and professional memberships
Paid attendance at business, professional and other outside meetings
Company medical department
Outside medical services
Psychiatric services
Company-provided or subsidized travel
Recreation facilities
Tuition refunds
Matching educational donations
Scholarships for dependents
Personal hotel and travel reservations
Tickets for theater and sporting events
Barber and beauty shop
Social-service sabbaticals

Perquisites

Financial counseling
Legal assistance
Tax assistance
Low-interest loans
Physical examination
Medical reimbursement plan
Company-provided automobile
Company-provided plane
Company-provided boat
Company-provided apartment
Home entertainment allowance
Club memberships
Personal use of expense account
Personal use of business credit card
Extra paid vacation
Chauffeur
Executive dining room

INTANGIBLES

Title
Job status
Opportunity for growth
Opportunity for recognition
Supervision
Training programs
Job challenge
Geographic location
Organizational climate
Job security

MANAGING MANAGEMENT RESOURCES THROUGH CORPORATE CONSTITUTIONALISM*

ROBERT GRANFORD WRIGHT**

There is a void in policy guidelines for the responsible treatment of lower and middle management employees. While a "constitution" to protect the rights of these people may seem problematical in terms of what it should cover, and who would administer it, it may be the least troublesome of all the possible alternatives now facing us.

Contemporary managers have met the challenge of maintaining workable human relationships in large-scale organizations. These evolving organizations are the most inventive social arrangements of our age and of civilization. It is a marvel to know that tens of thousands of people with highly individuated backgrounds, skills, and interests are coordinated in various enterprises to pursue common institutionalized goals. The credit for this social phenomenon goes to skilled, professional managers. It is thus strange that these managers are now being charged with the ills of organizations that came as a by-product of their meeting the requirement of society for major enterprises.

Critics of the quality of life within complex organizations

---

*Human Resource Management, Summer 1973, pp. 15-23. Reprinted with permission.
**The author is Associate Professor of Management at Arizona State University and the Visiting Professor in Manpower Studies at Cornell University. He was formerly the Assistant Dean for Graduate Programs in Economics and Business Administration at Arizona State and is now a consultant in organization planning and management development to such enterprises as AT&T, Motorola, and the U.S. Government. He has had eleven years of line management experience with General Telephone and Electronics Corporation.

assert that men in positions of unbridled power often become arbitrary and capricious; that men with unconstrained authority commonly impose unreasonable conformity and injustice upon subordinates. The critics—though they merely underscore the longstanding fact that living with authority has never been easy—are now being heard with renewed interest. Not since the philosophical struggles of men like Locke and Nietzsche has man been as concerned with the persistent and paradoxical problem of organized life: freedom versus authority. People, particularly in the burgeoning youthful segment of society, have a revitalized interest in the uneasy balance required to fill man's ambivalent needs for self-determination and the inevitable personal restrictions required for cooperative efforts.

Though the issue neither began, nor will it end with the corporation, corporate leadership is involved. The corporation continues to function more or less as an independent power center in its governance over employees. As such, it has become the natural target of many of the disaffected members of society when they address this issue of social justice; that is, the quality of life in a corporation. In private enterprises, inequities do exist, injustices do occur, and processes for review of decisions are often unavailable. At times, unnecessary interest is directed to the private lives of employees and unreasonable demands made for conformity to some set of norms, simply because requirements for effective contribution to organizational activity have not been developed. As the social scientist and consultant, Leonard R. Sayles, puts it:

> Not knowing how to assess Jones' contribution to effective management, we evolve irrational fetishes and taboos. The striped tie, the ivy-league suit, the sheepskin, the appropriate tone of voice, automobile, wife and home location, even the testing program designed to exclude all but the "safe" pedestrian types: these are all manifestations of imperfect knowledge about how to evaluate employees.[1]

Though Sayles is quick to point out that such behavioral patterns are not the inevitable, or inescapable products of life

---

1. Leonard R. Sayles, *Individualism and Big Business*, (New York: McGraw-Hill Book Company, Inc., 1963), p. 182-3.

in a large organization, they do exist. Nonsensical demands for conformity, according to someone's set of norms (sometimes idealized and sometimes perverse) will continue until we recognize that major enterprises need people with diverse patterns of thought and behavior, and until we give explicit franchise to individuality through written policies.

The purpose of this article[1] is to encourage reflection on the idea of corporate constitutionalism to preserve the rights of corporate "citizens," consistent with the requirements of the enterprise for some degree of coordinated direction toward preset goals. The thrust of these constitutionalized processes is primarily aimed toward management employees— from first-level supervisors to upper managers—for it is this group that is customarily disenfranchised by lack of contractual arrangements.

"Constitutionalizing" corporations would provide the means through which employees at all levels of authority are ensured the right to reasonable treatment and due process. A constitution would include written codes of ethical personnel practice, and a quasi-judicial procedure and structure to review decisions and resolve disputes. The conditions set forth would apply to all employees not now protected by similar statutes.

> For example, corporate constitutionalism might be made operational in the following way: Suppose that a decision were made by a line manager to demote a subordinate supervisor. The manager "feels" that the action is justified by abundant evidence (for example, the subordinate's inability to attain goals). Further, the superior believes that under the codes of ethical conduct, he has given the subordinate adequate time *and* sufficient support to correct the deficiency; yet, acceptable performance does not occur. At this point, under constitutional processes, the manager must review his decision and the conditions leading to the decision with a higher board before taking action. The supervisor subjected to the demotion decision has the right to challenge it; due process provides the

---

1. The writer expresses his appreciation to Judge Harry Krauss (retired) for his valuable advice on certain legal points in this paper.

means to have a full hearing before final action is taken.

You will note that corporate constitutionalism does not usurp corporate power. Rather, it distributes power so that it is used responsibly to ensure reasonable and equitable treatment of employees. Constitutionalism could be made a binding obligation through contractual provisions agreed to by both the corporation and employees upon their advancement into management.

Orthodox constitutional doctrine considered only two entities—the State and the individual; it must now be recognized that concentrations of corporate power produce a society that is not totalitarian, but is pluralistic, and constitutional, in structure. We are urged by Richard Eells and Clarence Walton in their book, *Conceptual Foundations of Business*, to recognize "That another formidable entity has intervened between the individual and his government—*the organized group.*"[1] It is inevitable that there is an accompanying danger that the importance of the individual and concern for his rights will decline.

If business leaders are to become socially as well as economically responsible; if business leaders are to be concerned with the quality of life within corporations, as well as economic and technical considerations; if business leaders are to accept responsibility—then, they would wish the group most intimately influenced by institutional power—the employees—to be protected. The pattern of corporate governance begins with its employees—whether the emerging behavior is dictatorial or democratic, integrated or isolationistic, responsible or irresponsible.

The Problem

Many daily wage employees are provided a form of constitutionality through a labor agreement. Most contracts are designed to provide regulations to assure justice, equity, and due process. Perhaps the strongest appeal of all unions is their ability to *contractually* protect the individual employee against arbitrary and capricious acts by preventing discrimina-

---

1. Richard Eells and Clarence Walton, *Conceptual Foundations of Business.* (Homewood, Ill.: Richard D. Irwin, Inc., 1969), p. 408.

tory treatment. Almost all current agreements include provisions for hearing grievances—a procedural structure to provide a review process so that each individual employee is ensured a full hearing of his complaints.

When an employee proves himself to be promising, he is often encouraged to accept promotion to management. If he is willing to accept attendant responsibilities, he typically *loses* the protection of his individual rights. As a consequence, he now becomes exposed to those same decisions and actions that constitutionality is designed to restrain. He may then be subjected to the will of men in superior power positions without representation or recourse. Fair treatment is ensured through the protection gained in contractual agreements or through personal power. When employees are advanced into management positions, the protection provided by contractual agreements (union or other) is lost, and power sufficient to protect their own interests is not acquired until managers move into upper echelons of the hierarchy.

Thus, since the sum of protection and power is inadequate to enforce equitable arrangements—a security gap occurs for lower and middle managers. The security gap might be illustrated in graph form. If one hundred equals the degree of power and/or protection necessary to absolutely ensure fair treatment, then employees in lower and middle positions of authority are exposed to possibilities of unfair treatment; the human resources are not secure from misuse or abuse. A security gap results. (See graph on facing page.)

Managers who lack security, and do not have the means to gain it, might devise ways to bridge the gap. They might attempt to gain support from those in more powerful positions through political strategies and conformity to expected behavior.

Managers might protect their positions through empire-building—toward becoming indispensable. Or, they might keep a constant vigil on developments in the labor market as a possible escape hatch.

Whatever tactic is employed, it can be injurious to sound human relationships, and in turn, to a sound enterprise.

Though top management may strive to preserve "fair treatment" for employees in management, those formal procedures that apply to organized employees are not guaranteed to managers. They become privileges, not rights. Hence, the treatment of a management person may become haphazard. It will depend largely on the predisposition—the attitudinal, moral, and ethical temperament—of his immediate superior. Herein lies the problem.

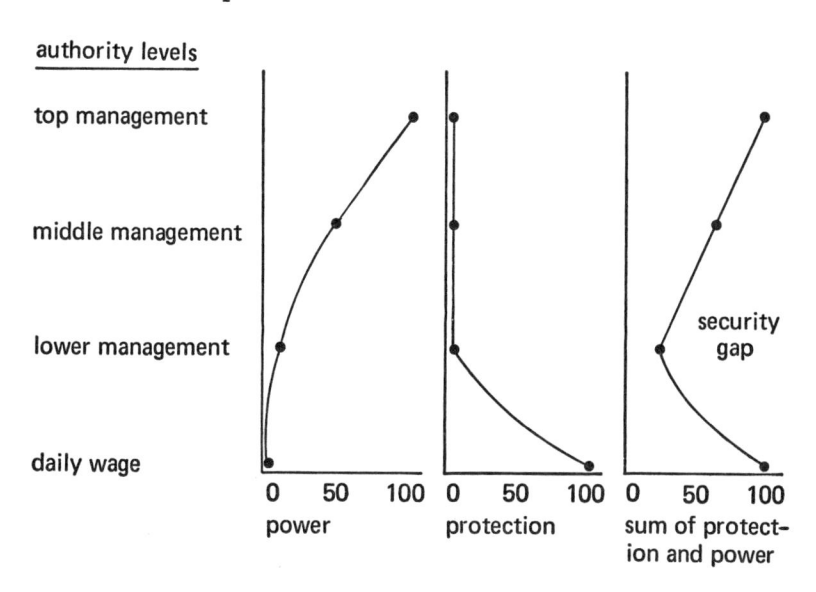

authority levels

[Chart showing three plots across authority levels (top management, middle management, lower management, daily wage) against: power (0–100), protection (0–100), and sum of protection and power (0–100), with "security gap" labeled on the third plot.]

TYRANNY OF AD HOCISM

Ad hocism is a useful term to refer to managerial decisions that are made for a particular situation or matter at hand without giving consideration to its broader or continued application. The decisions are unprecedented and do not establish precedence. They appear tyrannical because they are arbitrary in that they upset the continuity of treatment from which equitable human relationships stem. So, on a certain issue, one decision would be made for one subordinate, and a different decision might be made for another employee under the *same* set of circumstances. The consequence is inequity.

For example, consider the situation in which two equally qualified men are being considered for advancement. In the absence of written policies, differentiation between the candidates is left to the inclinations of the superior authority responsible for the selection decision. The basis for distinguishing one candidate over the other may thus degenerate to personal prejudices involving such irrelevant characteristics as mannerisms, personableness, rapport, or even length of hair. The stated criteria of professional competence is, as a consequence, subordinated to the whims of a superior, but rationalized away by his reinterpretation of the requirement for the advanced position. Since whims tend to change, on the next decision a new set of criteria may be imposed. The erratic behavior that ensues can only be seen as inequitable treatment by those subjected to it.

Ad hocism is a favored form of discrimination used by some superiors in the treatment of management employees. Without policy guidelines, prejudices and preconditioning rise to fill the void in the network of authority. And from particularized judgments (often emotionally laden) stem such crucially important matters as decisions on promotions, merit reviews, wage increases, assignment of resources, provision of opportunities, and degrees of cooperation. Though some residual power may be required by top management to make delicate differentiations, policy guidelines are also needed to provide continuity to decisions of a recurring nature.

ABHORRENCE OF DISSENT

Far too often (once is too often), the superiors of managers find dissent in thinking, or different behavior, repugnant. Disagreement becomes a threat to institutionalized processes, and a challenge to individual authority. Though some leaders actively encourage nonconforming thinking and action commensurate with coordinated effort, some others demand compliance to accepted norms when it is not required to preserve order or to protect authority. Yet, the right of dissent is not only the irreducible test of democracy, it is also prerequisite to nudging an enterprise to change: to assuring the viability necessary for institutional survival.

Most organizations fall short of their intended promise not because of misguided purpose, faulty doctrines, or stupidity, but rather because of introspection, rigidity, and the internal decay stemming from unquestioning obedience.[1] To some it seems the mature, secure corporation develops a condition of chronic myopia.

> A corporation is a social system . . . that tends to develop within it pressure groups and empire builders. It develops taboos, prejudices, policies, and rules of thumb. It develops sacred cows and scapegoats. It has pride in every corner. Instead of being oriented toward the conquest of some aspects of the external environment, it has an inclination toward introspection. It is overly concerned with its internal problems of communication, organization, and lines of command. The energies of the more talented, more aggressive, more ambitious employees often seem to be taken up with internal problems of power, prestige, and position. The corporation which is well established tends to become complacent and set in its ways. At times, this may make it appear to suffer from a kind of intellectual incest.[2]

Dissent is necessary to avoid the limited outlook, to overcome the functional blindness that keeps leaders from solving problems in their enterprises because they cannot see their problems. Some would advance the basic principle of human organizations that men in positions of power cannot trust themselves to be adequately self-critical (no more than the rest of us), that the danger of self-deception is great, and that rationalizing faults as virtues or necessities is common.[3]

The only protection is to create a cultural atmosphere in which management employees can speak out without fear of reprisal or coercion. The right of free speech is fundamental to a healthy society (including corporate enterprise). Specific provisions to allow for vigorous criticism must be made if an enduring system is to be ensured, and the tyranny of the limited outlook is to be prevented.

---

1. See Chapter VIII, "The Life and Death of Institutions," John W. Gardner, *No Easy Victories,* Harper & Row, 1968, pp. 39-47.
2. Thomas M. Ware, "An Executive's Viewpoint," *Operations Research,* Vol. 8, 1959, pp. 3-4.
3. Gardner, pp. 42-43.

ABSENCE OF CHECKS AND BALANCES

As the right to free speech protects the innovators and reformers, due process as an important corollary to constitutionalism provides checks and balances on power. It does not usurp power, but rather procedurally channels its responsible use so that individual interests are protected from unreasonable or arbitrary acts.

Today, few management employees enjoy the right of due process. Personnel policies may provide the privilege of review for decisions and actions affecting managerial employees, but few guarantee the right of due process afforded employees represented by a union. As a result, a decision by a superior concerning a subordinate in management is usually not reviewed and often not even known to others who might be in a position to be critical.

No procedure for checks and balances is operationally effective. If checks are made, superiors understandably defend their subordinate managers' decisions in the interest of preserving a unified stand and the integrity of the managers' authority. For example, say that a superior decides that a subordinate manager should be demoted. He then builds a "case" to justify, or rationalize, his decision. After gaining support from higher management, he demotes the subordinate. The subordinate may feel that he has been treated unjustly, yet, if he considers appealing to higher authorities, he believes (probably correctly) that they will back his immediate superior in his decision. Thus, he looks to other alternatives open to him. He can resign, but he feels entrapped by accruals of fringe benefits such as retirement, sick leave, medical and life insurance. He may be able to transfer, but necessary approval is another prerogative of his superior. He can decrease his participation in the enterprise so that contributions and rewards are in closer balance. Or, he can become discontent, alienated, or even vindictive in his future relationships with the enterprise.

Whatever tack he takes, the losses over the span of his career are immense. And this waste may have been caused by the arbitrary use of the largely unchecked power of a superior over a subordinate.

The Concept of Human Resource Management

Let us tighten the problem down further by considering the idea of managing men as valuable corporate *assets*,[1] and by considering shortly thereafter the areas in which constitutional processes may help the enterprise to gain a satisfactory return on its investment in human resources. Conventional accounting practices are undergoing somewhat unconventional changes on a test basis to make possible measuring man as a capital resource. Beyond technical considerations, human resource accounting holds significant implications for the treatment, and the management, of human assets. The concept points up the necessity, if not urgency, for reliable means to both protect the assets and to ensure that irresponsible decisions on personnel matters do not impede or lessen returns on investments.[2] Assume that through some generally accepted way of capitalizing assets—acquisition costs, replacement costs, or economic value—it is found that the management employee to be used here for illustrative purposes represents a capital investment of $200,000. The enterprise naturally expects an acceptable return on this outlay. Under current practices, appropriate treatment is largely left to the discretion of the employee's superior. If he is effective, payoff results. If he is ineffective, yield on the investment is lessened or lost.

RESPONSIBILITY FOR DEVELOPING THE HUMAN RESOURCE

Today, a line manager is typically responsible for the lion's share of the development of his subordinates. The arrangement produces questionable results for several reasons. First,

---

1. For a discussion of the accounting model for human asset accounting, see R. Lee Brummet, Eric G. Flamholtz, and William C. Pyle, "Human Resource Measurement—A Challenge for Accountants," *The Accounting Review*, Vol. 43, No. 2, April, 1968, pp. 217-224, or Eric Flamholtz's "Human Resources Accounting: Measuring Positional Replacement Costs," *Human Resource Management*, Vol. 12, No. 1, Spring, 1973, pp. 8-16.
2. These implications are discussed in my earlier article, "Managing Man as a Capital Asset," *Personnel Journal*, Vol. 69, No. 4, April, 1970, pp. 290-298.

his business day is absorbed by pressing operative or administrative work. More urgent tasks drain his time and intellectual energies, so that he defers the task of developing his subordinates (often the only aspect of a manager's work that can be deferred). Second, there are currently no rewards to a line manager for adding value to human assets. And third, top management does not now possess the procedural guidelines to approve capital budgets for human development, and thus, it does not insist upon the programs toward developing personnel.

As a consequence, developmental leadership is popularly espoused but erratically implemented. The $200,000 human investment in our example, for which the line manager is responsible, may be neglected and become obsolete, or lose incentive, which results in a financial drain from the management resource. If, on the other hand, top management explicitly recognized the individual value of its managers and supported written policies to maintain and attempt to increase the value of its human assets, its managers directly responsible for training would allocate their time and energies to include the continuing development of human resources.

Moreover, greater concern should be directed to assure that employees, once "developed," are assigned activities that are sufficiently challenging to realize a maximum return on investment. Yet, employees are often "under cast" in a role not requiring their full capabilities—for example, in a management position estimated to match the skills of a manager who represents an investment of $100,000 which is of necessity filled by a manager who represents a $200,000 investment. In a word, he is "cast too low" to bring a desirable rate of return. With promotions currently based predominantly on attrition, "under casting" is widespread.

With greater awareness of the implications of human-resource accounting, superiors would be alerted to underutilized talents. Astute managers would provide work-related activities to fill the disparity between present demands of the job and the capabilities possessed by the person holding the job. The employee's contributions would be broadened on the basis of potential competence; he would not have to stagnate until a more suitable position became available through attrition. Deliberate steps would be taken to provide opportunities to those persons whose upward progression is blocked. Job enlargement, expansion, and enrichment would be designed; special assignments would be provided; and a participative setting to encourage involvement in enterprise goals could be moved from theory to practical reality.

Given an awareness of unused human talents (achieved through human resource accounting), managers would strive to broaden the spans of responsibilities of employees who represent major investments. It would be done not only to provide the opportunity to realize a sufficient return on a valuable asset, but also to create a work atmosphere in which individual enterprise can flourish.

DEALING WITH THE INEFFECTIVE HUMAN RESOURCE

Today, when a management person becomes ineffectual for some reason, a number of alternatives are available to his superior. Among the relevant prerogatives, he can: a) replace the person by relegating him to a less sensitive position, b) terminate him, c) continue to tolerate substandard performance, or d) re-orient and redevelop the person so that he can meet the demands of the situation. Without the knowledge that the employee represents a sunk, or irretrievable investment (in our example, $200,000), and without the personnel policies to protect the investment—all alternatives mentioned are truly relevant. Often, the alternatives of replacement and termination appear to be the most appropriate.

If, by contrast, the superior of the underproductive subordinate had considered the employee as a $200,000 asset and had enlightened policies to guide him toward attaining an optimal return on that investment, all alternatives but one become irrelevant. The alternatives of replacement, downgrading, termination, and continued tolerance of subpar performance are unsuitable because they fail to maximize return on investment. Only one alternative stands the test of this definition of the problem: Efforts must be made to refurbish and retool the $200,000 human asset, in the same way that management would reinvest in any other valuable asset (equipment, plant, or technique) when for some reason it becomes ineffective or underproductive.

On other valuable fixed assets, however, the means have been developed, first, to financially account for them; and second, to provide standardized operating procedures for their treatment to protect the enterprise from irresponsible losses. At this time, managers lack information on the value of employees and guidelines for appropriate treatment of this—the most valuable, and only vital asset of the enterprise.

The Means to Social and Economic Responsibility Within the Enterprises

Responsible behavior always implies that the behaver knows something about the ramifications of his decisions, and that he has a standard against which his actions can be judged. Human asset accounting provides the leader with an estimate of the ramifications of his decisions concerning people. Constitutionalism provides the standard for action, and a firm's personnel policies provide an extension and expression of the guarantees secured by constitutionalism.

Constitutionalism is a means to protect human resources. It does not erode power (or authority), but defines conditions for its responsible use. Constitutionalism seeks to establish a basis for government to resolve the major problem in all forms of human association: how to *preserve* the authority required by an organization to reach its goals in a practical, orderly, and efficient way; and how to *limit* authority to those areas rather than to permit it to overflow into matters that are beyond its sector of basic concern.

A framework of constitutionalism is urgently needed for contemporary organizations to enhance their compatibility with the broader society from which they attract human resources.[1] Indeed, it is apparent to a number of thoughtful persons that unless corporations adopt guidelines for the treatment of personnel which closely parallel their treatment in the broader society, the powers of corporations will be usurped. The following observation by Eells and Walton is representative of this view:

> The assumption of the economic organization that, with the help of technology, it is furthering the pristine

---
1. Benjamin M. Selekman, *A Moral Philosophy of Management*, (New York; McGraw-Hill Book Company, 1959), p. 206.

American vision of the good life may be mistaken. The American way of life is a way not of status but of equal opportunity, not of media persuasion but of free choice, not of organization but of individualism. Any private government in the United States that fails to take into consideration this aspect of its history may find its private character altered to fit the simple, uncompromising, and still perennial demands of the men who drew up the Mayflower Compact.[1]

The drafters of the Mayflower Compact agreed to submit to authority required by the enterprise, but only through rules of conduct, duly constituted, with which *they were agreed*. This is the spirit behind constitutionalism. Though the philosophy of constitutionalism has found application predominantly in political governments, it is now "finding its way into other larger organizations as a result of social pressures to assure that power is used justly."[2] Corporate constitutionalism is needed to ensure decisions and actions to protect valuable human assets.

WHAT WOULD IT COVER?

The constitution would take the form of written policies and rules setting forth standards, embodied into binding form, for the treatment of *all* personnel. Rules would prescribe the terms of common transactions between employees and superiors in advance and thus minimize bargaining power over them. Though some bargainable transactions are, of course, necessary to retain organizational flexibility, those transactions "in which the cost of flexibility is too great must be covered by rules."[3] The cost of mishandling valuable human resources is indeed "too great" to be left to ad hoc decisions. To bargain where conformity holds a premium is particularly dangerous when procedures for checks and balances on the outcomes of such issues are often operationally

---

1. Eells and Walton, p. 412.
2. Keith Davis and Robert L. Blomstrom, *Business, Society and Environment: Social Power and Social Response*, 2nd ed., (New York: McGraw-Hill Book Company, 1971), p. 97.
3. Alfred Kuhn, *The Study of Society: A Unified Approach*, (Homewood, Ill.: Richard D. Irwin, and The Dorsey Press, 1963), p. 506.

ineffective. Constitutional rules provide a set program for uniform treatment of personnel. More important, in this instance, rules also stabilize bargaining power relationships.

The constitution governing corporate citizens should include the following minimum written provisions:

Protection of human resources from arbitrary or unreasonable practices.

Pronouncement of codes of ethical management practices to be used in dealings with employees.

Remedies for abuses of constitutional provisions.

Procedural checks and balances on the use of authority through a review process for appeal.

Judicial review through which issues receive impartial review, and whose deliberations are binding to the parties involved.

Designing the provisions for corporate constitutionalism is scarcely an easy or neat project. Indeed, it necessitates the design of new subsystems of standards and review so that the firm can be more consistent with the broader society in its treatment of people. Yet, management has ably met similar challenges in the past. It has designed *elaborate* subsystems for the protection and preservation of other corporate assets.

HOW WOULD IT BE ADMINISTERED?

Even after constitutional processes are designed, persistent questions will remain as to their implementation: What circumstances constitute violations of constitutional rights? How is the right to due process assured for a manager without the fear of reprisal? What penalties are appropriate for managers who violate the integrity of the constitution? And, finally, who serves on the "supreme court" of a corporate society to hear and deliberate cases? Alas, as Selekman observed, "the carrying out of social and moral responsibility in complex situations is hardly ever a tidy, roseate affair except in utopian narratives."[1] But, orderly or idealistic progress may be sacrificed in the interest of the broader urgency of resolving the problem for two reasons. First, constitutionalism is necessary if human resources are to be treated

---

1. Benjamin M. Selekman, *A Moral Philosophy for Management*, (New York: McGraw-Hill Book Company, 1959), p. 219.

responsibly. And, second, it is commonly believed that there are only two major possibilities for the control of corporate power: Controls of managerial power by external agencies and internal controls through institutionalized devices within the firm, designed to secure responsible corporate government.[1]

Alternatives to Corporate Constitutionalism

There are a number of alternatives to assuring responsible governance of management employees other than through corporate constitutionalism. 1) Many believe that the time is ripe for lower and middle managers to be organized into unions. 2) It may be that if conciliatory means are not developed, fringe benefits will be tied to national associations of managers rather than to specific firms so that greater freedom of movement will be made possible. 3) Lacking due process under a constitutionalized arrangement, management employees are more frequently taking their grievances and appeals to the civil courts for redress. 4) There are those who agree that the way to meet the problem of governance lies in the long tradition of the law—both common law and constitutional law: "Corporate action may in the not distant future be held to the controlled by the provisions of the Fourteenth Amendment . . . Where the corporation is actually working under state regulation, . . . the tie-up between corporate authority and state authority becomes clear."[2]
5) Still others believe that moderation of abusive uses of power will occur in less explicit ways through organized management, litigation, or further governmental intervention. They observe that in organizations where illegitimate authority is used, employees counter with more subtle tactics. Consider, for instance, a firm that has built an image as one that uses its power only in the legitimate sense, and acts as the protector of the interests of its management personnel.

Imagine further that the leaders of this company unilaterally impose a major cutback in employees or a reorganization, which changes the major bargain it made with its employees

---
1. Eells and Walton, p. 509.
2. Adolf A. Berle, *The 20th Century Capitalist Revolution*, (New York: Harcourt, Brace and Co., 1954), p. 104.

as they view it. The management employees sense that their immediate bargaining power is seriously affected so that a possible threat exists to their job, status, salary, security, and progress. Employees may retaliate by illegitimate evasions of authority and a negative, defensive stance toward any proposed changes until their own positions are assured.[1]

> The organization's assertion of its freedom to make important changes without prior staff approval can therefore be expected to reduce the organization's flexibility in gaining ungrudging assent in the details of daily life thereafter. Single large, or repeated small, uses of illegitimate authority often lead to malingering, efforts to evade or thwart instructions, and a general un-enthusiasm toward the organization's goals.[2]

In the absence of constitutionalized arrangements, decisions arbitrarily imposed can weaken the effectiveness of a leader with his subordinates. A leader bargains on his own behalf for, say, a raise, promotion, or acceptance of an idea. Rejections of his requests indicate that he is a relatively weak bargainer, or of little relative value, and this reduces his status with subordinates and peers. Likewise, a reprimand or censure for presumed or actual misconduct lowers his status and bargaining power over those under his authority.[3] Thus, if the chain of management is no stronger than its weakest link, unrestrained uses of power can bring on less effective leadership due to losses of status; such a condition will reverberate downward throughout the organization.

Conclusion

Though corporate constitutionalism for the protection of human assets is difficult to frame and tedious to administer, it appears to be superior to other alternatives available. Management unions create bi-allegiant leaders and forced relationships. Court settlements bring unwarranted costs and notoriety. Government concern is often followed by government control. Counteracting behavioral patterns inject ineffi-

---

1. Kuhn, pp. 506-7.
2. Kuhn, p. 507.
3. James G. March and Herbert A. Simon, *Organizations*, (New York: John Wiley and Sons, 1958), p. 78.

ciency and rigidity into organized arrangements. It seems apparent that responsible executives would find these alternatives repugnant. In response, they would develop and administer the means to measure the value of human resources and frame an operationally functional charter to ensure employee's responsible—fair and reasonable—treatment.

It appears that as nature abhors a vacuum, so do organizational relationships. When voids appear in power and responsibility relationships, these voids tend to be filled. We are here concerned with the common void in policy guidelines for the responsible treatment of lower and middle management employees. History teaches that when responsibilities are not met, power is lost. The growth of legislation to assume responsibility for employee safety, health, compensation, unemployment compensation, and civil rights, all bear abundant evidence to support this fact. And in turn, they give credence to the idea that, "in the long run, those who do not use power in a manner which society considers responsible will tend to lose it."[1]

To act responsibly, both fiscally and socially, leaders need to reconceive the true nature of human resources. Management employees, rather than representing drains on operating funds, are valuable corporate assets. Once recognized *explicitly*, leaders will become crucially concerned with the development of personnel policies and practices to protect each valuable resource. To "protect" assets, in this sense, means maximizing future returns on the investment to the corporation. Because returns from human resources are encouraged by ensuring equity, justice, harmony, identification, and commitment, policies need to be extended and adapted from constitutional principles and applied to corporate citizens.

---

1. This is the so-called "Iron Law of Responsibility." See Davis and Blomstrom, Chapter 6.

Scene 2

LEADERSHIP — MOTIVATION

In "Delegation: Key to Involvement," the author begins from the position that employee involvement in the decision-making process is important for both worker productivity and job satisfaction. He claims that one way to attain the necessary involvement is through delegation. The vital questions that he attempts to answer include: Why aren't managers more willing to delegate responsibility? When managers are willing to delegate, how can they best accomplish their objectives? What will be the end results of adequate delegation for both the manager and the organization?

Dr. Feinberg analyzes, in the next article, the phenomenon of decision-avoidance that plagues so many managers and companies. First, he examines the excuses for delaying decisions which range from "going by the book" to "ideologizing the issue." Then, assuming that an individual wishes to overcome his propensity for indecision, he prescribes methods of self-examination which can help alleviate the problem.

In an article which covers both leadership and motivation,

William J. Morgan asks the question: "Do You Really Know Your Employees?" The essence of his treatise is that the things which the employees really want are based on their backgrounds and needs, and that unless management has an accurate assessment of these it will be impossible to lead and motivate effectively.

The scene concludes with Vincent J. Byrne's article which attempts to narrow the gap between motivational theory and the practice of employee motivation. Mr. Byrne lists six skills, which, if implemented, will aid the manager in developing his ability to motivate. Can you expand on the list? In other words, if a particular manager was already competent in the areas discussed, what recommendations would you make that could help him attain the next level in motivational management?

DELEGATION: KEY TO INVOLVEMENT [*]

MARION E. HAYNES[**]

When you pick up a business-oriented periodical today, you will probably be exposed to someone's urgent appeal for employee involvement. Much of the meaning has been taken out of jobs, according to observers of the business scene. Employee talents, skills and abilities lie fallow due to the constraints of the bureaucracy. Involvement in decision-making is often proposed as a means of increasing both productivity and employee satisfaction.

How can such involvement be achieved? One way is through delegation. Delegation, as a principle of management, is still not used to its maximum by many managers. Why do they hesitate to use this proven tool? Some simply believe that the work won't be properly done unless they do it themselves. Others who are, or at least feel they are, less competent than some members of their staff fear the consequences of being out-performed. While it is necessary to recognize that these attitudes exist, they represent only a small portion of the total problem. There are many more reasons.

A manager may enjoy doing a task to the extent that he is reluctant to let someone else handle it. This is especially true

---

[*]*Personnel Journal*, June, 1974, pp. 454-456. Reprinted with permission.

[**]*Marion E. Haynes* received his B.S. degree from Arizona State University and the M.B.A. from New York University. He joined Shell Oil's employee relations organization sixteen years ago and now serves as a staff specialist in management and organization development. Mr. Haynes' work has been published in other periodicals, such as *Personnel Management Review* and *Public Personnel Management*.

when he is promoted within the same department so that he is now expected to manage work he formerly performed. Some managers do not delegate because they don't fully understand their roles. A manager's superior may expect him to know every detail of a project, thereby making it difficult for him to delegate. Or his staff may resist accepting more responsibility because of its own insecurities or lack of motivation. Many managers who endorse delegation in principle do not delegate because they mistakenly believe it is an all-or-nothing arrangement.

Degrees of Delegation

There are degrees of delegation ranging from fact-finding to decision-making. As manager, you decide which degree is appropriate by considering the nature of the task, the ability of the person doing the work, the amount of top management interest, and the time available for task completion. W. H. Nesbitt of Westinghouse Electric Corporation[1] is credited with detailing these degrees of delegation:

1. *investigate and report back.* You make the decision and take appropriate action.
2. *investigate and recommend action.* You evaluate the recommendation, make the decision, and take action.
3. *investigate and advise of action you intend to take.* You evaluate the decision made by your staff member and approve or disapprove.
4. *investigate and take action; advise of action taken.* Here you display faith in your staff's ability but want to be kept advised of what's going on.
5. *investigate and take action.* This is full delegation and displays complete faith in your staff's ability.

Full delegation should be your goal in the delegation process. It means the staff member has been given an area of decision-making and his decisions are accepted. To reach this level you must be willing to give up a portion of your authority. You must support decisions after they have been made whether you feel they are the best ones or not. You must

---

1. Harvey Sherman, "How Much Should You Delegate," *Supervisory Management*, October 1966.

be willing to gamble that your staff can do a better job when left on its own than when closely supervised. To play it safe and avoid risk by not delegating merely makes your staff an extension of yourself rather than (a group of) separate, complete individuals.

How to Delegate

Delegation must be both personal and individual. As such, it depends to a large extent on the relationship between you and each member of your staff. However, there are some general guidelines to follow:
— delegate by results expected, not by the method to be used in performing the task.
— set performance standards to measure accomplishment against results.
— give the staff member all of the relevant information you have about the task.
— delegate only to qualified members of your staff. (This may mean that you will have to train some of your staff in preparation for further delegation.)
— establish controls that will alert you to exceptions to normal operations.

Identifying Work to Be Delegated

The first thing to do, if interested in delegating more work, is to analyze your own involvement in the work of your department. In this analysis you should categorize all of the work you now perform into three groups:
1. work which can be done only by you, the manager.
2. work which can be delegated as soon as someone is trained to do it.
3. work which can be delegated immediately.

Work which only you can perform includes your leadership role and your duties as coordinator. Other duties in this category are those which you may not be authorized to delegate, such as personnel and cash disbursement decisions. As far as possible, you should delegate all of the routine work of your job. As manager, you should confine yourself as much as possible to the unique action—to doing things the first time.

When you have identified work which can be delegated,

but which no one is trained to perform, you have identified training needs to be accomplished by you or other appropriate people. Start immediately to provide the necessary training to prepare someone to take over these duties. Then proceed to delegate by degrees until full delegation has been achieved.

Work you are now performing which can be delegated immediately should be assigned to staff members in accordance with the currently appropriate degree of delegation. Then, as you acquire confidence in your staff's abilities, you can increase the delegation until you have accomplished as near complete delegation as possible.

Effects of Delegation

One of the most marked effects of delegation is the feeling of importance it gives staff members. When you give someone a job to do and let him make his own decisions as to how it should be done, you make it plain that he is capable and important. If, on the other hand, you expect him to come to you for each decision, it is apparent that you have very little faith in his ability. Giving your staff the authority to make its own decisions gives it a vested interest in the results produced. There is no greater motivating force than to put someone in charge of a portion of the department's work, give him the authority to make decisions which spell success or failure, and then reward him in terms of his accomplishment. An employee working for a manager who delegates as much as possible has an excellent opportunity to learn. Since it is an accepted fact that people learn by doing, the best way to prepare for a position that requires decision-making is to have delegated responsibility for making decisions. This training can be instrumental in helping a person grow within the organization.

As manager you also receive benefits from delegating. The most obvious benefit is the time that is freed for managing—more time for planning the future of your department, coordinating the efforts of your staff, developing new and better techniques to do the work, and establishing better relationships with those you deal with in your day-to-day contacts. When your staff is properly trained and performing the duties assigned, you will have a well-managed, smooth operation. What better recommendation could you receive for a more responsible managerial position than that you are an excellent manager who motivates his staff to peak performance?

MANAGEMENT PSYCHOLOGY*

MORTIMER R. FEINBERG, PH. D**

Many executives are not aware that events are forcing them into making many more decisions than were customary in the past. A period of rapid change compels the formulation of more judgments. With sudden sharp rises in costs, followed by zigs and zags in government anti-inflation policies, past decisions urgently demand review.

In a period such as this, the cardinal business sin is decision-avoidance. The most extreme form of this practice has been tagged by psychiatrists as aboulia, a Greek word meaning lack of resolution. Nobody can estimate how costly this mental state can be to a business; in many cases, more damage may be wrought by the failure to make a decision than by making a wrong one.

Executives, reviewing failures down the line as well as their own, would do well to paraphrase the poet's line: "Aboulia ben Adam, may his tribe decrease!"

Tactics of Aboulacs

The disease survives and spreads, because it has ready devices at hand for concealment. The list of techniques used is almost inexhaustible. Writing in the *Defense Management Journal*, Dr. Jitendra M. Sharma and Dr. George R. Carnahan, of North Michigan University, describe some of the ploys.

Restaurant Business (formerly *Fast Food*), April 1974, pp. 44-52. Reprinted with permission.
**Dr. *Feinberg* is president of BFS Psychological Associates, Inc., New York. This material is drawn from his management psychology letter, *OBI Interaction*.

We list here an expanded *catalogue of equivocation:*
1. *disowning the problem.* One sure way to avoid making a decision is to deny the very existence of the problem. If sales are dropping, wishful thinking tells you, "Things will pick up in the fall." If an employee is in a slump, "Give him a chance; he'll snap out of it." In either case, it's the executive's responsibility to make things happen, not wait for them to happen.
2. *going by the book.* You can avoid making a decision by simply saying, "What's company policy? Okay, that's what I'll do." When policy becomes a substitute for judgment, the tendency is to ignore the unique elements in the situation that require a flexible approach. Similarly, the effort to evade responsibility results in a refusal to reevaluate policies that once had utility but have now become irrelevant.
3. *reverence for tradition.* This kind of error comes easy. Usually, traditions have a justification; they represent a body of successful experience painfully accumulated over the years. But the wisdom of the ages becomes the folly of the moment, if change has occurred. "We've always done it this way," is a convenient excuse for shirking fresh decision-making.
4. *trivialization.* If you can't face up to the burden of making a decision, you can tell yourself: "This issue isn't important." But you don't really get off the hook; instead the hook sinks deeper.
5. *denial of the facts.* This is one of the common managerial faults charged against government agencies. The current Congressional investigation of cost overruns on military contracts has revealed that Pentagon executives have sometimes avoided painful decisions by isolating or discharging the individual who insists on presenting the gory details and demands a decision. "Fire the man who discovered the facts, and maybe the facts will go away with him."
6. *ideologizing the issue.* Men of strong convictions find it hard to abandon a theory. Psychologically, the function of an ideology is to make it unnecessary to reexamine our basic premises. It operates like a pair of eyeglasses that force reality to take on the coloration we want. In effect,

the ideology predetermines our conclusions, and we don't have to rethink our way to a new decision.
7. *consultation.* We can put off the moment of truth by telling ourselves that we need the thinking of others. We set up committees, invite prolonged discussion, hoping that the problem will solve itself before decision is necessary. Of course, there is value in consultation, but to reap its benefits be sure to set a *deadline for decision.*

Pressure and Anxiety

Psychiatrists, who have been working with executives, tell us that these terms are being mentioned with greater frequency on the analytic couch or in the therapy room.

That feelings of pressure and anxiety are mounting in private as well as political and social matters is clear. Executives, harried by a multiplicity of obligations, are bound to experience such stress from time to time. An understanding of its nature may be helpful.

Usually it is accompanied by a sense of powerlessness. The victim is overwhelmed by the idea that things are beyond managing. For some, it leads to apathy, immobility, surrender. Its worst aspect is that it may even lead to a complete loss of feeling, may even lead to a complete absence of feeling.

Most of us, fortunately, experience anxiety on limited occasions and in a limited degree. But if it is not so deep-rooted as to require therapy, suggestions will help:
1. *put some order into the chaos.* Since the major symptom is the pressure of "things out of control," try to sort out specific problems. Fix your focus on a few concrete, immediate tasks.
2. *persuade yourself that the mood is temporary.* Recalling that you survived such feelings in the past will make a difference. Lincoln, who was a frequent victim of anxiety, found help in the line, "This, too, shall pass away."
3. *take some action.* By listing the specific challenges you are facing, deciding which of the problems are more serious and which are less, you demonstrate to yourself that you can still function. You overcome inertia and start into motion.

4. *look for diversion.* Take a coffee break. But don't look for relaxation that means withdrawal from your problems— like opening a bottle.
5. *talk to someone about it.* Anxiety that is pent up feeds on itself. By discussing it, you release some of the steam. Remember, too, that pressure and anxiety are not altogether negative forces. Without the tension they create, we might not be moved to take creative action. Dr. Hans Selye, in his very useful book, *The Stress of Life*, makes this important point: "Stress is not even necessarily bad for you; it is also the spice of life."

Problem with Part-Timers

"You are correct in saying that part-timers can be less expensive than full-timers," writes a reader of this column. "We have saved substantial sums by using them and have avoided premium pay for overtime shifts and fringe benefits that would have been required by law and our union contract. But the difficulty has been that we find a higher amount of turnover among part-timers, with loss of output when needed and the nuisance and cost of new hirings. We still use part-timers, but is there anything we can do to reduce the turnover?"

Our correspondent's experience is shared by others. Statistics do show a higher turnover rate among part-timers than among full-timers. This one factor alone may more than nullify the cost savings that justify the use of part-timers.

But there is an answer: *the turnover can be reduced by better hiring criteria.*

Who stays on the job?.. Two researchers, Martin J. Gannon and Joseph C. Nothern of the Behavioral Science Division of the University of Maryland, have come up with specific data based on a study of short-lived versus long-lived part-time employees. Their sample consisted of 552 checkers in 14 supermarkets.

They concentrated on two factors: (1) *attitude towards the job* and (2) *attitude towards one's self* as revealed by a standard self-description inventory. The findings shed light on both full-timers and part-timers.

A striking conclusion was reached in the matter of job attitudes: among *full-time employees*, it is well established that *job satisfaction is a strong predicter of lower turnover.* But with part-timers, job satisfaction is not as significant. The reason would appear to be that, with fewer hours on the job, dissatisfaction is less burdensome.

It follows that expenditures aimed at increasing part-timers' job satisfaction bring back a lesser return to the company than similar expenditures on full-timers.

Gannon and Nothern, however, indicate that proper selection criteria can reduce turnover even among part-timers. They contrasted the turnover rates among part-time employees by setting up two categories: short-term (those who lasted less than two years) and long-term (those who lasted more than two). The short-term, turnover-prone part-timers scored worse on the Self-Description Inventory than the long-termers.

For instance, as compared with the way long-termers rated themselves, the short-termers were more self-disparaging on these qualities:

▫ intelligence;

▫ initiative;

▫ self-assurance—in this factor they showed the widest disparity with the self-perception of the long-termers;

▫ perceived occupational level—that is, their level of aspirations;

▫ decision-making;

▫ "sociometric popularity"—their perception of how readily they are accepted by others.

Thus, even though the job-related attitudes are not predictive of job tenure, psychological tests can reveal the personality traits of those part-timers who are not likely to stay on the job.

Such testing, of course, requires the participation of the psychologist. But some factors indicative of continued service are readily observable by the layman. For example, as age increases, turnover-proneness declines among part-timers as in the general working population. So, too, an expressed willingness of the part-timer to work longer hours suggests greater continuity on the job.

Taking Criticism

Logic says that criticism is desirable—how else can we learn? But feeling says that criticism is something to be avoided—isn't it a threat to self-esteem?

The challenge is to reconcile this conflict by using criticism constructively—that is, to elicit guidance, apply it effectively, improve performance, and thus heighten social and self approval. But if the initial reaction to hearing criticism is resistance and rejection, good counsel will be overlooked, performance will deteriorate and the precious "image" eroded.

The starting point for the individual who wants to *take criticism constructively* must be an examination of how he has responded to it in the past. Here are some of the alternatives:

1. *fear.* The symptoms are an accelerated heartbeat, a change in breathing-rhythm, a desire to flee from the situation. Obviously, under such circumstances it is more difficult for the mind to grasp the objective content of the criticism. The victim may then defend himself by minimizing the facts or exaggerating them. By minimizing, he can shrug them off; by exaggerating, he can deny their accuracy.

2. *automatic resistance.* This reaction pattern is often the result of an irrational self-confidence that flows not from competence but from a closed mind. The refusal to examine any new ideas, however, is inimical to good performance.

3. *prompt acceptance.* The individual who swallows all criticism without hesitation obviously sets a low value on his own abilities. By selling himself short, he, too, undermines his future behavior.

4. *judicial evaluation.* This is the open mind, the self-respecting personality, in action. He knows that no matter how good he is, there is always a chance to be better, and he is willing to listen and appraise. He receives criticism with these questions in mind:

> what are the facts at the core of the criticism?
>
> what are the feelings with which the criticism is being communicated—are they hostile? friendly? or neutral?
>
> what should be *my reaction to the facts?*
>
> what should be *my reaction to the feelings?*

This kind of analytical approach may result in a variety of responses: affirmative action taken on the facts and a decision to ignore the feelings; a rejection of the factual assertions and an effort to alter the feelings, and so on. Whatever the choice, however, the individual has the advantage of knowing that his response is thoughtful and not just emotional.

The other side of the coin, of course, is the giving of criticism. You'll do a better job of dishing it out if you know how to take it yourself.

DO YOU REALLY KNOW YOUR EMPLOYEES?*

WILLIAM J. MORGAN, JR., PH. D.

Do you know how the workers in your establishment really feel about important matters? Test yourself. How do you think they feel about the ten factors shown in Chart I?

Now that you've estimated some figure as to how many of your employees are pleased with your program—or unhappy or neutral about it—check with Chart II, which shows the success that 46 managers of food service organizations had in assessing their employee attitudes. Chart III on page 188 gives the figures for 254 restaurant employees who work in 37 different food service establishments. Few managers were able to make correct predictions.

The managers' predictions were best for mechanization (make the work easier), job security, and training programs. But they woefully underestimated how their employees felt about convenience foods, their supervisors, and their own image of their jobs. And the employees were far less contented with their wages and fringe benefits than the managers thought.

Some managers and supervisors of food service operations believe that by virtue of their long experience in the industry, and because of their close association with food service workers, they can tell the attitudes of most of their workers. Many actions they take in supervising their employees are

---

*The Cornell Hotel and Restaurant Administration Quarterly, May 1973, pp. 36-40. Reprinted with permission.

This article is based upon Professor Morgan's doctoral thesis, completed at Cornell University in 1971: "The Sensitivity of Managers to the Attitudes of Non-Supervisory Food Service Workers and Its Effect upon the Attraction and Retention of Industry Workers."

I – HOW DO YOUR EMPLOYEES FEEL ABOUT THEIR JOBS?

	Positive Attitude %	Negative Attitude %	Neutral %
1. Use of convenience foods?			
2. Mechanization of food service procedures?			
3. Wages paid?			
4. Fringe benefit offers?			
5. Security in his job?			
6. Working environment?			
7. His image of his job?			
8. His opportunity for advancement?			
9. Training which is given him?			
10. The type of supervision he receives?			

II – ABILITY OF MANAGERS TO PREDICT SPECIFIC ATTITUDE FACTORS

(See discussion on the following pages.)	No. of Managers Making Correct Prediction	%	No. of Managers Over-Predicting	%	No. of Managers Under-Predicting	%
1. Convenience Foods	16	34%	11	24%	19	42%
2. Mechanization	29	63%	11	24%	6	13%
3. Wages	23	50%	17	37%	6	13%
4. Fringe Benefits	25	54%	9	20%	12	26%
5. Security	36	78%	6	13%	4	9%
6. Working Environment	12	26%	21	45%	13	29%
7. Job Image	14	30%	13	28%	19	42%
8. Opportunity for Advancement	21	45%	15	32%	10	23%
9. Training	42	91%	4	9%	0	—
10. Supervision	16	34%	11	24%	19	42%

46 Managers responding; percentage rounded to equal 100%

based upon these pre-conceived determinations of employee attitudes. This is done, in many cases without adequate knowledge of the attitudes they project into their employees, which are not often those actually held by the workers.

Can a manager really afford to make incorrect assumptions? If he makes the wrong projection, will it affect other aspects of the management-employee relationship?

In *The Polish Peasant in Europe and America* (1918), U. L. Thomas and F. Znamiecki, equated attitudes toward the study of social psychology and suggested that an attitude was a state of mind toward a value.[1] Joining the term with the job satisfaction being experienced, Mayo, in his classical Hawthorne studies, highlighted the important relationship between these two factors.[2]

In view of this close association between how a worker views a factor and how he feels toward his job, can a manager really guess how a worker sees his job within the organization? Or how the worker views some change which has been instituted by management in an attempt to improve production?

Industry Efforts to "Make the Jobs Better"

The food service industry has experienced a sales growth of some 80% in the past ten years, and an employment growth rate of 50% during the same period. It is projected that the industry will need some 250,000 new employees each year to keep pace with planned growth. Ninety percent of these workers will be required in non-supervisory positions such as kitchen helpers, waiters, countermen, and cooks. As the industry attempts to attract these necessary workers, many establishments find it difficult to hire new workers, and experience high turnover rates with those workers whom they do employ.

Many managers and supervisors appear to regard these job vacancies, turnover rates, and the low pay scales paid in many establishments as inevitable. Some, however, have attempted to take positive action to correct the labor problems which exist.

---
1. W. L. Thomas and F. Znamiecki (Boston, Massachusetts: Badger Press)1918.
2. F. J. Roethlesberger and others, *Management and the Workers* (Cambridge, Massachusetts: Harvard University Press)1919.

Of those establishments surveyed in an Industry Manpower Survey in 1969, one-third of the operations reported that they raised wages for food service workers; 25% had begun to use part-time help; and 10% instituted the use of convenience foods and other methods of mechanization to help solve the gaps in the labor ranks.[1]

Some companies have restructured jobs and changed the basic methods of food preparation or reduced the scope of the menu. Because of a scarcity of both skilled and non-skilled personnel, a "systems approach" has been developed by some establishments, utilizing a fully or partially prepared food item, prepared by a central commissary type of facility and requiring a minimum amount of on-site equipment, personnel or procedures.

Manufacturers serving the industry have attempted to provide assistance by the introduction of new food forms, new equipment, and by a plethora of disposable aluminum, plastic, and paper goods—all offered in the cause of requiring fewer personnel, less space, and fewer procedures.

Vocational training programs for food service workers at either a local level, or in connection with funds made available under the Federal Manpower Development and Training Act, have been tried. Despite an increase, some 50% since 1967, in vocational training programs for food service workers, one study showed that less than half of those who received the training remained in the industry after one year.

With the prospects for increased business, due to more leisure time for Americans and a general propensity of the population to eat out more often, looming just over the horizon, what can an operator do to solve his labor problems and capture his fair share of this new business?

Many managers have always felt that there would be a surplus of workers willing to do a hard day's work for a good day's pay. It doesn't appear that there are now adequate numbers of these people available to staff the food industry establishments. Because of this shortage, as well as to meet minimum wage requirements, pay scales in the industry have

---

1. P. L. Gaurnier and W. P. Fisher, *A Study of Career Ladders and Manpower Development for Non-Management Personnel in the Food Service Industry*, Chicago, Illinois: National Restaurant Association, 1969, ch. 3.

been raised an average of 48% in the past ten years, and fringe benefits have been widely introduced.

Citing these actions as important improvements, many references in recent literature identify the factors of job image, working environment, type of supervision, lack of training, and the inability to receive advancement as being the most important reasons for the lack of adequate manpower.

Do these factors really make a difference? Are measures which are taken by management to improve the effectiveness of the worker actually seen by the worker as measures to help, or are some—such as the introduction of convenience foods or new machinery—seen as threats to their jobs or dilutions of their culinary skills?

What do the workers really want? Does management really know what the workers want? Is it possible to show any relationship between managers who appear to really know their workers and the ability of these managers to keep their job positions filled?

Industry Attitude Survey

In late 1971 a pilot research study was conducted to explore these types of questions. In order to provide meaningful information to the restaurant industry, the study sites were selected on the basis of representativeness and accessibility. Restaurants in a northern industrial city and in a southern resort-type location were selected to insure that both geographical and economic base boundaries would be crossed.

From a total population of 934 establishments and 7,433 workers in the northern city, and from 395 establishments and 8,000 workers in the southern location—and accepting a tolerance error level of 10% and a desire to meet this tolerance 19 out of 20 times—a sample of 96 establishments was selected. At each location, 200 workers were included in the sample.

Utilizing a Likert type scale of statements, which gives high reliability, and a full range of attitudinal determinants, statements to indicate attitudes in the ten areas of concern noted in the literature were constructed. These statements were pre-tested on a sample population of 54 employees, similar in all respects to those who would later participate in the study.

Scale Value Difference Ratios and an Odd-Even method of correlation were utilized to test the validity and reliability of the statements to be used. When completed, a total of 42 statements was constructed which sampled attitudes in the following 10 factors:

Convenience Foods	Fringe Benefits
Wages	Working Environment
Security	Opportunity for
Job Image	Advancement
Training	Supervision
Mechanization	

Using pre-trained interviewers, a total of 254 workers was sampled from a total of 37 restaurants, resulting in a response ratio of 63.5%.

In addition, 75 managers from each geographical location were asked to predict the attitudes of food service employees by using a like list of statements which was mailed to them to insure anonymity. They were also asked to provide information on the turnover rate experienced at their establishments in accordance with the following formula:

$$\text{Turnover rate} = \frac{\text{Accessions} + \text{Separations}}{\text{Average No. of Employees}} \times 100$$

Out of a total of 150 forms which were submitted to managerial personnel, 46 were returned for a response ratio of 30.6%. (See Table II, p. 183.)

Survey Findings

Standard errors of attitude percentages and resulting attitudinal confidence limits were constructed. Means and Standard Deviations of all attitudes to specific factors were also computed. Ranges to be permitted for managerial projections, turnover rates, correlations between projections and turnover rates and a critical ratio were also arrived at.

The data collected indicated that although some differences were noted in sub-groups arranged according to age, sex, race, and years of service and by type of position, that the food service workers responded as a homogeneous group in demonstrating positive attitudes to convenience foods, mechanization, job security, job image, training and supervision.

III — WORKERS HOLDING POSITIVE ATTITUDES

Factors	% Positive
1. Convenience Foods	60.16%
2. Mechanization	93.36%
3. Wages	34.38%
4. Fringe Benefits	21.48%
5. Security	88.67%
6. Working Environment	48.63%
7. Job Image	60.16%
8. Advancement	46.09%
9. Training	100.0 %
10. Supervision	52.73%

Of those managers missing the projections, the majority overestimated the workers' attitudes on mechanization, wages, security, working environment, opportunity for advancement, and training; they underestimated the attitudes on the remainder.

Turnover rates, for establishments of managers reporting, indicated percentages from 0% to 560% with a mean average of 141%. A correlation between the ability to predict attitudes and a lower turnover rate was computed at +.32 with a critical ratio of 2.0 which indicated that a practical and significant relationship existed at the 4.5% level of confidence.

Implications for Management

This study should indicate to food service managers that the attitudes of food service workers, expressed as either a verbal opinion or a non-verbal behavior, indicate problems for the food service industry unless some action is taken.

It is time that the restaurant owners and/or managers realize that the standard studies of personnel behavior, to which many of them have been exposed as a result of their middle-class backgrounds, do not necessarily hold for many of the workers whom they employ. It is important that they learn to recognize the backgrounds of the workers and their specific needs, so that policies and procedures may be instituted to gain satisfaction for the worker and increased efficiency for the manager.

In the case of the disadvantaged worker (the majority class of food service workers) the basic attitudes and values of their subculture, learned in the crowded home of the ghetto, do not always equate with the predicted attitudes or actions as seen through the eyes of the average middle-class, college-educated owner or manager.

As suggested by the study, pay and fringe benefits may be of even greater importance to many food service workers than had been first believed, because of the deprivations and constant fight for survival they have experienced in their homes and in their social groups. The "Now" orientation which they possess, and their desire to spend, consume and enjoy, may make the working environment, the pay scale, and the fringe benefit of much greater importance to them than to the "average" American workers.

The study implies that the introduction of convenience foods and new equipment (which would normally be expected to result in dissatisfaction for the "classical" industrial worker) apparently holds little threat for the average food service worker. Oriented only toward the present, he views his work as a necessary evil which should be either avoided or completed with the least amount of effort. The disadvantaged worker—because of his previous life of insecurity—has the ability to expect and accept challenges to his future and to his security. He works in order to gain monetary rewards which he may spend elsewhere in his "Now" search for the visceral, genital, or emotional gratifications. These are more available and more practical for him "Now" than his "Future."

The data also suggests that managers must consider that such factors as "training"—which is meaningful to an individual motivated by achievement—may have another meaning to a food service worker who sees his future chance for advancement blocked by inadequate education, discrimination, or managerial apathy. Perhaps the positive attitude displayed by workers toward training indicates that training is now adequate—or it may simply show they believe that this is the attitude they *should* have. It is also possible that it isn't important to improve worker satisfaction in many restaurants by giving additional training—workers may believe they now have all the training they will ever need in view of their limited chances for advancement.

The positive attitude to "job image" might be a surprise for many managers in the food service industry. However, in addition to the cognitive dissonance theory which may apply as the worker attempts to justify his job, the attitude may be "positive" because—from the vantage point of his family and social situation—the food service industry does look good. This departure is certainly somewhat different from the image held by the average middle-class member, or even by the average black who aspires to some improvement in his social situation. It may be, however, this is the image many workers have who see their future as "Now."

Much of the behavior accepted in the culture of poverty goes counter to the ideals of the middle-class member of American society. It is important for managers to realize this as they make policy, institute changes, or administer personnel programs. The traits of punctuality, responsibility, and the desire to get ahead are not as basic to many disadvantaged people as they are to other types of industrial workers, and to other members of the food service industry.

The daily battle for food, privacy, attention, and survival may dictate more importance to the "hygienic" factors of wages, temperature of the working area and the like, than would normally be expected. This importance may be experienced at the expense of many of the factors which many of us have believed to be more important in making our industry more attractive.

It may be timely for owners and operators of food service establishments to question their "sound" personnel theories in relations with many workers now employed in the industry. Some of these theories may apply to certain classes of workers.

By identifying the specific characteristics of the workers employed in a particular establishment, it may be possible to structure the individual incentive and motivating systems to meet their particular needs. It might be possible to increase productivity, reduce turnover, and achieve better customer satisfaction and employee morale without patterning every plan upon the "classical" base of current personnel theory.

Flexibility of schedules, monetary motivating principles to increase productivity, attendance or tenure, or a new locker, air conditioning or a fan may be more important to the success of a restaurant and the tenure of the employees than providing job enlargement opportunities or improving the image of the industry.

We will only know and be able to do the correct thing if we really learn the attitudes of our employees and learn how they feel about a specific matter.

How did you do in the questionnaire?

SIX SKILLS PUT MOTIVATION THEORY INTO ACTION*

VINCENT J. BYRNE

A serious gap exists between the theory and practice of motivating employees. At best, motivation is an elusive and abstract concept which managers find difficult to understand and cope with.

Studies have shown that most employees genuinely want to move ahead and demonstrate their effectiveness on the job. But often they do not know how to translate their hopes and aspirations into action.

On the other hand, although managers know they must unleash the human potential within their employees if productivity is to be increased, many of them don't know how.

"I've attended some of those seminars on motivation," one manager told me, "and the theories sound great. But once I get back to my desk, I don't know how to apply those theories, and somehow they just get lost."

Managers need guidelines—no matter how humanly imperfect—to put motivation theories to work. To date, few such road maps which combine theory with practice are available.

In the last few years, Xerox Learning Systems Div. has developed a learning program to help managers do a more effective, rewarding job which will result in more satisfied, committed employees.

It is based on a study of more than 5,000 managers conducted by Synectics, Inc., Cambridge, Mass. The study shows what successful managers do to motivate effectively and what unsuccessful managers are doing wrong.

The program concentrates on developing specific skills

**Industry Week*, March 11, 1974, pp. 42-44. Reprinted with permission.

which, building on each other, provide managers with motivation techniques. At least six such skills can be practiced by managers with their employees.

Learn to Listen

A basic managerial skill is proficiency in listening to an employee. To find out what makes another person "tick," and to motivate him, the manager must first communicate with him.

This means not merely an exchange of words or facts, but an exchange of ideas—an understanding. By the very act of listening to a person, a motivating effect is created: "I respect your ideas and opinions enough to want to listen to them."

A major barrier to interpersonal communications is the natural tendency to judge and evaluate before the speaker is finished. We think much faster than we speak—and tend to make lightning-fast judgments which block concentrating on what else he has to say.

Responses must clearly indicate that the manager is listening to the employee, but they must not be judgmental.

Criticize, but Do It Effectively

The ability to criticize is also necessary for a manager to motivate his employees. When a worker's performance is unsatisfactory, he expects and needs feedback. And when he makes a poor suggestion, he wants to know how it can be corrected.

To improve his performance, a subordinate needs to know what aspects of his activity or thinking need changing. He also needs to know what aspects should not be changed. When criticism focuses on what's wrong with someone's work or idea—but doesn't include any mention of what he's done well and should continue to do—additional mistakes are an increased probability.

Also, criticism that is one-sided is likely to produce defensiveness. Properly understood and executed, criticism can have positive motivational consequences. When a manager provides the kind of criticism that enables people to improve their performance, he is helping them to grow.

Further, criticism is one means by which a manager can prepare a subordinate for greater job responsibility.

Increase Employees' Value

Building—the process of increasing the value of another person's work or idea—is an important managerial skill. In building, a manager acknowledges the importance of a subordinate's work by making it more useful.

For example, he takes an idea that won't quite work and then makes it workable. Or, he listens to the intent behind a suggestion or innovation and finds a way of making the intent a reality.

Building often follows naturally from listening, because both are based on assuming there is value in someone's work. This leads directly to increasing its value.

Building is difficult, because the immediate impulse to judge must be suspended. Instead, managers must take the time to clarify and confirm their understanding of a situation.

Often managers use their employees' work and ideas as springboards for their own creativity. They forget to acknowledge the value of contributed ideas—and occasionally even minimize someone else's efforts.

True building begins when a manager tells a subordinate that his idea or way of doing things was in some way the source of the manager's own idea or activity.

By building in this fashion, the manager answers a subordinate's need for achievement, recognition, self-esteem, and the esteem of others. In short, he motivates him.

Diverse Opinions: Asset or Liability?

To develop a successful working relationship with employees, the manager must learn to cope with differences of opinion, and make them work for him.

Depending on how managers deal with them, differences can be an asset or a liability. On one hand, they can lead to the kind of disagreement and conflict that results in inefficiency, frustration, and unsatisfactory compromises.

On the other hand, they can be the source of increased cooperation and better alternatives, through the productive use of the different experiences and capabilities that people bring to a situation.

One way in which differences can create conflict is by leading the manager and employee into a win-lose position.

When two people have different points of view about something, each tends to have an investment in his own view.

To counter the win-lose situation, managers should realize that the differences between two people, which tend to set up a vertical barrier between them, can be changed to a difference about which the two can agree to differ.

When such an agreement has been reached, it is then possible for them to look for new alternatives that had not occurred to either. And because the new alternative selected is likely to have been built on both points of view, it becomes possible for both to "win."

The process of managing differences—whether it results in agreement or not—will have emphasized the manager's willingness to give employees' opinions due consideration. This creates a feeling of mutual interdependence between a manager and his subordinates.

Give Credit Where Credit Is Due

A favorable management-employee relationship can also be furthered when the manager learns how to extend recognition.

Many workers never see the results of their efforts, and recognition from his superior becomes an important indicator of an individual worker's competence and achievement.

While crediting would seem to be something that managers would do almost automatically, many fear overdoing praise even when it is earned.

To be effective as a motivator, esteem must be related in some way to a specific achievement. "Joe, you're doing a terrific job," tells the employee little. It is better to say, "Joe, that order you brought in from XYZ Corp. has improved our revenue picture by 10%."

Crediting an employee's work also provides him with feedback on what the manager expects. A worker's past behavior is used to illustrate what the manager wants him to do in the future.

Atmosphere Is Key In Discussions

A manager's proficiency at leading group discussions also can have important effects on employee motivation. Meetings are a necessary evil in business because a manager either needs to give information to his subordinates—or wants information from them to help him solve a problem, make a decision, or carry out a plan.

But the study of task-oriented discussions conducted by the 5,000 successful and unsuccessful managers (the Synectics study), reveals that most managers do not create an atmosphere which minimizes defensiveness and encourages openness, mutual support, and a willingness to offer imperfect ideas.

Three techniques can prevent managers from creating such an atmosphere.

First, productivity in a discussion can be impaired by a lack of objectives. Ideally, a discussion leader should inform his group, at the outset, of his objectives. They need to be precise and definite.

Second, some managers do not appreciate their influence on the readiness of others to voice ideas or opinions. Because the manager's opinion matters the most, group members have a natural tendency to defer to what he says, even when he doesn't want them to.

Other managers do realize the power they hold and use it to give their own ideas precedence. When a manager favors his own ideas, he competes with his team and creates defensiveness.

Third, group members may exert counterproductive influences on each other. They may judge and evaluate each others' ideas as soon as they are offered, without asking for clarification and confirmation. A good manager assumes the burden of keeping people's ideas alive. He can use all his skills to make sure that members do not de-motivate each other.

As these six skills build on each other, managers can use each separately and also interrelate them. With practice and experience, managers will discover that motivation is not as mysterious as they perhaps once thought, and that theory can indeed be put to work effectively.

Scene 3

COMMUNICATION

This scene is concerned with the field of communications, a vital component of all managerial functions. The initial article, "Labor-Management Communication," is divided into two sections. The first explains a communication behavior model based on the concept that the problems which develop during communication processes often come from the people rather than the subject matter itself. The second section applies the model to the difficulties that are encountered during labor negotiations, with basic problems highlighted and possible solutions given.

The concluding article by Athanassiades studies a very specific area of managerial communications: upward communication (i.e., from subordinate to superior) of female employees. His article is based on the joint concepts that behavior is motivated by a hierarchy of unsatisfied needs and that it is always directed towards goal-achievement. The method employed is an analysis of the distortions that are created in upward communications and the ways in which those distortions can affect the achievement and security needs of those involved. Pay particular attention to the methods employed by the author in reaching his conclusions.

LABOR-MANAGEMENT COMMUNICATION*

LOTHAR A. KRECK

Introduction

I would like to focus your attention on the communication that goes on between management and labor unions in general, and particularly between top management and top union officials during negotiations. What seems to happen during negotiations, as conveyed by news services, should be described as an unimpressive spectacle rather than communication. This does not mean that there is not an attempt to communicate.

Based on observation over a period of time, it would seem that the general public also views the negotiating process as a spectacle and is little impressed with it. If the negotiators possessed the same point of view, a single letter would probably be more effective than their extended sessions. When they try to discuss matters, they only get deeper into trouble, as their attempts to communicate seem doomed to failure.

In talking about this area of communication, it might be helpful to define "communication" first. I presently define it as "interpersonal contacts to affect the behavior of the communication partner(s)."[1] The heart of the definition is "...to affect the behavior of the communication partner(s)."

---

*Previously unpublished.
1. Thayer calls it communication "to some end." Lee O. Thayer, *Administrative Communication* (Homewood, Ill.: Richard D. Irwin, Inc., 1968), p. 144. Merrihue expresses it as "...desired response behavior from the receiver." Willard V. Merrihue, *Managing by Communication* (New York: McGraw-Hill Book Co., 1960), p. 16.

The union tries to affect management's behavior, and management tries to affect the union's behavior.

As we know to begin with, it is very difficult for two members of management—such as an executive chef and a headwaiter—to affect each other successfully, even if (or because) they are on the same hierarchical level. Add to this customary difficulty the fact that union members and management belong to two different ideologies, and the implications can clearly be seen. However, it is not the purpose of this introduction to go into an analysis of the problems. It will be more beneficial here to take a closer look at the human being involved, without regard, at this point, to whether he is a representative of the unions or of management.

Early Influences

While growing up, a young person is molded by a number of influences, influences which have their origin in the society in which he lives. A person of Italian parentage born in the U.S. does not automatically become a member of the U.S. society. Rather, he may remain for a period of time a member of the Italian society, depending on the strength of the influence of his parents' heritage or the weakness of the surrounding society.

The social environment in which any person lives is composed of a number of factors: education, religion, social stratum or economic level, race, philosophy, politics, among others.

Thayer refers to these factors as "normative reality."[1] Some of the molding of a person's life takes place at home, some outside his home.[2] The "product" which results from this molding is unique, and two persons will never have identical background "mixes."

Out of each specific background "mix" comes a particular

---

1. Lee O. Thayer, *Administrative Communication* (Homewood, Ill.; Richard D. Irwin, Inc., 1968), p. 46.
2. Katz and Lazarsfeld say that "... seeking acceptance in a new circle may lead an individual to bring his opinions and attitudes into line with the new group ..." Elihu Katz and Paul F. Lazarsfeld, *Personal Influence* (New York: Free Press, 1955), p. 67.

type of verbal or non-verbal communication behavior.[1] This can be observed, for example, in the use of the language, in the ability to generalize, to reason, to predict, to make statements of fact, to organize one's thoughts, to listen.

An example of verbal communication behavior is the use of certain words, such as, "hell," and "God damn." They are considered by some people as foul language; other people do not feel that way. "Neat" and "groovy" are clearly understood by some people, by others not at all. The jokes of teen-agers are understood by them but not by the older generation because of a difference in reasoning. Mentally maladjusted persons, even when their difficulties are not necessarily noticeable, lack the ability to generalize, to predict, to listen.

Two examples of non-verbal behavior not familiar to Americans are the following: in Pakistan if you want to call someone over to you who is looking at you, you use our hand signal for "go away"; or if you agree with someone, you would shake your head. This can be rather confusing for newcomers at first. I believe that to recognize that different backgrounds result in different communication behavior is of vital importance to understanding the communication process.[2]

If the above statement can be accepted, then it is not difficult to see why communication so often fails.[3] Suppose that

---

1. Fearing describes this behavior in the following way: ". . . responses to stimuli in communication situations are not automatic and mechanical, but rather are dependent on the totality of cultural and personality factors which each respondent brings to the situation . . ." Franklin Fearing, "Human Communication," *Audio-Visual Communication Review*, Vol. 10, No. 3, 1962, p. 80. Weaver, in dealing with Labor-Management Communication, calls any resulting difference in communication "semantic distance." Carl H. Weaver, "The Quantification of the Frame of Reference in Labor-Management Communication," *Journal of Applied Psychology*, Vol. 42, 1958, pp. 1-9.
2. For an example of what grave consequences background "mix" can have if involving intercultural communication, refer to the following: Lothar A. Kreck, "Communication: A Dimension of International Relations," *ETC. A Review of General Semantics*, Sept. 1972, Vol. 29, No. 3, pp. 233-242.
3. Another way of stating it: we should be pleasantly surprised to find communication going right so often.

Mr. A. is joined now by Mr. B., who comes from the same social environment (or background "mix"); who acts according to the same sets of values and reference groups[1] and uses the English language—supposed to be "common" to most U.S. nationals, including Mr. B.—to communicate. It is probable that the first differences will show up in the area of language as Mr. A. tries to communicate a meaning to Mr. B.

"What do you mean?" is a frequent reaction, with the receiver blaming the originator for communicating poorly. Pei says that ". . . a truly complete system of meaning involves an analysis of the universe . . . A word or sentence is not merely a bundle of sounds; it is also a bundle of associations. These associations are not quite identical for any two speakers; neither will the words or sentence hold for them exactly the same semantic content."[2]

In the example, it was presumed that Mr. A. and Mr. B. had the same social status, and that they were willing to communicate. Suppose that Mr. A. is a boss and four levels removed from Mr. B. If Mr. B. were willing to communicate with Mr. A. (for example, some information vital to Mr. A.), the communication would somehow reach Mr. A.; but if Mr. B. is unwilling to communicate, the message will never reach Mr. A.[3] Conversely, it is known that about eighty percent of a message gets lost or is changed when traveling three or four levels down in an organization.

To mention just one more problem: the size of a group will determine the number of relationships possible. "Relationship" should really be translated as "power play," the way in which power can be utilized to achieve personal ends. These relationships are totally out of proportion, as can be seen from the following examples based on Kephart's formula on intra-group relationships: three persons can have six different relationships, four can have 25 relationships, five can have 89, with similar increases as the number of persons

---

1. Both are part of a particular ideology.
2. Mario Pei, *The Story of Language*, (Philadelphia: Lippincott, 1949), pp. 138-139.
3. Thayer calls this "information ownership." Lee O. Thayer, *Administrative Communication*, (Homewood, Ill.: Richard D. Irwin, Inc., 1961), p. 146.

increases.[1] Taking into consideration what has previously been brought out—that each of the members is himself an entity with his own goals and desires—we can be sure that people will use all possible relationships to satisfy those goals and desires.

The introduction of "goals and desires" into the model brings the discussion to another area of why humans react the way they do. Originating with Maslow, and later somewhat modified by Douglas McGregor, is the concept of need fulfillment. This concept can be simply expressed as the idea that, in order to live, people have to have certain needs fulfilled, and that those needs are in hierarchical order.

The most basic need is the physiological need for food and shelter, followed by the need for the safety of one's life generally, one's family, and one's job. However, once the threats of hunger and the threats to safety are gone, people seek fulfillment of other needs. Among these needs are: meeting people, talking to them, and taking part in interpersonal activities.

A place of work very often becomes the social meeting ground. It is the job of the supervisor to see that this socializing does not get out of hand, but a wise supervisor will never shut it off completely. In a society like ours, these needs are fulfilled for a majority of the people.

Next, we have to look at two needs which are not so easily fulfilled or will never be fulfilled. The first one is the ego need: this is fulfilled through the power over others which results when high status is achieved in an organization. Brown in his excellent paperback, *The Social Psychology of Industry*[2] expresses it this way: "For some, work becomes an avenue for securing ego satisfaction by gaining power and exerting it over others."

Another way of fulfilling the ego need is recognition received for something done or said. Not everyone will admit that he does something simply to satisfy his ego needs. I have

---

1. William M. Kephart, "A Quantitive Analysis of Intra-Group Relationships," *American Journal of Sociology*, May 1950, pp. 544-549.
2. J. A. C. Brown, *The Social Psychology of Industry*, (Baltimore: Penguin Books, 1954), p. 189.

a good friend who at one time was in an administrative position in an organization and at the same time served as president of the local hospital board of a small community—needless to say, without pay. After we had talked for some time about need fulfillment, he had the courage to admit that he undertook the burden of the hospital job for his ego need fulfillment.

It takes a strong individual to admit this. Others would have stated that they did it "for the community," "to help out," or say, "I was pressed into this." Later it will be shown what influence such feelings could have on the communication.

Finally, there is the highest of all needs that man has—one out of reach for most of us: self-fulfillment. By this we mean, to attain something in life about which most of us can only dream, i.e., to have the opportunity to develop our potential to its fullest. This can be done through reaching a position, or status that permits one to realize his full potential. The farther we are away from satisfying this need, the less it hurts. The closer we come to the "dreamed of" position or status, the more we want to have our need fulfilled. For some people, satisfying this need becomes not just a motivation but an obsession.

In this introduction, two aspects have been discussed which may have seemed, to some people, to have little to do with communication: (1) each individual was described as unique, since no two individuals have the same background "mix" and, consequently, they differ in their communication behavior; and (2) all people have certain needs which they try to fulfill throughout their lives. Some needs can be fulfilled easily and some not so easily.

For more clarity, and only for that reason, the two ideas, or parts, of the communication behavior model were treated separately. At this point it should be made very clear that need fulfillment (especially fulfillment of those of a higher order) originates in the social environment (micro or macro) in which the person lives.[1]

---

1. Actually this is only a personal hypothesis, and I wonder whether the saying "keeping up with the Jones" doesn't explain some of this feeling. It might be interesting to speculate on what might motivate Charles, the Prince of Wales, both in his present and in his future life?

A person with poor, uneducated parents will probably have a greater need for ego satisfaction than, for example, a person who comes from an affluent family which has always had secure social standing in the community. A person from such a family has probably had part of his ego needs continuously fulfilled from childhood on (because "he is the son of the banker, Mr. A...."). Couldn't this need for ego satisfaction on the part of the majority be contributing to our present social unrest?

Analysis of the Problem

We are now ready to begin the analysis of the communication problem for management and union leaders during labor negotiations. The problem by now should be rather obvious, if one accepts the points made in the Introduction.

Concentrating first on the human beings involved, it can safely be assumed that there exists a difference in ideology. "Ideology," as I see it, is a way of life which is governed by a particular set of values based on one or more reference groups.[1]

How strong can an ideology be? Wars were/are fought because of differences in ideologies; people will set themselves ablaze because of an ideology; people will live in seclusion all their lives because of an ideology; revolutions, political and religious movements will be started because of an ideology. This should answer any question about the strength of an ideology.

"Management" is an ideology, "The Labor Union" is an ideology. Unfortunately, these ideologies are at opposite ends of the scale. What put them in these positions? People who have different background "mixes," who come from different micro societies or reference groups.

Most of our business leaders today have college educations. This alone makes it safe for us to assume that they must come from at least a lower-middle class family and have been

---

1. C. E. Larson, Speech Dept., Univ. of Denver, in a discussion speaks about "dogmatism," which he defines as closed-mindedness. "Ideology" and "dogmatism" have this closed-mindedness in common; they differ only in degree.

influenced by whatever goes with that life style. Such influences might be neighborhood, primary education, primary social groups and, of course, a style of communication which is in accordance with the environment.[1] Going to college continues the trend away from "The Labor Union" ideology.

What follows is a generalization: I do not believe that colleges of business today are "Labor Union" oriented; they stress profit and as such are "Management" oriented. Most of the graduates in business start out as management trainees and stay in management. Communication behavior develops parallel to an individual's professional development. This is the usual background of the person who will one day sit across the table to communicate with a labor union leader.

How does the labor leader's communication behavior develop? Labor leaders usually come from the ranks.[2] They have stayed very much in a particular stratum of society and have had very little exposure to influences of other strata. They probably close themselves off from any influences which are not in harmony with their present thinking or that of their reference group. As a person matures he is less likely to be remolded; his beliefs harden; he develops prejudices, and makes value judgments. (This is equally true, of course, of the executive.)

Problems of Negotiation

The union leader, because of his different development, will bring his own style of communication behavior to the conference table. What will be the results when he meets with the executive? There may, and often will be, a difference in meaning of language used; opposing prejudices and biases will be brought in; opinions will be stated as facts without labeling them as such; intolerance will prevail; each side

---

1. Alland thinks that "... human behavior is in large part adaptive ..." An example of this would be the executive who comes from a lower class family and who, later in his development, changes his speech to conform to that of his new reference groups to decrease the semantic distance between the new groups and himself. Alexander Alland, Jr., *Evolution and Human Behavior* (Garden City, N. Y.: The Natural History Press, 1967), p. 159.

2. Even national labor figures, like Haney, Reuther, and Hoffa were at one time laborers, as reported in *Who's Who in America* (1968-69).

will be unable to see the other's point of view, and there will be a difference in the definitions of key terms.[1]

As if all of the above were not enough to ruin communication efforts—each person's need fulfillment will also be a factor. Nothing needs to be said about the primary needs, because executives as well as union leaders are extremely well off when it comes to financial rewards. We do not have to concern ourselves with the social needs either: they are fulfilled, although in different ways for people in each group.

Troubles start with attempts to satisfy the ego need fulfillment. Whoever loses in the negotiations loses ego satisfaction, or to reverse it: only the one who can convince his "followers" that he won gets the ego need fulfillment essential for every person.

It is vital to the labor union leader that he win, because his job and the existence of labor unions in general depend on his winning. This last statement is also true for the executive, but only to a degree: an executive will seldom lose his job if he is unsuccessful, even in a number of negotiations. Further, in only a few cases has the existence of an organization been threatened. (However, one should not forget the consequences of the newspaper strike in New York which occurred a few years ago.)

Parallel at the beginning but accelerating in importance more for one group than the other as negotiations continue, is the last need: self-fulfillment. As was pointed out earlier, only a few people are able to fulfill this need during their lives but the closer people come to fulfillment, the harder they will work. In looking at the executive who successfully directs an enterprise of 100,000 people and who comes from a lower-middle class family, one can say that he has had this need fulfilled. The job ahead from him is only to keep it fulfilled. Under normal circumstances this should not be too difficult.

---

1. Weaver found out that a ". . . significant semantic distance between the two groups . . ." existed. "Labor stereotyped more than management . . . thus, the semantic distance seemed to have resulted more from labor's position than from management's . . ." Carl H. Weaver, "The Quantification of the Frame of Reference in Labor-Management Communication," *Journal of Applied Psychology*, Vol. 42, 1958, pp. 1-9.

The union leader who heads a group of 100,000 members has his self-fulfillment need satisfied. However, trying to hold on is much more difficult; one or two unsuccessful negotiations, an unsuccessful strike, or a conflict with the law, and he will lose the next election and be succeeded by someone

The loss of the position keeps him not only from self-fulfillment but also from satisfying the next lower need, the ego need.

These then are the characteristics of the two groups of persons, representing two ideologies, who face each other across a table in an attempt to come to a mutual agreement.[1] Contrasted with these communication difficulties inherent in man, the subject matter—for example, "increase in benefits"—appears rather insignificant. A letter would probably do the job, as suggested previously.

Solutions

We are faced with two basic problems: (1) the communication behavior of the individual who, over a period of time, has developed both a stereotype about his communication partner and at the same time has developed his own biases, opinions and prejudices; and (2) the desire of people to fulfill, or keep fulfilled, certain needs of a strictly personal nature that have no relation to the needs of the people they lead.

The idealistic solution to the first problem is the use of scientific language. It is intended to destroy stereotypes in the minds of communication partners; to permit them to meet at an agreed-upon level of language; to encourage them to discard prejudices and biases and replace them with statements of fact, as described by Vardaman.[2]

Scientific language is also said to encourage the labeling of opinions as such and prevent their use as facts; to encourage tolerance of a communication partner's behavior and attempt

---

1. Another way to analyze interpersonal communication is to use the systems approach. L. A. Kreck, "Communication: A Dimension of Tourism Promotion," *Revue de Tourisme*, Vol. 24, No. 3, July-Sept. 1972, pp. 86-92.
2. In conversations with G. T. Vardaman and L. E. Glorfield, professors at the University of Denver.

to see his point of view; and, finally, to leave out value judgments.[1]

How far and how fast this idea of a "scientific language" can be instilled in people is difficult to predict. One thing is certain: if something like this could be made operational, many of the communication problems, both during management-labor negotiations and in many other situations, would be eliminated. Expressed differently: with the help of scientific language, communication effectiveness could be increased significantly.

This leaves one problem still to be dealt with: need fulfillment. Unfortunately, needs cannot be replaced, they can only be re-directed; instead of fulfilling the ego needs on the job, they can be fulfilled at the bowling alley outside the job. This, or similar suggestions, would not be applicable to the problem we face here.

My suggestion is (and it should be said that it is highly idealistic) that the communication partners, before attempting to communicate on the subject matter, e.g., "increase in benefits," should meet in a number of informal group sessions.[2] The desired result of the sessions should be recognition (bringing out into the open) of these facts: (1) representatives of both groups seek fulfillment of a number of needs within their respective organizational environments, that is, the company and the union; and (2) the desired fulfillment must be continuous, i.e., no threat of terminating the need fulfillment exists.

A legitimate question could be asked: what does this process have to do with communication? The answer is, it clears the air for a discussion of the subject matter, which with the help of the scientific language, can now begin. Perhaps a letter, even though it has the disadvantages pointed out by Aranguren,[3] would, after all, be sufficient to affect the behavior of the communication partner.

---

1. Bertrand Russell supported the idea that political controversies ought to be conducted in quantitative terms. B. Russell, *The Future of Science* (New York: Philosophical Library, 1959), p. 18. A similar suggestion could be made in regard to labor-management issues.
2. Despite my efforts, I was not able to find a "high-powered" term for such sessions.
3. J. L. Aranguren, *Human Communication* (New York: McGraw-Hill Book Co., 1967), p. 47.

Conclusion

An attempt has been made to bring into focus the problems which seem to exist during management-labor union negotiations. It is now apparent that the communication problems originate with the people involved and not with the subject of the negotiations. The communication model suggested that problems are based on: (1) the uniqueness of each individual which he derives from his background "mix," and (2) certain needs which each person tries to fulfill. For each of the two problems, a solution was recommended. Both solutions were idealistic. But fifty years ago, so were most of today's proven principles in human relations.

BIBLIOGRAPHY

Alland, Jr., Alexander. *Evolution and Human Behavior.* Garden City, N. Y.: The Natural History Press, 1967.

Aranguren, J. L. *Human Communication.* New York: McGraw-Hill Book Co., 1967.

Brown, J.A.C. *The Social Psychology of Industry.* Baltimore: Penguin Books, 1954.

Fearing, Franklin. "Human Communication," *Audio-Visual Communication Review*, Vol. 10, No. 3, 1962.

Haney, William V. *Communication and Organizational Behavior.* Homewood, Ill.: Richard D. Irwin, Inc., 1967.

Katz, Elihu, and Lazarsfeld, Paul F. *Personal Influence.* New York: Free Press, 1955.

Kephart, William M. "A Quantitative Analysis of Intra-Group Relationships," *American Journal of Sociology*, May, 1951.

Kreck, L. A. "Communication: A Dimension of Tourism Promotion," *Revue de Tourisme*, July-September, 1972, Vol. 24, No. 3.

Kreck, L. A. "Communication: A Dimension of International Relations," *ETC. A Review of General Semantics*, September, 1972, Vol. 29, No. 3.

Maslow, Abraham H. *Motivation and Personality.* New York: Harper & Row, 1954.

McGregor, Douglas. *The Human Side of Enterprise.* New York: McGraw-Hill Book Co., 1960.

Merrihue, Willard V. *Managing by Communication.* New York: McGraw-Hill Book Co., 1960.

Pei, Mario. *The Story of Language.* Philadelphia: Lippincott, 1949.

Thayer, Lee O. *Administrative Communication.* Homewood, Ill.: Richard D. Irwin, Inc., 1961.

Thayer, Lee O. *Communication and Communication Systems.* Homewood, Ill.: Richard D. Irwin, Inc., 1968.

Thayer, Lee O. *The Future of Science.* New York: Philosophical Library, 1959.

Weaver, Carl H. "The Quantification of the Frame of Reference in Labor-Management Communication," *Journal of Applied Psychology*, Vol. 42, 1958.

Who's Who in America, 1968-69.

AN INVESTIGATION OF SOME COMMUNICATION PATTERNS OF FEMALE SUBORDINATES IN HIERARCHICAL ORGANIZATIONS*

JOHN C. ATHANASSIADES**

Communication in its broadest sense[1] is a major element of interpersonal relations. As such, it has been viewed as "instrumental behavior"[2]—i.e., behavior that is goal-motivated and goal-oriented.

One aspect of communication that clearly fits the instrumental theory of communication is upward communication— that from subordinate to superior.[3] A recent study has not

---

*Human Relations, Vol. 27, No. 3, pp. 195-209. Reprinted with permission.

**Dr. John C. Athanassiades is an Associate Professor of Management at Georgia State University in Atlanta, Georgia, where he has taught for the past 3 years in the Graduate and Undergraduate Schools of Management. A native of Greece, Dr. Athanassiades took his undergraduate degree in Chemical Engineering at Georgia Institute of Technology in 1951, spent 12 years as an executive in industry, then took his M.B.A. at New York University GBA ('67) and his Ph.D. ('71) at New York University GBA. His writings have appeared in journals here and abroad, his most recent work, an empirical research in upward distortion in hierarchical organizations, appearing in June 1973 issue of the *Academy of Management Journal*. His special study on distortion in Police Organizations, which appeared in *Police Chief* in May, 1972, has led to a major research which Dr. Athanassiades is now concluding on that subject and which will appear in a book on the subject which Dr. Athanassiades is now writing.

1. Verbal and non-verbal communication, i.e., the flow of information, impressions, and understandings from one individual to others.
2. E. Goffman, *The Presentation of Self in Everyday Life* (Garden City, New York: Doubleday, 1959), pp. 2-4.
3. J. Thibaut and H. Riecken, "Authoritarianism, Status, and the Communication of Aggression," *Human Relations* 8, 1955, pp. 95-120; A. Cohen, "Upward Communication in Experimentally Created Hierarchies," *Human Relations* 11, 1958, pp. 41-53; W. Read, "Upward Communication in Industrial Hierarchies," *Human Relations* 15, 1962, pp. 3-15.

only confirmed that distortion of upward communication by subordinates is instrumental behavior on the part of the subordinate, but has also uncovered a close relationship between some personality, as well as environmental, factors and the degree to which a subordinate distorts his upward communications. For example, significant relationships have been shown to exist between a subordinate's distortion of upward communication, his level of insecurity, his drive to ascend, as well as some aspects of the organizational climate.[1]

However, these and earlier findings were based almost exclusively on male populations, obviously reflecting current employment realities. Thus, a legitimate question can be raised as to the projectibility of such findings to female populations. Although there are conflicting views today about any real differences between sexes (besides the physiological ones),[2] the fact remains that women at work very often face a cool, if not openly hostile, male-oriented and male-dominated environment.[3] Therefore, aside from the ongoing argument about *real* differences between the sexes, the work-environment of men and women is different, and will very probably have some differential bearing upon their respective behavior.

Today, an increasing number of women are entering managerial and other executive ranks and the trend is likely to accelerate this decade.[4] This expected influx of women into

1. J. Athanassiades, "The Distortion of Upward Communication in Hierarchical Organizations," *Academy of Management Journal*, June, 1973.
2. T. Alexander and J. Krause, "There Are Sex Differences in the Mind, Too," *Fortune*, Feb., 1971, pp. 76-79, 132-135.
3. It has been pointed out that although women today constitute about one-third of the U.S. work force, they are, as a rule, relegated to lower occupational echelons. And those few women who have challenged the male job market and reached for the higher jobs have been viewed with suspicion, hostility, and ridicule, even though they may have all the qualifications necessary to hold those jobs. C. Epstein, *Woman's Place* (Berkeley, Calif.: University of California Press, 1971), pp. 2-3. A somewhat similar view regarding career opportunities for women in Great Britain is presented in M. Fogarty, et al., *Women in Top Jobs* (London: Allen and Unwin, Ltd., 1971), pp. 18 and 308.
4. G. Bowman, N. Worthy, S. Greyser, "Are Women Executives People?" *Harvard Business Review*, July/Aug., 1965. Also C. Orth, and F. Jacobs, "Women in Management: A Pattern for Change," *Harvard Business Review*, July/Aug., 1971.

executive ranks suggests the need for better understanding of their behavior in an organization.

This study is concerned with one aspect of women's behavior in the organization—the distortion of upward communication by female subordinates, and its relation to the female subordinate's achievement and security needs. It is also concerned with the differential effect of the work-environment on the distortions by males and females, inasmuch as the assumption that women and men face differing environments is basic to the understanding of this study.

The model of upward distortion used in this study is similar to that of an earlier study of male populations, also conducted by this writer.[1] Briefly, the model is based on two aspects of motivation theory:

(a) that behavior is motivated by a hierarchy of unsatisfied needs in such a way that higher order needs do not become operant as motivators of human behavior until the lower order needs become relatively satisfied;[2] and

(b) that behavior is goal-directed, i.e., the individual attempts to engage in activities that he/she considers instrumental to the attainment of his/her goals. However, since an individual very often must choose alternative courses of action in the face of uncertainty, one's behavior would be affected not only by one's perception of path-goal instrumentalities but also by higher expectation of achieving the desired goal. Yet, personal expectation (or subjective probability) is related to one's propensity to take risks.[3]

Finally, an important situational variable affecting subordinate behavior by affecting the subordinate's perception of path-instrumentality is the organizational climate.[4]

Looking, then, at the distortion of upward communication as instrumental behavior on the part of the subordinate, one

---

1. J. Athanassiades, *op. cit.*
2. A. Maslow, *Motivation and Personality* (New York: Harper & Row, 1954).
3. For an elaboration of this, see V. Vroom, *Work and Motivation* (New York: Wiley, 1964).
4. W. Bennis, et al., "Authority, Power and the Ability to Influence," *Human Relations*, 11, 1958, pp. 143-155.

would expect it to be related to the subordinate's unsatisfied needs, his/her perceptions of path-goal instrumentalities of achieving those goals (as affected by the situational variable), and the subordinate's risk-taking propensity.

Since need-satisfaction studies have shown that the two most important needs in the minds of employees are security and achievement needs, these needs are used as two of the variables for the model.

DIAGRAM A—Model of the Distortion of Upward Communication

situational variable(s) perceived path-instrumentality

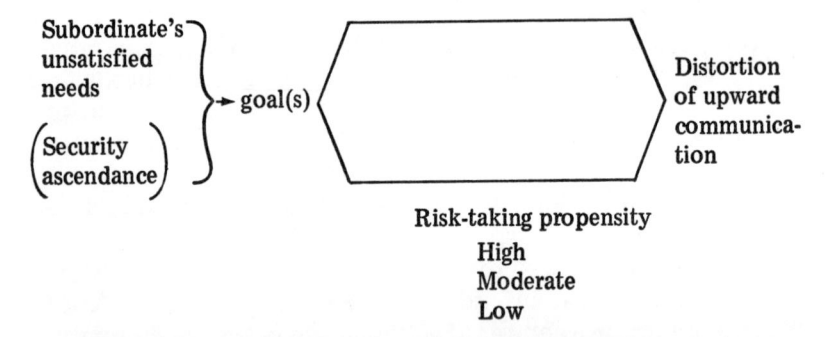

Subordinate's unsatisfied needs
(Security ascendance)
→ goal(s)

Distortion of upward communication

Risk-taking propensity
High
Moderate
Low

The above model (Diagram A) suggests the following possible types of subordinates, represented by each of the numbered cubes: (See Diagram B on p. 215.)

Typology of Subordinates

1. Low Security—low ascendance—low risk taking.
2. High Security—low ascendance—low risk taking.
3. Low Security—high ascendance—low risk taking.
4. High Security—high ascendance—low risk taking.
5. High Security—high ascendance—high risk taking.
6. High Security—low ascendance—high risk taking.
7. Low Security—high ascendance—high risk taking.
8. Low Security—low ascendance—high risk taking.

DIAGRAM B—Typology of subordinates in terms of security, ascendance and risk-taking propensity

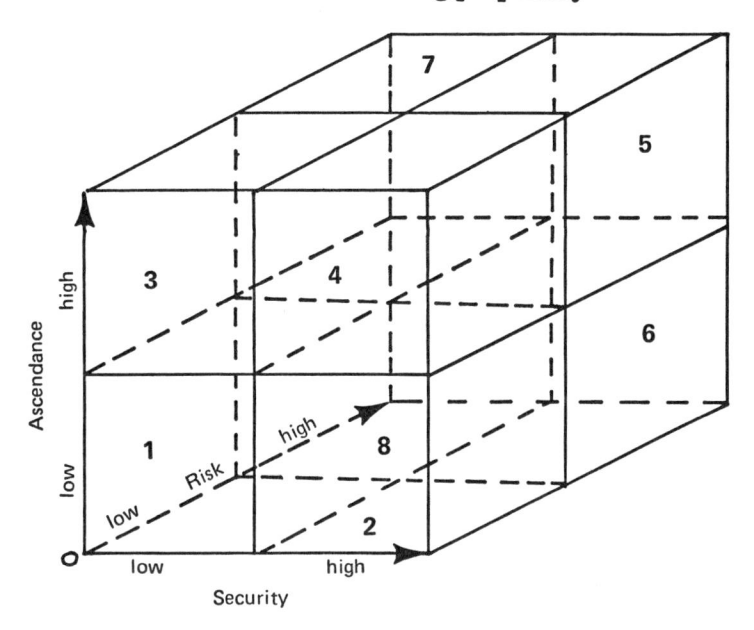

However, on the basis of Maslow's prepotency of the lower order needs, mentioned earlier, the eight types merge into the following:

A. Low Security—low risk taking (from 1 and 3).

B. Low Security—high risk taking (from 7 and 8).

C. High Security—low ascendance (from 2 and 6).

D. High Security—high ascendance (from 4 and 5).

To test this model of distortion by female subordinates, the following hypotheses were formulated:

HYPOTHESIS 1

Among insecure female subordinates, those with low propensity to take risks will distort their upward communications more than those with high risk-taking propensity.

HYPOTHESIS 2

Among secure female subordinates, high ascenders will distort their upward communication to a greater degree than low ascenders.

HYPOTHESIS 3

Female subordinates perceiving an autonomous work environment will distort their upward communications to a lesser degree than those perceiving a heteronomous environment (*ceteris paribus*).

HYPOTHESIS 4

Female subordinates will distort their upward communications to a greater degree than their male counterparts (*ceteris paribus*).

DEFINITIONS

Communication: the flow of information, impressions and understandings between members of an organization—whether directly related to the functioning of the organization or incidental to it.

Upward Communication: communication from subordinate to superior.

Distortion of Upward Communication: the difference between upward communication *as it occurs*, and *as it would occur* if the subordinate were not distorting.

Ascendance: a drive or striving to ascend, to rise above others in a hierarchy, as measured by the "A" scale of Gordon's *Personal Profile*.

Security: a feeling or feelings resulting from, or associated with, the relative satisfaction of one's security needs as measured by Maslow, et al., *Security-Insecurity Inventory*.

Risk-taking Propensity: willingness to take chances, as measured by the "C" scale of Gordon's *Personal Inventory*.

METHODOLOGY

POPULATIONS AND SAMPLES:

Members of a Business Women's organization, employees of a large firm, and a group of career women from the paramedical field in a major Southern city of the United States were the populations from which samples of 25 each were taken. In addition, a sample of 25 male employees was also taken from the above-indicated firm.

MEASUREMENTS

A battery of questionnaires was administered to each respondent in each sample, under the pretext of measuring communication accuracy. The questionnaires were given in a certain order, and each questionnaire except the last one was administered with the promise to participants that their answers would be anonymous. Before administering the last questionnaire, however, each participant was informed that the answers to this particular questionnaire—and this one only—would be shown to his/her superior for the purpose of obtaining a counter-evaluation of the participant's responses to this questionnaire. Thus, with regard to this last questionnaire, participants were given the strong impression that their superiors not only would see the responses but also would counter-evaluate them.

From the above battery of questionnaires, the following indices were constructed to measure the pertinent variables of this study:

Index of Ascendance: Each participant's score on the "ascendancy" scale of Gordon's *Personal Profile* was used as an index of that participant's drive to ascend. This scale was selected because it is consistent with our view that achievement and "success" in society today are practically synonymous with ascendance or "climbing up" the organization ladder; also, because it is a forced choice questionnaire which reduces the fakeability of responses.

Index of Autonomy: A seven-point scale of the agree-disagree type was used to register each participant's perception of openness or closeness of supervision, participation in decision-making, and freedom to express disagreement with one's superiors. The scores from this questionnaire were used as an index of the participant's perception of autonomy.

Index of Upward Communication as It Would Occur if the Subordinate Were Not Distorting: This index was constructed from the sum of the subordinate's scores on Gordon's *Personal Profile* and *Inventory* scales. These scales, of the forced-choice type, measure the respondent's self-image in terms of eight personality factors which have been found to play an important role in the functioning of people in everyday situations.[1]

Index of Upward Communication as It Occurs: This index was constructed by asking each participant to rate herself/himself on a min-max type scale on the same eight factors of ascendance, responsibility, etc. This was the last questionnaire to be administered, and, as indicated earlier, the participants had—prior to responding here—been made aware that these responses would be counter-evaluated by their respective superiors. It is assumed that through this procedure, a participant would respond as if one were communicating to a superior the image one wants to convey.

Index of Distortion of Upward Communication: This index is the absolute difference between the index of upward communication as it occurs and the index of upward communication as it would occur if the subordinate were not distorting.

Security-Insecurity Index: Each participant's score in Maslow's, et al. *Security-Insecurity Inventory* was used for this index.

Index of Risk-Taking Propensity: Each participant's score on the "C" scale of Gordon's *Personal Inventory* was used to construct this index. The "C" scale measures the individual's degree of cautiousness. Thus, a person scoring high on this scale is thought to be a cautious person; therefore, a low risk-taker.

Index of Perceived Discrimination: Each participant's score on the following two questions was used as an index of perceived discrimination against women;
   1. It is easier for a man to be promoted than for a woman.
      (agree) 7,6,5,4,3,2,1 (disagree)

---

1. These factors are: ascendance, responsibility, emotional stability, sociability, cautiousness, creativity, personal relations, and vigor.

2. Most business firms and government agencies discriminate against their female employees. (agree) 7,6,5,4,3,2, 1 (disagree)

Analysis of the Data

It was indicated at the beginning of this paper that women in managerial positions today are still working in a male-oriented and male-dominated environment, an environment which not only appears to discriminate against women, but which also may color their outlook towards the organization, their work, and even themselves, differently from that of men.

To ascertain whether these assumptions were warranted or not, a series of questions was addressed to these points. One set of questions was designed to probe the participants' perceptions of discrimination against women; another, the perceptions of autonomy in the organization, and a third to probe the participant's perception of, and self-image in, the organizational framework, i.e., the amount of self-esteem the participant perceives deriving from his/her position, and the amount of prestige one believes one enjoys inside the organization.

Table 1 (see following page) summarizes the responses of males and females in supervisory and executive positions. The data shows that there is agreement ($a = 0.85$, t-test) between male and female subordinates; that, indeed, there is discrimination against women in business and government organizations. Subsequently, the sample mean of the combined male and female scores on discrimination was tested against (a) an assumed population mean of no discrimination against women ($\mu_0=0$) and (b) an assumed population mean equal to the midpoint of the scale ($\mu_0=7$). One tail t-tests were performed in both cases, and in both instances the null hypothesis (Ho: $\bar{X}=\mu_0$) was rejected and the alternate (Ha: $x \rangle \mu_0$) was accepted at $a=0.005$, and $a=0.01$, respectively.

The results summarized in *Table 1* further show that women in managerial positions do perceive the organizational climate as less autonomous than do the men in the same organizations, ($a=0.05$). This means that women feel that they have less opportunity to participate in decisions than men; feel more than men that they do not have sufficient

TABLE 1

Perception of discrimination against women, autonomy, and self image of male and female employees in managerial positions

	Sample Means Males	Sample Means Females	$t^{(5)}$
Discrimination against women $^{(1)}$	$8.4^{(2)}$	$8.2^{(2)}$	0.174
Autonomy $^{(3)}$	20.00	16.80	2.506
Self-image $^{(4)}$	9.00	8.20	0.736
n	(5)	(5)	

1. No significant difference between males and females in perception of discrimination against women at $a=0.85$;
2. Male and Female scores on discrimination against women were combined, and the combined sample mean (11.54) was tested against the null hypothesis Ho: $x=\mu_0$; where $\mu_0=7$. The null hypothesis is rejected at $a=0.01$.
3. Significant difference between male and female autonomy scores at $a=0.05$.
4. No significant difference between male and female scores at $a=0.6$.
5. Critical ratio of t-test.

authority in their jobs; that too often, decisions are imposed on them from above; and feel less free than men do to express disagreement with superiors. In light of these findings, then, the assumptions expressed at the beginning of this paper about the different work environments faced by men and women seem to be justified. Interestingly, though, the data in *Table 1* also shows that no significant differences ($a=0.6$) between the self-images of men and women in terms of prestige and self-esteem derived from their positions in the organization.

Table 2 summarizes data regarding the distortion of upward communication of insecure female subordinates. The Mann-Whitney test was used to test for any significant difference here because it is known that security scores are not distributed normally but are skewed towards the secure side, and, therefore, a non-parametric test is required.

The data of *Table 2* show that a significant difference

TABLE 2

Distortion of upward communication of female insecure-low risk takers vs. insecure-high risk takers

	(Mann-Whitney U Test)		
	Means	$U^{(1)(2)}$	n
Insecure-high risk takers	83.45	63	(8)
Insecure-low risk takers	54.40	2	(8)

1. U is the Mann-Whitney statistic. The smaller the U, the greater the distortion.
2. Significant at $a=0.006$.

TABLE 3

Distortion of female secure-ascenders vs. secure non-ascenders

	(Mann-Whitney U Test)			
	Means	$U^{(1)}$	n	$z^{(2)}$
Secure-Ascenders	72.63	17	(16)	2.543
Secure Non-Ascenders	55.13	103	(13)	

1. U is the Mann-Whitney Statistic. The smaller the U, the greater the distortion.
2. Significant at $a=0.005$.

($a=0.045$) exists between low- and high-risk takers, i.e., insecure low-risk takers distort their upward communications to a greater degree than insecure high-risk takers. Thus, the data support *Hypothesis 1*.

Table 3 summarizes data regarding the distortion of upward communications of secure female subordinates. It shows that a significant difference ($a=0.02$) exists between the distortions of secure ascenders and secure non ascenders —secure ascenders distorting significantly more than secure non ascenders. The data, therefore, support *Hypothesis 2*.

TABLE 4

Distortion scores vs. perception of autonomy of matched pairs of female subordinates (matched with regard to security and ascendance scores)

	High Autonomy						Low Autonomy				
#	$Sec.^1$	$Asc.^2$	$Auton.^3$	$Dist.^4$	R^5	#	$Sec.^1$	$Asc.^2$	$Auton.^3$	$Dist.^4$	R^5
91	1	20	46	52.00	3	29	1	19	35	64.72	1
7	2	20	51	41.56	2	25	2	23	45	62.90	6
30	4	24	45	59.54	5	38	4	29	32	103.33	10
45	7	16	60	53.75	4	31	7	30	38	80.90	9
18	11	20	56	34.90	1	81	11	24	36	74.31	8
					15						40

1. Security scores
2. Ascendance scores
3. Autonomy scores
4. Distortion scores
5. Rank of Distortion scores

To test *Hypothesis 3*, that subordinates perceiving an autonomous organizational environment will distort their upward communications to a lesser degree than those perceiving a less autonomous one (*ceteris paribus*), pairs of subordinates perceiving high and low autonomy were matched as closely as possible with regard to their security and ascendance scores. Their distortions were then tested for significant differences. *Table 4* lists the matched pairs and the relevant scores. The Mann-Whitney U-statistic was calculated from the ranked scores and used to test for any significant difference between the high- and low-autonomy groups. It was found that the distortions of these two groups differ significantly ($a=0.008$). Female subordinates perceiving high autonomy in their organizational environment distort their upward communications to a lesser degree than those perceiving a less autonomous environment. The results, as summarized in *Table 5*, support *Hypothesis 3*.

It was assumed throughout the study, and confirmed by the data shown in *Table 1*, that women in managerial positions face a male-oriented and male-dominated work environment different from that faced by men, i.e., women view it

TABLE 5

The difference in the distortion of upward communication between two groups of female subordinates—one group perceiving high autonomy, the other perceiving low autonomy in their organizations[1]

Perceived Autonomy	Distortion Mean	U [2]	n	$P(U \leq U)$ [3]
High	48.35	25	5	0.008
Low	77.23	0	5	

1. Female subordinates in the two groups were matched as closely as possible with regard to their security and ascendance scores, as shown in *Table 4*.
2. The Mann-Whitney U-statistic was used to test for significant differences in the distortions of these two groups of subordinates. The higher the distortion, the smaller the value of the U-statistic.
3. $P(U \leq U_o) = 0.004$ for 1-tail test. Therefore, for a 2-tail test $a = 0.008$.

as discriminating against women; as providing them with fewer opportunities for decision; with less freedom for expression, etc., than men view the same environment under which they work. In effect, it seems as if we were looking at two different organizations—one male-oriented and male-dominated, and therefore discriminating against, and less hospitable to, women — the environment in which women work. The other environment would seem to be more autonomous, non-discriminating against men — the environment in which men work. Were this to be the case, according to *Hypothesis 4*, female subordinates would distort their upward communications to a greater degree than their male counterparts *(ceteris paribus)*. *Table 6* shows the distortion scores of pairs of female and male subordinates matched as closely as possible with regard to ascendance, autonomy and security scores.

The Mann-Whitney U-statistic was used to test for any significant differences in the distortion of the two groups. *Table 7* summarizes the results, which seemingly support *Hypothesis 4*. The data show that, other things being equal, female subordinates distort upward significantly more ($a = 0.095$) than male subordinates.

TABLE 6

Distortion of upward communication scores of male and female subordinates, matched with regard to their security, ascendance and autonomy scores.

Male

#	Sec.[1]	Asc.[2]	Aut.[3]	Distn.[4]
9	1	20	46	58.00
29	1	19	46	64.72
26	1	25	29	93.56
10	8	23	49	53.00
8	11	24	41	74.31
34	14	30	45	56.22

Female

#	Sec.[1]	Asc.[2]	Aut.[3]	Distn.[4]
22	1	33	46	52.36
—	—	—	—	—
2	1	21	29	81.76
14	8	25	49	43.35
3	12	23	41	49.00
1	14	24	42	49.44

1. Security scores
2. Ascendance scores
3. Autonomy scores
4. Distortion scores

TABLE 7

The difference in the distortion of upward communication between male and female subordinates[1]

	Distn. Means	U[2]	n	$P(U \leqslant U_o)$[3]
Female Subordinates	66.64	4	6	
Male Subordinates	55.18	21	4	0.026

1. Subordinates in the two groups were matched as closely as possible with regard to their security, ascendancy and autonomy scores.
2. The Mann-Whitney U-statistic was used to test for significant differ-

ences in distortion between the two groups. The higher the distortion, the smaller the value of the U-statistic.
3. $P(U \leq U_0)=0.026$ for a 1-tail test. Therefore, for a 2-tail test, $a=0.052$.

TABLE 8

Security, ascendance, risk-taking and distortion of upward communication of women in managerial and clerical positions

	Sample Means		$Z^{(1)}$
	Managerial	Clerical	
Security[2] ($\bar{X}_S$)	12.00	14.28	0.27 [4]
Ascendance ($\bar{X}_A$)	20.77	21.45	0.265 [4]
Risk-Taking [3] ($\bar{X}_R$)	27.11	27.50	0.94 [4]
Distortion ($\bar{X}_D$)	67.18	67.66	0.60 [4]

1. Critical ratio of Mann-Whitney U-test.
2. The lower the security index, the more secure is the individual.
3. The higher this index, the lower the risk-taking propensity (the more cautious) is the individual.
4. No significant difference.

TABLE 9

Security, ascendance, risk-taking and distortion of upward communication of professional women and women in managerial positions

	Sample Means		$Z^{(1)}$
	Professional	Managerial	
Security[2] ($\bar{X}_S$)	9.69	12.00	0.230
Ascendance ($\bar{X}_A$)	24.00	20.77	1.726 [3]
Risk-taking [4] ($\bar{X}_R$)	24.42	27.11	1.682 [5]
Distortion ($\bar{X}_D$)	58.12	67.18	1.439 [6]

1. Critical ratio of Mann-Whitney U-test.
2. The lower the security index, the more secure is the individual.
3. Significant at $a=0.04$, 1-tail test.
4. The higher this index, the lower the risk-taking propensity (the more cautious) is the individual.
5. Significant at $a=0.05$, 1-tail test.
6. Significant at $a=0.08$, 1-tail test.

The data were also grouped into the following categories:
1. Women in managerial positions
2. Women in clerical positions
3. Professional women in the paramedical field

These groups were analyzed for any significant differences in the relevant variables by means of the Mann-Whitney test, and *Tables 8* and *9* summarize the results. *Table 8* shows no significant differences between women in Managerial and Clerical positions. *Table 9* shows no significant differences in the security levels of Professional and Managerial women. But the two groups are found to differ significantly in terms of the other variables. That is, Professional women score higher in ascendance, are less cautious, and distort less than Managerial women.

Finally, *Table 10* summarizes the scores of all three groups.

TABLE 10

Security, ascendance, risk-taking, distortion of upward communication of professional, managerial and clerical women

	Sample Means		
	Professional	Managerial	Clerical
Security[1.] ($\bar{X}_S$)	9.69	12.00	14.28
Ascendance ($\bar{X}_A$)	24.00	20.77	21.45
Risk-Taking[2] ($\bar{X}_R$)	24.42	27.11	27.50
Distortion ($\bar{X}_D$)	58.12	67.18	67.66

1. The lower the security index, the more secure is the individual.
2. The higher the risk-taking index, the more cautious (the lower the risk-taking propensity of) the individual.

DISCUSSION

The data generated by this study lend support to the hypotheses stated in this paper. These findings are in general accord with other studies that have shown consistently that subordinates tend to screen, withhold, and, in general, distort in various ways the communications directed upwards. Furthermore, these findings are in close agreement with a recent study of male subordinates, showing that such upward distortion is need-motivated and goal-oriented; that it is related to the subordinate's security and ascendancy needs, to the propensity to take risks, and to the organizational climate.

However, although these findings confirm the applicability of such models of upward distortion of communication to both male and female populations, it should be kept in mind that these data were drawn from limited populations of subordinates and their projectibility to large populations of female subordinates is not warranted. Therefore, any generalizations based on these data must be viewed as such at all times and treated accordingly.

Nevertheless, such generalizations have some useful function in the sense that they may focus attention on some special points of interest and help direct further research in those areas.

Of particular interest, therefore, are the findings of this study regarding the female subordinate's perceptions of sex discrimination, autonomy, self-image, and the subordinate's distortion of her upward communication.

The findings show that subordinates (of both sexes) are clearly aware of the existence of job discrimination against women. These findings also show that women in managerial positions feel more suppressed—less autonomous, less independent—than men do in similar positions. Further, they show an inverse relationship between perceived autonomy and the distortion of upward communication by female subordinates. Finally, these findings show that there is no significant relationship between the female subordinate's perception of discrimination, autonomy, and her self-image.

The implications of these findings are important for both the individual and for the organization.

First, let us look at job discrimination based on sex. Whether real or imaginary, it is acknowledged almost unanimously and, therefore, cannot be ignored. What, then, are its effects on female subordinates? Do they rebel and protest, or do they become apathetic? What are the *real* costs to the individual and to the organization for one to perceive oneself as a second class organizational citizen?

One may also wonder what may be the effect on male

subordinates. Does this sex favoritism shown by the organization give him a sense of superiority, a greater sense of loyalty to the organization? Or does such discrimination, in effect, turn even the lowest male employee into a brahmin of organizational society? Does this increase his productivity?

Regarding the differences in perceived autonomy between male and female subordinates: do women perceive less autonomy because of their feelings of discrimination? Or do organizations really allow more autonomy to men than to women? Again: what are the effects of such differences in perceived autonomy, whether real or imaginary? What are their costs, for both the individuals involved and for the organization?

Let us look, too, at the inverse relationship between perceived autonomy and the distortion of upward communication by female subordinates. If this is so, then one may visualize a spiraling situation. The less autonomous a subordinate feels, the more likely is she to distort her upward communications; the closer, then, the superior may tend to supervise, the less autonomous the subordinate will feel; etc., etc.

One may ask, what is the net effect of such a state of affairs? Is the superior's decision-making ability impaired by (a) having to spend more and more time and effort on supervising one's subordinates closer and closer? (b) relying on the distorted information that flows upwards from one's subordinates? One may wonder further how this relationship may vary, if any, if the sex identities in the superior-subordinate relationship change, i.e., male superior/female subordinate, female superior/female subordinate, or female superior/male subordinate.

Finally, one should note that the findings show no relationship between a subordinate's perception of organizational climate—in terms of discrimination and autonomy—and her self-image. Obviously, organizations are capable of eliciting behavior on the part of female subordinates which may be at variance with the subordinate's self-image. Thus, it is perfectly conceivable that female subordinates may choose to feign submissiveness, loyalty, enthusiasm, frivolity, or low intellect —simply because they may feel that this kind of stereotyped behavior is prescribed by a male-oriented and dominated organizational culture. Obviously, since the female subordinate's self-image does not differ significantly from that of a male subordinate's, her upward behavior is a "put-on," a means to the attainment of her goals. One may ask, again: what are the costs to the organization in terms of utilization of its human resources?

QUERIES

1. In 1922, J. W. Wood stated that a "fixed scale of wages" should be avoided. Do you think that this is possible and/or desirable in today's world? What are the justifications for your position?

2. Compare the "Tyranny of Ad Hocism" with the concept of human resource management. If you feel that one is preferable, how would you eliminate the undesirable one from your organization?

3. What would be an alternative to McMurry's Machiavellian approach to management survival? Which do you find preferable? Why?

4. Think of a recent decision that you have put off, and list (according to Feinberg's classification) the basic reasons behind your indecisiveness.

5. According to Morgan, why do managers so often misinterpret the real feelings that employees have towards their place of employment?

6. Utilizing the type of analysis employed in "Labor-Management Communications," examine a communication problem that you have with some other individual or group.

7. Explain the differences between the three forms of communication networks (Mean's article) and discuss which type would be the most appropriate for a small restaurant operation.

ACT III

The Actors—

THE EMPLOYEES

INTRODUCTION

The vital link between The Director, or Management, and The Gallery, or The Guests is formed by The Actors, or The Employees. Without actors there is no play—without employees there is no hospitality service. In this chapter we will take a good look at the personnel administration function and the proper utilization of human energy. In the previous chapter we talked about how a manager can be a leader, motivator and communicator; this involved concepts which were largely intangible.

The personnel administration function (actually there are many functions involved) which we will introduce now is quite tangible. Before going into the functions, it may be advisable to trace briefly the historical development of the personnel department. The department evolved from a record-keeping function; records were needed which contained hiring dates, wages, transfers, penalties, and similar information. It involved clerical skills and lessened the paper work of the line supervisors.

In the early '20s, the term industrial relations came into vogue; at that time, the emphasis was on providing services to the employees. Management felt that this was one way to combat employee discontent which made itself noticeable in aggressive unionization efforts. However, by this time, most states had passed workmen's compensation laws which held the employer financially responsible for all injuries occurring to employees while working. Union membership actually declined during this period.[1] *These developments resulted in new responsibilities which were passed on to the personnel department. The department was charged now with tasks quite different from mere record-keeping and began to be involved in negotiating with unions, operating cafeterias, planning recreational programs and running first aid clinics.*[2]

During the '30s, unions charged management with setting substandard wages, discharging employees unjustly, letting favoritism be the basis for promotions and transfers and many other acts they considered unfair. Unions launched a concerted effort to organize employees and this now proved to be highly successful. Since the personnel departments or industrial relations departments had so far been involved in handling unions, they were charged with the responsibility of negotiating labor contracts, handling grievances, etc. This, without doubt, increased the status and power of the departments and gave them a respected voice, if not an authoritarian position, in all matters relating to the labor force vis a vis the line supervisors.

Today, it is difficult to generalize about the specific functions of the personnel departments, if only because organizations of different sizes will require different tasks. However, in general, the following functions[3] *are involved in a medium to large-size, single hotel, a large club, or a food service corporation (with a number of outlets).*

The foremost function is the employment function. After the executive chef or the club manager has established the need for an additional employee, a requisition is passed on to the personnel department. Using previously developed and

---

1. D. S. Beach, *Personnel—The Management of People at Work*, 2nd ed., (New York: MacMillan Co., 1970), p. 29.
2. While personnel departments in U.S. companies soon became involved in policy determination and even decision-making, the "service state" that had prevailed in the U.S. during the '20s, as just described, was actually still very much in evidence in Europe during the late '50s. For a glimpse into the conditions in German industry at that time, see L. A. Kreck, "The Philosophy of German Management," *Pakistan Management Review*, May-June, 1966, pp. 4-22.
3. The discussion follows an outline used by D. S. Beach, *Personnel— The Management of People at Work* (New York: MacMillan Co., 1970), pp. 69-74.

up-to-date sources of prospective employees, the department will contact applicants for further interviews. If no ready sources are available, the available position can be advertised in newspapers, trade journals, state and private employment services, labor unions, and schools and colleges. Further, the opening can also be announced on the hotel's or club's employees' bulletin board, or "walk-ins" can be considered.

Based on the job content and job qualifications established by the chef or club manager, the personnel department is now charged with carrying out the selection process. This may involve interviews, selection tests, medical examinations, and reference checks. The ideal result should be more than one suitable candidate for the position. Those candidates are then presented to the line management, e.g., the chef, who makes the final decision to hire or reject. The idea behind this procedure is that it is he, not the personnel manager, who has to work daily with the new employee; therefore, the chef should have the final say.

Administering transfers is another function of the personnel department. Transfers are reassignments of employees to another job with the same pay, status, and responsibility. The employee himself can ask for a transfer because he is not happy in his present position or because he feels that promotional opportunities are limited. For example, a waiter in a hotel might ask to be transferred from the speciality restaurant to room service because he wants to work the morning shift.

The operation can also initiate transfers because of changes in sales volume, changes in operating hours, new openings, etc. For example, a fast food chain might want to transfer one or two experienced cooks from a present unit to one which will open soon. International hotel companies quite often relocate managerial personnel from one continent to another, depending on the need of the company.

Promotions are also carried out through the personnel department. Quite often in our industry, promotions are based on seniority, or at least seniority plays an important part in the decision to promote. This is the case whether a food service worker is unionized or not. Traditionally, unions were little interested in pursuing a policy on promotion. But today some unions think that seniority, or length of service, *should be the only criterion for promotions and have set up grievance procedures to take over this former management prerogative.*

Sometimes temporary business conditions require an organization to lay off some of its employees. Layoff is beyond the control of the individual employee and can be for a nonspecified period of time. Before layoffs actually take place, a reduction in employees' working hours will often be put into effect. For example, in order to maintain a reasonable labor cost, a large convention hotel might ask some maids, waiters, cooks, and bellboys to take one or two additional days off without pay during a slower part of the month in order to avoid layoffs. Unions, of course, are highly interested in controlling layoffs. Many contracts state that seniority should be the primary consideration for layoffs. This is one of the reasons the personnel department, with its records, is involved in the above.

Together with line management, the personnel department determines training needs, from induction training to senior management seminars. While actual on-the-job training is carried out by the supervisor, pre-opening and classroom-style training is quite often the task of the personnel department. Anyone who has been involved in the opening of a food service, club, or lodging operation knows about the tremendous training task which the personnel department has to accomplish. If the training activity takes place across national boundaries, training becomes a study in sociology.[1] Any training beyond classroom-style training, such as training for job rotation and understudies, while the responsibility of line management, is very often coordinated by the personnel department.

The whole matter of wage and salary administration, which includes designing and installing job evaluation programs, and surveys of wages and salaries in the local labor market, is done by the personnel department with the help of line management. However, the final decision rests with top management since wages and salaries have a direct bearing on the profitability of the organization.

---

1. L. A. Kreck, "Personnel Planning for Foreign Hotels," *The Cornell HRA Quarterly*, Vol. 9, No. 4. Feb. 1969, pp. 32-86.

Today, two subjects are very much in the news, preserving the health and assuring the safety of employees. Constant reference is made to the "Occupational Health and Safety Act of 1970." The personnel department is especially involved with activities centering around health and safety. These activities include pre-employment health examinations, treatment of first-aid cases, treatment of minor ailments, and health and first-aid education.

The aim of the safety program is to prevent work injuries, such as cuts, burns, and other injuries. The personnel department prepares educational material and displays, develops safety instructional material, organizes safety meetings and keeps records of injuries in compliance with the federal law. Since the frequency of injuries determines the company's insurance rate, management is quite concerned about safety. Some older food service and lodging operations encounter problems in complying with the above act.

Disciplining and discharging employees are two necessary evils in business. While these are line functions, it is quite often the personnel department which establishes rules and penalties which are then used by the supervisors. Not only does the personnel department establish rules, but sometimes line management even has to get approval[1] from the department before any dismissal can take place. This is done for at least two reasons: first of all, to stay in line with a companywide standard for dismissals and, second, to make certain that the case is severe enough to stand up under grievance procedures, which latter involve the personnel department.

Handling grievances is only one of the tasks the personnel department has to carry out in its labor relations function. The primary tasks are contract negotiations, interpretation, and administration. While it is top management's decision to accept or reject a contract, a representative of the personnel department is quite often management's representative during negotiations.

Another important contribution of the personnel department is the establishment and administration of benefits and services which include such items as pensions; life, hospital

---

1. C. A. Myers and J. G. Turnbull, "Line and Staff in Industrial Relations," *Harvard Business Review*, July-August, 1956, pp. 113-124.

and medical insurance; loan funds; credit unions; social and recreational programs. While again it is top management's prerogative to start or stop certain benefits, it is surely not done without consulting the personnel department.

Next comes organizational and manpower planning. This involves advising top management on changes in the organization, such as answering the question as to whether a food service management company should be organized according to geographic locations or types of food services, i.e., health care, fast food, etc. This type of planning also assures top management of the needed manpower during times of expansion.

Finally, there is the task of personnel and behavioral research, i.e., trying to find answers to questions dealing with motivation, leadership, job satisfaction, and others. While the hospitality industry, with few notable exceptions, has not yet concerned itself with these questions, companies in other industries have. If the hospitality industry wants to stay competitive as an employer, and there are indications that it is not presently competitive, then some major efforts have to be made now. It is the personnel department's job to remind top management regularly of the importance of an urgent commitment to such research.

In the last few pages we have been concerned with the "actors," or the "employees," of the company. The administration of these people necessitated, in many cases, the formation of a department, the personnel department, staffed more often than not with college graduates. The discussion so far has set the stage for two scenes in the present "Act," namely personnel administration and labor relations. One scene remains to be discussed: human engineering.

Human engineering has as its goal ". . . the adaptation of human tasks and working environment to the sensory, perceptual, mental, physical and other attributes of people. This adaptation for human use applies to such functions as the design of equipment, instruments, man-machine systems . . . and to the development of optimum work methods and work environment."[1] *To apply this to the food service/lodging*

---
1. E. J. McCormick, *Human Engineering* (New York: McGraw-Hill Book Co., 1957), p. 1.

industry would mean, for example, arranging for a cook to work in an environment which preserves his energy, yet at the same time allows him to produce efficiently.

To achieve the above, a technique, the motion and time study, is used. The "father" of a portion of this technique was Frederick W. Taylor who more than 90 years ago tried to find "the best way to do work." Taylor, after he became general foreman of a steel plant, was authorized to involve himself with scientific study of the time required to do various tasks. He stated that ". . . in these experiments we were not trying to find the maximum work that a man could do on a short spurt or for a few days, but that our endeavor was to learn what really constituted a full day's work for a first-class man; the best day's work that a man could properly do year in and year out, and still thrive."[1] This was the beginning of the time study.

Motion studies were first carried out by F. B. Gilbreth who, in 1911, published his results in a book appropriately called Motion Study.[2] He, together with his wife Mary Gilbreth, a psychologist, by using the motion picture camera, studied such concepts as fatigue, monotony, and transfer of skill. Today, neither of the two techniques is used by itself but industry has found them inseparable.

In the hospitality industry, the value of the technique of motion study has also been recognized, and many food service operations throughout the U.S. are witnesses to that fact: they are planned, designed, and executed to save human energy in efficient production.

---

1. F. W. Taylor, *The Principles of Scientific Management* (New York: Harper and Bros., 1942), pp. 54-55.
2. F. B. Gilbreth, *Motion Study* (Princeton: D. Van Nostrand, 1911).

Scene 1

PERSONNEL ADMINISTRATION

When we read the short selection "Why Hotel Employees Fail to Rise," does it seem applicable only to 1907? On the contrary, it offers some very timely suggestions.

In "Employee Responsibility, a Key Goal for Managers," the old saying "a fair day's work for a fair day's pay" is questioned and new dimensions are suggested for an employee's responsibility. The results of the survey showed that employees, managerial as well as non-managerial, regard many of those suggested responsibilities as legitimate but also reject some.

Buchanan in "How a Supervisor Wins Employees," gives some practical suggestions and makes the point that the art of supervision can be learned.

In the next selection "Labor Supply, Payroll Costs and Changes," the author traces the development of the cost of labor over the past years and compares it with productivity. He suggests further that generous welfare benefits have reduced the work force with subsequent hardship for the hos-

pitality industry. To overcome the problem of labor supply (connected with high costs), he thinks that every operator should ask himself, "What satisfaction does the guest require and how can I offer that satisfaction at a realistic cost?" Power thinks that some mechanization may make the "re-personalization" of some service possible by eliminating hand labor.

WHY HOTEL EMPLOYES FAIL TO RISE*

MARY E. PALMER

The reasons why some people never rise above commonplace positions should be made clear to all who seek employment or better conditions. In every field there are those who never take the initiative and they make up the great majority. They are apparently afraid of doing too much work, or of making themselves generally useful, or of doing some bit of work that has not been assigned them, for which they might not be paid, forgetting that the world's greatest prizes are generally bestowed upon the individual who does the right thing without being told.

If we wait to be told our duties, we cease to be moral agents and are mere machines, and, as such, stationary in place and pay.

If you would succeed, cultivate self-confidence, which is one of the foundation stones of success. Rest assured your employer knows the difference between "bluff" and the real thing. "Nerve" will not win in the long run. It may accomplish temporary advantage, but there must be something back of "nerve."

Practice self-control. If you cannot control yourself, you cannot control others. When the commander riding in front of his army takes to the woods in the face of the enemy, he can but expect his troops to follow his example. Anger is an unbecoming mood. In serenity lies power.

Keep busy. Improve each moment. Do not be afraid of too much work. The office boy who sits around watching

---

**The Hotel World*, June 1, 1907, p. 22. Reprinted with permission of *Hotel and Motel Management.*

the clock, as if he might be waiting for his automobile to take him home, will never own the hotel.

The superintendent who has not enough patience to instruct a beginner properly may lose valuable assistants and cannot hope to achieve a great enterprise.

Do not become discouraged and resign your position because it is not up to your ideal. It may be better to bear with the ills you have than fly to others you know not of.

The man hanging on to the tail gets there as sure as does the man riding on the horns. But he must hang on. The other fellow's place only seems to be the best. *Hang on to the tail.*

EMPLOYEE RESPONSIBILITY, A KEY GOAL FOR MANAGERS*

JOHN P. LOVELAND**
JACK L. MENDLESON***

Question: Why does overtime work bother employees so much when, to top management, the need for the overtime work is so obvious?

Question: Why do employees have such negative reactions to some training programs while managers see the training as an attempt to "help" the employees?

Question: What can be done to enforce necessary rules when employees refuse to be "informers" and supervisors "look the other way" during violations of rules?

The literature of organizational behavior and personnel management abounds with concepts which emphasize the responsibility of the organization to the employee. What seem to be missing, at least explicitly, are concepts which focus on the responsibility of the employee to the organization. Traditionally, a "fair day's work for a fair day's pay" is assumed to be the standard for determining and evaluating the employee's responsibility to the firm.

One must question whether a fair day's work is sufficient or meaningful measure of employee responsibility, especially

---

*Human Resource Management, Graduate School of Business, University of Michigan, Spring, 1974, pp. 32-35. Reprinted with permission.
**John P. Loveland is an Associate Professor of Management in the New Mexico State University. He received his doctorate in business administration from Arizona State University.
***Jack L. Mendleson is an Associate Professor of Management at Arizona State University. He received his doctorate in business administration at Michigan State University and has published extensively, in this journal and in others.

in an environment of complex, dynamic organizations vying for survival and growth. The purpose of this article is to present an alternative concept of employee responsibility which is more relevant to understanding the responsibilities that complex organizations require of individuals.[1] The paper also discusses the implications of this new concept for personnel selection and evaluation.

Traditional approaches to defining an employee's responsibility deal with certain individuals in given jobs or positions, but support exists for a looser definition:[2] individuals are obligated for certain broad behaviors which are not limited to a given job or positions, but rather which apply to *all* employees in three separate categories of behavior:

> at-work behaviors directly related to job performance
> at-work behaviors peripheral to job performance
> away-from-work behaviors related to the organization

These required behaviors provide a basis for effective organizational functioning, or result from organizational norms of behavior.

How Workers Define Their Responsibilities

A questionnaire was given to 112 full-time employees in the banking industry in a southwestern state, asking them to indicate the extent to which they accepted various behaviors as part of their legitimate responsibility as employees of their firm. The employees were divided into management and nonmanagement groups and the behaviors were presented in the three categories mentioned above.

At-Work Behaviors Directly Related to Job Performance
1. To seek greater responsibilities.
2. To accept overtime whenever asked, if the firm pays the established overtime rate.

---

1. For more detail, see "An Investigation of Employee Attitudes Toward a Concept of Employee Responsibility," (unpublished dissertation, College of Business and Economics, Arizona State University, 1971).
2. For example, see, Keith Davis and Robert L. Blomstrom, *Business and Its Environment* (New York, McGraw-Hill Book Company, 1966), pp. 136-138.

3. To follow instructions from individuals in positions of authority over him.
4. To seek assistance in job situations with which he is unfamiliar.
5. To accept overtime work even though the firm does not pay an overtime rate.
6. To answer truthfully all job-related questions asked by management.
7. To accept greater responsibilities if offered.
8. To exercise care when using organization property.
9. To seek better ways to perform his job.
10. To employ the most efficient work methods within his command.
11. To maintain a consistent rate of work during established hours.

At-Work Behaviors Peripheral to Job Performance

12. To arrive at work at the established times.
13. Not to engage in theft of organization property, no matter how small.
14. For any actions on the job which could harm the reputation of the firm.
15. To cooperate in organization-sponsored training programs.
16. To return to work promptly after all established work breaks.
17. To dress neatly and appropriately for the position and/or nature of the work.
18. To tell management whenever he observes another employee breaking a rule.
19. To respect all confidences associated with organization position.
20. To depart work no earlier than the established time.
21. To make known personal ideas or methods that could benefit the firm regardless of whether he is compensated for those ideas.
22. To notify the firm two weeks in advance of an anticipated change of employment.
23. To safeguard information which may be beneficial to competitors.
24. To accept transfers within the firm which do not require relocating himself or his family.
25. To safeguard his own health and the health of fellow employees.
26. To prepare for greater responsibilities.
27. To accept short-term "speed-ups" at work if necessary to achieve the goals of the firm.
28. To accept retraining if requested by the firm.
29. To follow all organizational rules and regulations.

30. To carry out all orders and directives which the organization considers legitimate.
31. To provide an accurate account of background and personal information required for employment.
32. To make known personal ideas or methods that could benefit the firm, if he is compensated for those ideas.

Away-From Work Behaviors Related to the Organization

33. For any actions off the job which could harm the reputation of the firm.
34. To work for only one employer at a time.
35. To speak favorably of the firm and its management to outsiders.
36. To move to another city or state if it would further the goals of the organization.
37. To be active in groups and clubs which promote the general interests of business.
38. To hold the goals of the organization above personal non-work goals which affect the job.
39. After changing employment, to keep all information confidential that may hurt the competitive position of his former employer.
40. To further his formal education whether or not the firm makes funds available.
41. To work at home on his own time if necessary to finish a job.
42. To avoid careless actions, either on or off the job, that could compromise or weaken the competitive position of the firm.
43. To study information related to the job/position on his own time.
44. To purchase his firm's products or services rather than those of competitors.
45. To insure that his family's conduct reflects favorably on the firm.
46. To seek retraining on his own time when it becomes necessary.
47. To vote for individuals and issues which support the interests of the business community.
48. To get enough rest and sleep necessary for effective performance on the job.
49. To refrain from unfavorable public criticism of the firm and its management while employed by the firm.
50. To spend time off the job with those in higher positions than his own.
51. Not to drink alcoholic beverages immediately before or anytime during the working day.

Summary of Item Responsibility Index Scores for Managers and Non-Managers by Category of Behavior

Responsibility Index Score

Item No.	At-Work Behavior Directly Related to Job Performance Manager	Non-Manager	Item No.	At-Work Behavior Peripheral to Job Performance Manager	Non-Manager	Item No.	Away-From-Work Behavior Related to Organization Manager	Non-Manager
1	91.07	92.86	12	94.64	100.00	33	96.43	79.46*
2	80.36	69.64	13	98.21	94.64	34	87.50	29.46*
3	96.43	99.11	14	99.11	96.43	35	96.43	91.07
4	100.00	99.11	15	100.00	90.18	36	42.86	37.50
5	91.96	37.50*	16	94.64	100.00	37	81.36	48.21*
6	100.00	100.00	17	100.00	100.00	38	86.61	67.86*
7	95.54	94.96	18	67.86	40.18*	39	87.50	92.86
8	100.00	100.00	19	100.00	99.11	40	66.96	62.50
9	100.00	100.00	20	64.29	64.29	41	91.07	40.18*
10	100.00	100.00	21	97.32	93.75	42	98.21	98.21
11	86.61	94.64	22	100.00	100.00	43	91.96	59.82*
			23	100.00	99.11	44	66.07	60.71
			24	83.93	76.79	45	79.46	74.11
			25	100.00	99.11	46	95.54	66.07*
			26	97.32	99.11	47	72.32	60.71
			27	97.32	91.07	48	96.43	95.54
			28	94.64	91.07	49	100.00	99.11
			29	91.96	95.54	50	18.89	14.29*
			30	89.29	87.50	51	79.46	77.68
			31	98.21	96.43			
			32	80.36	84.32			

The results of the survey show evidence of strong support for including many of the items within the scope of an employee's obligation to the organization. In fact, only one of the fifty-one items was rejected by a large percent of the managers (75%) as part of their obligation; this was the item suggesting that they should spend time off the job with those in higher positions than their own. Only three items received low scores from the non-management participants (numbers 5, 34, and 50); this return indicates a very high degree of acceptance of a broad range of obligation on their part.

These results are significant in themselves, for they provide a basis for suggesting that employees recognize and accept a much broader concept of employee responsibility than that of a fair day's work. The results also provide an additional criterion for employee selection and evaluation if one accepts the importance of this new concept of employee responsibility for effective organizational functioning.

Moreover, the attitude study identifies areas where differences exist between managers and non-managers. Whether these differences produce conflicts within the organization is undetermined; however, they do identify areas where potential conflicts could develop. This would be especially true if a manager expected a certain behavior of a subordinate and the subordinate did not feel obligated in the area or was unaware of the expectations of his superior.

While the results in the banking industry indicate that both managers and non-managers accept a broad range of obligations, non-managers feel much *less* obligated in the following areas:

at work behavior
5. working overtime without pay
18. informing management about a rule breaker

away-from-work behavior
33. avoiding actions off the job which could harm the reputation of the firm
34. working for only one employer (not moon-lighting)
37. being active in clubs and groups which promote the general interests of business
38. holding organizational goals above personal non-work goals which affect the job

41. working at home for the organization
43. studying work-related material on one's own time
46. seeking retraining on one's own time

If there is one central message from the non-managers, it is this: "My free time is my free time!"

How to Build Employee Responsibility

Let's start with this assumption: employees feel a sense of responsibility to their employing organization. Unfortunately, employees often do not feel obligated to perform some specific activities which top management believes are essential to the effective performance of the organization. It is the job of the personnel manager to identify discrepancies between what employees acknowledge as their obligations and what the organization requires, and then help to eliminate these discrepancies.

The personnel manager has a threefold role in working with employee responsibility:

research in his organization to determine what general activities are required for effective performance and whether employees feel obligated to perform these activities;

communication to top management of discrepancies between requirements and employee feelings of obligation;

training of managers at all levels to understand and cope with existing employee feelings of obligation, and attitude training for employees throughout the organization to increase feelings of obligation where needed.

One point should be clearly established; an employee responsibility index is not another employee screening or selection test. Its usefulness is as a guide to identifying:

(1) areas where the acceptance of responsibility by employees has a direct impact on the effectiveness of the organization;
(2) types of behavior acceptable and unacceptable to the employees;
(3) areas where differences in attitudes toward responsible behavior may exist between managers and non-managers.

The items of behavior included on an employee responsibility index are directly tied to the organization's profitability and effective functioning, identification of these responsible behaviors may provide the basis for expanding existing reward systems to include a broad range of behaviors directly related to the success of the organization.

The areas of "acceptable" and "unacceptable" behavior as determined in this study are reflective of a specific industry, i.e., the banking industry. Differences may and probably do exist in different industries. Surveys by personnel departments in industries other than banking would reveal the dimensions of acceptability of employee responsibility in each industry. Further, the survey results would establish the boundaries for normative behavior, i.e., the framework for determining what is and is not expected of new and existing personnel . . .

GOOD TITLE

"That is a very polite waiter you have," remarked the new guest. "What do you call him?"

"Well," replied the hotel proprietor, "all the boys around here call him 'Scales.' "

"And why do they call him 'Scales'?"

"Because he is tipped so often."—
Daily News*

---

*The Hotel World, June 1, 1907, p. 35. Reprinted by permission of *Hotel and Motel Management*.

HOW A SUPERVISOR WINS EMPLOYEES*

ROBERT D. BUCHANAN**

Seventy percent of a foodservice supervisor's job involves human relations. Training programs, standardized recipes, convenience food components and convenience food items have reduced the technical problems of quality food production. The human side of the business, however, has become more important with the continued growth of the economy, increased labor rates and the increased level of education.

Interwoven with the supervisor's responsibilities of planning and coordinating tasks, seeing that they are done on time and interpreting objectives and policies to employees is the responsibility of building good employee relations. The supervisor can improve employee relations by knowing and following through on these old, time-tested guidelines.

Employees are largely what we make them. Let's face it, there never will be a supply of perfect employees. Each person has certain abilities and shortcomings.

---

*(Buchanan)©, *School Foodservice Journal,* July/August, 1973, pp. 96-101. Reprinted with permission.

**Robert D. Buchanan* is Associate Professor, Institutional Management, Purdue University, Lafayette, Indiana. He formerly was Associate Director of Auxiliary Service at Northern Illinois University, where he was responsible for the operation of six residence hall kitchens, three snack bars, central bake shop and a school lunch program in the University Laboratory School. Active in many professional organizations, Mr. Buchanan was president of the National Association of College and University Food Services in 1966-67 and received NACUFS Distinguished Service Award in 1971. Recipient of an international Foodservice Manufacturers Association Silver Plate Award in 1969, Mr. Buchanan also has received four *Institutions/VF* Magazine outstanding Foodservice Design Awards.

When confronted with an employee problem, many inexperienced supervisors first think of terminating the employee. This is an easy way—but usually the wrong way—to handle the situation. It costs money to hire and train new workers. In general, the supervisor who has an excessive number of terminations is at fault rather than the employees.

The supervisor's job is to mold the human weaknesses of his workers in the proper direction.

Ability to handle people is acquired. Some supervisors are much more skilled than others in gaining cooperation and enthusiasm from their workers. Such a skill is not some mysterious gift, but results directly from knowledge and training. First, you must have a sincere desire to be a good boss.

Anticipate your workers' needs. Look ahead and be prepared to answer employees' questions. Be ready at all times to interpret rules and policies of the organization to your workers.

The most dangerous approach to dealing with subordinates is ignoring them. Do not ignore. Impress each employee with the importance of his job and let him know that he has a vital part in the optimum functioning of the organization.

An employee whose work is not noticed may come to feel that his job is unimportant. If it is unimportant to the supervisor, it is certainly unimportant to the individual. The employee's efficiency may drop quickly. Wise supervisors, no matter how busy they are, find time to show an interest in their workers even on the most minor jobs. All jobs are important to the overall picture.

Give praise. Don't be afraid to give praise. We pay cash wages in weekly checks. We pay mental wages by expressing appreciation for a job well done. Mental wages pay dividends.

People need a word of encouragement now and then just as they need food. Most people feel inferior or insecure at times. In many cases employees will work just as hard for mental wages as for cash wages. Cash wages provide for our physical needs, but mental wages provide for our emotional needs.

Praise the work. Because management is interested primarily in efficient use of time, supervisors must emphasize using time efficiently. Let praise for efficient use of time or for a job well done come from you as a supervisor and representative of management, rather than from you as an individual. In other words, praise the work rather than the worker.

When it is possible, praise in the presence of others. This impresses the employee receiving the praise with your sincerity and encourages others to merit your praise.

Don't give your praise too freely. Save it for the unusual job. Constant praise loses its force and effectiveness.

Adjust your praise to the individual. A very few egotistic individuals get swelled heads over praise. However, these people are in the minority. An occasional word of praise is all that is needed by the average employee.

An indirect and effective method of praise is asking an employee for his ideas. This gives him a sense of importance and helps sustain his ego. You may learn something at the same time.

Sympathetic handling of grievances is a potent form of mental wage. When a worker comes to you with what may seem to you a small complaint or grievance, listen attentively to the entire story. Remember it is important to him. Don't cut him short. Hear him out. Keep in mind that just listening to a grievance often clears it up. If you do not listen the employee will consider you unjust, unfair and bullheaded.

If an employee is emotionally upset, first try to calm him down. Try to get a smile before you begin discussing his problem. Talk to him in private if possible.

If you fail to handle complaints and grievances the situation may become serious. It's the little things that count.

Do not let the aggrieved worker rush you into a decision. Explain that both sides are entitled to a hearing. But be sure to make a definite decision as promptly as possible. Delay causes the worker to lose faith in you.

Be sure to leave the door open for appeal. Offer to go with the worker to your superior to talk the matter over calmly. The employee will rarely take you up, but he will feel that you are not unfair or bullheaded.

Reprimands should always be constructive to help the individual improve his work. Be sure it is worth the time and effort to issue a reprimand. If it isn't—skip it. Do not act in anger. If an employee makes a mistake through ignorance, the situation calls for training.

Do not store up your resentment over a long time period and then take it out on the worker in a burst of anger. Correct each offense as it comes up. If you ignore several infractions before you reprimand, the employee will feel that you should have spoken about his conduct before. Remember that many people like to be led. They want leadership.

Do not hesitate to reprimand workers for fear that you will be disliked. The boss who is an "easy mark" neither earns the respect nor does he get the maximum production out of his workers. Nothing is more unfair to your subordinates than allowing them to continue making mistakes without correcting them.

Begin with a question. No matter how sure you are of the worker's guilt, you lose nothing by opening your remarks with a question. This gives the employee a chance to tell his story. Keep an open mind and hear the employee out. He might change your mind.

Adjust the severity of the reprimand to the individual. A sensitive, high-strung person may become quite upset by a reprimand that would have no effect on a more thick-skinned individual. Learn to know each worker through observation and experience. No two people are alike nor can they be handled in the same way.

Criticize methods but never criticize intentions. "Hell is paved with good intentions." Practically everybody has good intentions. Most of us don't mind our methods being criticized, but we do not want our intentions questioned. It is negative to imply that a man is not loyal.

There are times to reprimand in public. Reprimand before others *only* when the employee is openly violating an important rule. You must show other workers that such actions will not be tolerated. If you fail to do this, your employees will doubt your ability to lead.

After giving a reprimand, forget it. If the worker admits his mistake, you have gained your point. Hold no grudge. Tell him you are going to forget it and start again with a clean slate. Be big enough to forget and make a point of commending him on something in the next few days.

If the rules do not suit you, don't tell your subordinates. Be loyal. Even when you disagree with a ruling of the management, be loyal and have your workers carry it out with no adverse comment from you. How can you expect them to be loyal if you are not? Nothing is ever perfect, and there will always be imperfect rules in all organizations. But don't let your subordinates suspect it!

Make your discipline consistent. Workers do not mind strict discipline as much as they mind inconsistent discipline. If you let down the rules in one particular case you may have difficulty maintaining them in others. Make your discipline consistent. Don't let a worker get by with something today and then jump down his throat for the same thing tomorrow. Never let your instructions be forgotten. After you make a job assignment, check to see that it is being carried out.

Be a square shooter. You can't keep the respect of your employees unless you play fair. Shoot square. Don't play favorites. Don't chisel in anyway. Give employees the benefit of the doubt. Be sure you treat every employee alike. Don't favor those whom you like. Make a conscientious effort to understand and like those who "get on your nerves."

Don't be too lenient or too severe. New supervisors either tent to be too meek and mild in dealing with subordinates or else they tend to be too hard and severe. To discover if you are too lenient, check this list:

1. Your workers display a lax attitude toward their work.
2. They impose on your good disposition.
3. They show a lack of respect for you.
4. Your reprimands have little effect.
5. Your praise has lost its power to stimulate them.

If you tend to be too stern, watch for these signals:

1. Your workers avoid you.
2. They appear sullen or stubborn.
3. Turnover among your workers is higher than normal.
4. Your workers restrict their work.
5. Opposition to your goals is apparent—this shows up in decreased work.

Don't take yourself too seriously. Don't confuse dignity with seriousness. Be cheerful, and your whole organization will reflect your good nature.

Do not ridicule or be sarcastic or play practical jokes. Good-natured kidding is all right if you are sure the employee is taking it in the spirit intended. But, here again, you must know your worker.

Relax, don't be a stuffed shirt.

It all adds up to:

1. Do not ignore. Impress each employee with the importance of his job and let him know that he has a part in the optimum functioning of the organization.

2. Don't be afraid to praise. We pay cash wages by check. We pay mental wages by expressing appreciation for a job well done.

3. Praise the work—not the worker. Praise in the presence of others when possible.

4. Be sympathetic in listening to an employee's grievance. Hear his entire story.

5. Reprimands should always be constructive.

6. Do not hesitate to reprimand for fear that you will be disliked.

7. Begin all reprimands with a question.

8. People are different. Adjust your discipline to the individual.

9. Never criticize intentions—criticize methods.

10. Sometimes you will have to reprimand publicly—when an open violation of an important rule is committed, for example.

11. Don't harbor resentment. After giving a reprimand, forget it. Try to find something to commend the employee for at a later date.

12. Support departmental and organizational rules even if you don't agree with them.

13. Be consistent with your discipline.

14. Be fair with all employees. Give them all the same opportunities and discipline.

15. Don't be too lenient or too severe. Either is bad. Seek the middle ground.

16. Don't take yourself too seriously.

In the final analysis, the best rule to follow in establishing effective and efficient human relations is an old one—the Golden Rule.

LABOR SUPPLY, PAYROLL COSTS AND CHANGES*

*THOMAS F. POWERS, Ph.D.***

Labor is identified by economists as one of the three basic factors of production: land, labor and capital. It is clearly one of the most basic inputs to any kind of enterprise. Labor costs of the foodservice and housing industries have undergone seemingly radical change in recent years and structural developments in the labor market suggest that the pattern of change will not only continue but accelerate. A number of factors have bid up the price of labor in recent years. Principal among these are a growing economy coupled with a relatively tight labor market, and the social welfare policy of the state and national governments.

This article will review briefly historical trends in wage rates and in the minimum wage, examine new factors whose effect is only beginning to be felt from the social policy domain, and attempt to consider the probable impact of logical future developments on the work force and hence on foodservice and housing enterprises.

---

*Cornell Hotel and Restaurant Administration Quarterly, May, 1974, pp. 5-13. Reprinted with permission.
**Dr. Thomas F. Powers is Professor in charge of Food Service and Housing Administration and Associate Professor of Organizational Behavior at Pennsylvania State University, where he has served on the faculty since 1970. Previously he was an Assistant Professor of Hotel, Restaurant & Institutional Management at Michigan State University. Earlier, he directed the Food Production Management Program at Morris Brown College in Atlanta, Georgia and served as coordinator of Atlanta University Center's undergraduate program in business administration. For five years, he was a Holiday Inns manager. Dr. Powers received his A.B. and M.B.A. degrees at Harvard University and his Ph.D. from Georgia State University.

The Minimum Wage

Toward the end of the Great Depression of the 30's, the Fair Labor Standards Act of 1938 was enacted. "The goals of wage regulation were: 1) elimination of poverty resulting from substandard wages; 2) creation of the necessary purchasing power to maintain high levels of employment and output; and 3) establishment of a floor under wages to prevent repetition of the downward wage spiral experienced during the depression."[1] The minimum wage established by that act was 40¢ an hour. After World War II the act was amended in 1949 raising the minimum wage to 75¢ an hour. Overtime penalty pay provisions were clarified and spelled out in considerable detail in this set of amendments. In 1955 the minimum wage was raised to $1.00 an hour and in 1961 the basic minimum wage was raised to $1.25.

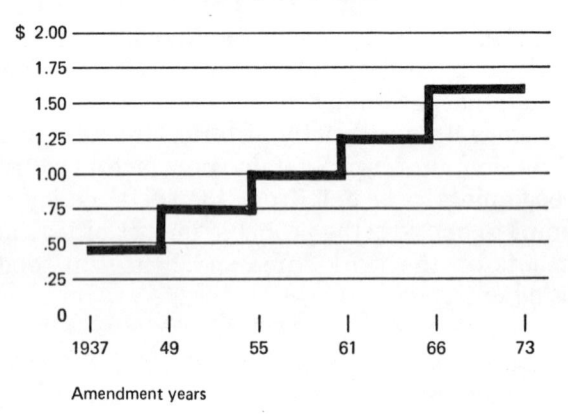

Fig. 1—INCREASES OF MINIMUM WAGE 1938 to 1973

Amendment years

Source:
Legislative Analysis: Proposed Minimum Wage Amendments, American Enterprise Institute for Public Policy Research (Wash., D.C.), Legislative Analysis #5, 93rd Congress, May 9, 1973.

1. John P. Henderson, *Labor Market Institutions and Wages in the Lodging Industry,* MSU Business Studies, 1965, Division of Research, Bureau of Business and Economic Research, Graduate School of Business Administration, Michigan State University, East Lansing, Michigan, p. 100.

The general trend, which is summarized in Figure 1, was clearly one of raising wages. During the same time, legislation was passed broadening the coverage to include more industries and to include smaller firms.

These tendencies reached the hospitality industries in 1966, when the national minimum wage was raised to $1.60 an hour and foodservice and housing establishments were brought under FLSA regulation at $1.00 an hour with fifteen-cent raises each year to bring the industry's wage to the national level of $1.60 an hour by 1971.

Fig. 2—AVERAGE HOURLY EARNINGS OF PRODUCTION (NONSUPERVISORY) WORKERS ON PRIVATE NONAGRICULTURAL PAYROLLS 1947 TO 1970

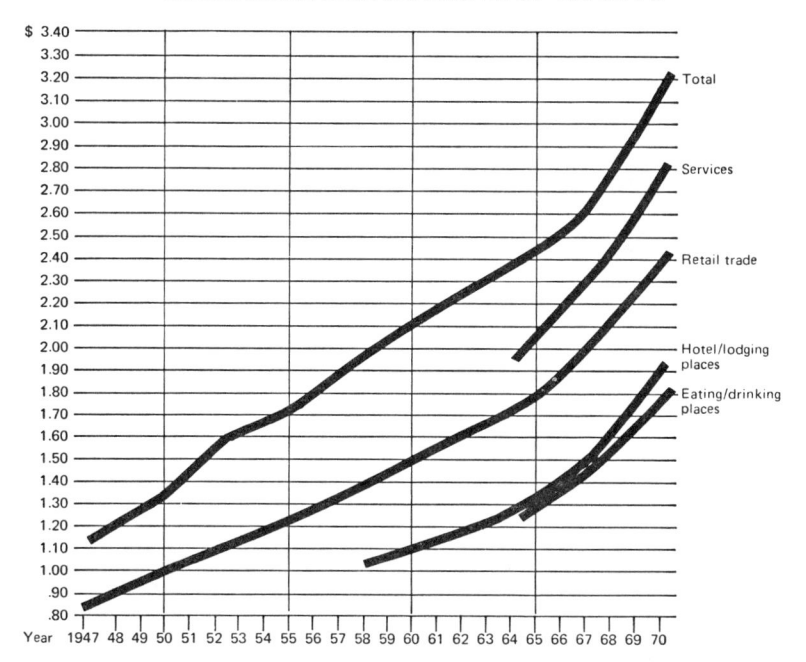

Source:
Employment and Earnings for the United States (1909-1971), Bureau of Labor Statistics, pp. 548 and 565.

THE RISE IN EARNINGS

As Figure 2 suggests, average hourly earnings have risen for hospitality industries, as have hourly earnings of other service employees and other retail employees and, indeed, as have wages for all employees. While the lines representing wages in these various groups are not perfectly parallel, an examination of the figures suggests that the rates of increase experienced by our industries have not been radically different than those of other industries.

Figure 3, which reflects not only hourly income but also the length (i.e., number of hours) of the work week, suggests

Fig. 3—AVERAGE WEEKLY EARNINGS OF PRODUCTION (NONSUPERVISORY) WORKERS ON PRIVATE NONAGRICULTURAL PAYROLLS, 1947 TO 1970

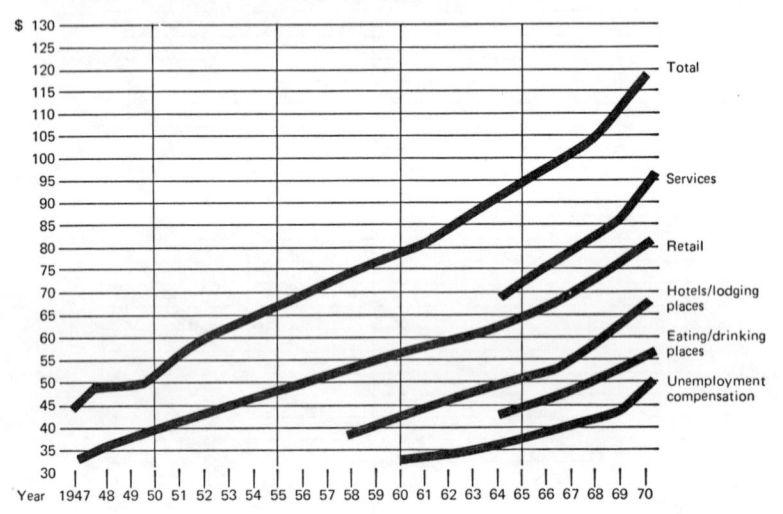

Source:
Employment and Earnings for the United States (1909-1971), Bureau of Labor Statistics, pp. 548 and 565.

that hotel and food service employees' weekly earnings have risen at a rate similar to other employee groups.

An interesting development shown in Figure 4 is that unemployment benefits (for all employees) begin to approach the rate of compensation for employees in the food service and housing industries.[1]

Fig. 4—AVERAGE WEEKLY EARNINGS OF FOOD/DRINK ESTABLISHMENTS AND HOTELS/MOTELS COMPARED TO INDICES OF ECONOMIC PRODUCTIVITY 1947 TO 1970

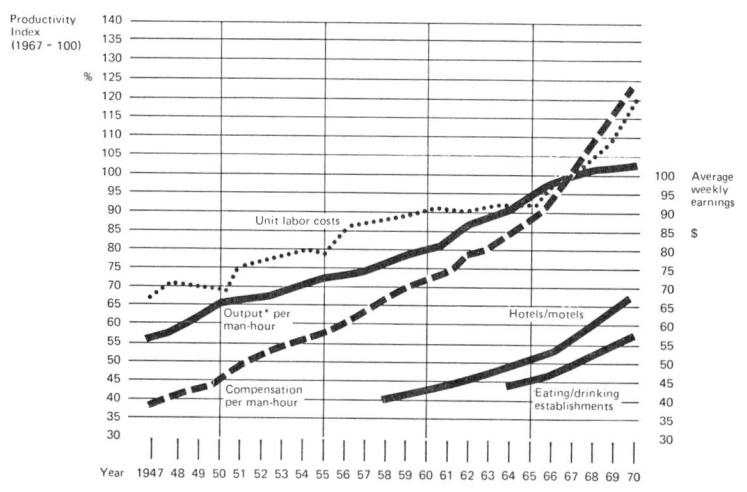

*Output refers to GNP in 1958 dollars

Sources:
Productivity indices
Economic Report of the President, 1973; Annual Report of the Council of Economic Advisers, Table C-32, "Output per Man-hour and Related Data, Private Economy, 1947-72," p. 230.
Average weekly earnings
Employment and Earnings for the United States (1909-1971), Bureau of Labor Statistics, pp. 548 and 565.

---

1. *Social Security Bulletin*, "Current Operating Statistics," December, 1972, p. 60. Unemployment benefits for many hotel and restaurant workers might be somewhat less than the average shown for all workers because in most states unemployment benefits have some relationship to the income of the worker when employed. Since employees in hotels and restaurants earn less, their employment benefit would probably be at the lower end of the range. On the other hand, average earnings shown in Figures 2 and 3 do not include tip income. Since something on the order of 15 to 20 percent of hotel and restaurant employees are tipped employees, the average income of hotel and restaurant workers may be somewhat understated.

Although wages have risen rapidly in our industries, that increase has, in fact, been less rapid than the rise of wages in the economy in general. Hotel wages rose 70% from 1958 to 1970, while wages for the whole economy rose 80%. Foodservice wages rose 30% from 1964 (the earliest year for which this data is available) to 1970. In the same period, wages for all employees rose 43%. On the other hand, the rise in wages in the economy as a whole was accompanied by an increase in productivity. Output per man hour in the United States rose 12% from 1964 to 1970 and 35% from 1958 to 1970. Unit labor costs for the entire economy rose 27% from 1964 to 1970, and 34% from 1958 to 1970. The relationship between output per man hour, unit labor costs, and compensation in the total economy is compared with wage data for hospitality industries in Figure 4.

THE PLATEAU IN PRODUCTIVITY

Although no separate productivity index is available for foodservice and housing industries, it is important to notice that the majority of the workers in our industries are engaged in either personal service work or in manual occupations in which only limited productivity increases are available through mechanization. While wages for hospitality industries rose at a slightly slower pace than in the economy as a whole, it seems reasonable to assume that productivity in traditional hospitality firms such as hotels and restaurants rose only marginally.

Some increases in productivity might be noted, for instance in the trend toward more self-service (for instance, in the use of buffets, reduction in bell staff services) and limited economies may have been realized from such automated devices as dial switchboards. The basic picture, however, remains one of a labor intensive, personal service industry. If this reasoning is correct, it follows that unit labor costs (i.e., the portion of revenue from each cover sold or room rented required to cover labor costs) in the hospitality industries have risen at a substantially higher rate than they have in the economy as a whole.

It is instructive to look at the firms in our industries which *have* improved productivity. In fast food, where the number of covers served per employee is surely radically higher than in the more traditional restaurant setting, what we have is not so much the introduction of automated equipment as the complete redesign of the foodservice system relying on a drastically simplified menu and self-service,[1] as well as the introduction of industrial engineering techniques accompanied by a certain amount of automation.[2]

As wages rise (along with other costs) the operator has really only two choices, aside from going out of business. Those are either to rework the system to eliminate labor (as in fast food, perhaps by drastically simplifying the system) or to incorporate the ever higher cost structure in the price offered to the consumer and maintain the traditional level of service. As prices in traditional service settings rise, that increased price structure offers an inducement to innovators to develop new, simplified formats, such as the fast food operations have done, to compete on a price basis with the traditional establishment.

Social Policy and Labor Supply

Writing in 1965 on the labor market of the lodging industries, John P. Henderson stated:

> But for the unskilled 50 to 60 percent of workers at the base of the lodging industry pyramid, there are few alternatives, and these workers do not have much opportunity to move into new occupations and industries. It is this lack of mobility that has allowed the industry to continue to pay such low wages to many employees, since it is obvious there has been no need to offer higher wages to attract the requisite number of workers.[3]

This condition, so recently described by Professor Henderson, may, in fact, be changing radically at the present time. Figure 5 (see following page) compares wages in the foodservice and housing industry to incomes available for "non work." While general assistance has never been competitive with wage

---

1. Thomas F. Powers, "The Only Constant," *Institutions Magazine*, January, 1972, p. 34.
2. Theodore Levitt, "Production Line Approach to Service," *Harvard Business Review*, September-October, 1972, p. 41.
3. Henderson, *op. cit.*, p. 55.

Fig. 5—AVERAGE MONTHLY BENEFITS: AFDC, GENERAL ASSISTANCE AND UNEMPLOYMENT* COMPARED TO AVERAGE MONTHLY WAGES* FOR FOOD SERVICE AND HOTEL/MOTEL ESTABLISHMENTS 1940 TO 1972

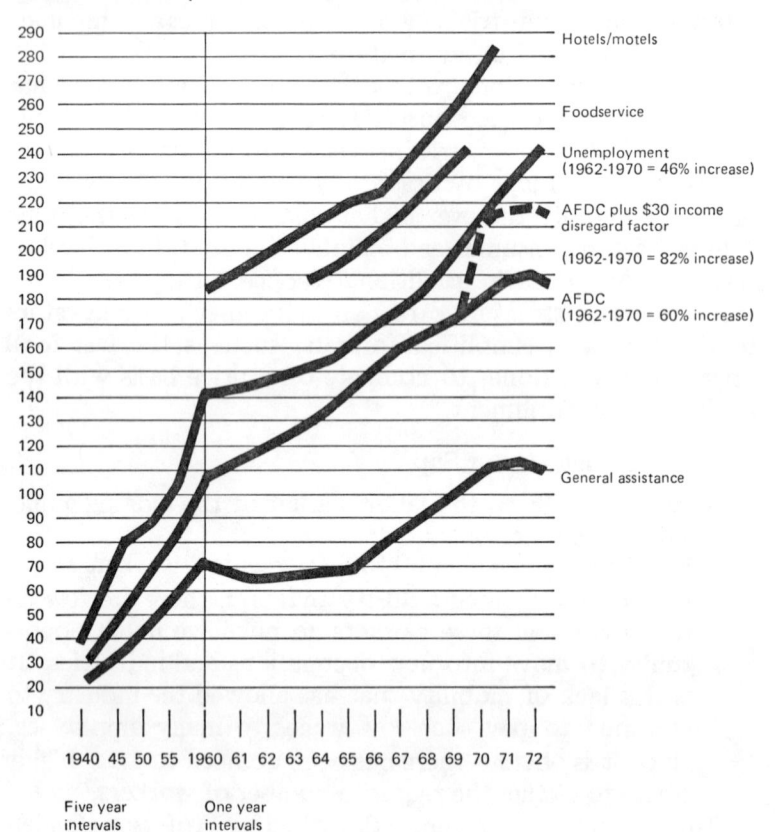

Hotels/motels
Foodservice
Unemployment (1962-1970 = 46% increase)
AFDC plus $30 income disregard factor
(1962-1970 = 82% increase)
AFDC (1962-1970 = 60% increase)
General assistance

1940 45 50 55 1960 61 62 63 64 65 66 67 68 69 70 71 72

Five year intervals   One year intervals

Notes
*Wages and unemployment data represented by weekly amount x (4.3)

General assistance and AFDC benefits per family

Wages and unemployment per individual

Welfare benefits measure cash benefits only—does not include other services such as counselling, medical services, food stamps and non-recurring grants such as special allowances for winter clothing or furniture.

Sources:
Food service and hotel/motel establishments
  Employment and Earnings for the United States (1909-1971), Bureau of Labor Statistics, pp. 548 and 565.
AFDC, general assistance and unemployment benefits Current Operating Statistics in the *Social Security Bulletin,* Dec. 1972.

earnings, patterns set by AFDC (Aid for Dependent Children) are clearly on the verge of being competitive with the wage scale of our industry.

WORK VS. WELFARE

In evaluating Figure 5 it is important to realize that the hotel or restaurant worker of interest is not the tipped worker but the 50 to 60 percent Henderson referred to as unskilled. Thus, understatement of tipped income is not a factor in the comparison. On the other hand, it is perhaps even more important to notice that the welfare benefits shown in Figure 5 are probably a *significant understatement* of the actual benefits available. In addition to the dollar income received from AFDC, generally included in those benefits are free medical care, food stamps (and free lunch for school children), and substantial free counseling services on economic, family, and social matters. As one authority has put it, "it is worth pointing out here that a job at the minimum wage level in New York City yields an equivalent annual income significantly lower than the scheduled welfare budget allowance for a family of four."[1]

Welfare benefits, as Figure 5 indicates, have increased dramatically in the past thirty years. Durbin, in a study of welfare benefits in New York states that "welfare benefits increased more than average wages in manufacturing, more than the minimum wage and more than the average or maximum unemployment compensation benefits."[2] Between 1962 and 1967 Durbin's study shows average wages rose 13% while the minimum wage rose 30% and the welfare allowance rose 40%. AFDC expenditures have grown 156% between 1965 and 1970. This growth was attributed to increased benefits (52%) and increased number of recipients (48%). These rates of change are summarized in Tables 1 and 2 (see following page).

Another point to recall in gauging the understatement of the welfare benefit is suggested by the dotted line in Figure 5

---

1. Elizabeth F. Durbin, *Welfare Income and Employment: An Economic Analysis of Family Choice, 1969*, (Praeger, 1969), pp. 13-14.
2. Durbin, *op. cit.*, p. 82.

TABLE 1
Changes in Average Minimum Wage and Non-Wage Incomes in New York State

1962-67	Increase
Average Wage	13%
Minimum Wage	30%
Welfare Allowance*	40%

*Average of all welfare programs
Source: Durbin, *Welfare Income and Employment*.

TABLE 2
Changes in AFDC Payments, Benefits and Recipients in New York State

1965-70	Increase
AFDC Expenditures	156%
Increased Benefits	52%
Increased Number of Recipients	48%

Source: Durbin, *Welfare Income and Employment*.

which begins in 1969 for AFDC, referred to as the "income disregard factor." Beginning in that year the first $30 of earned income (and a declining portion of all income over that amount) was disregarded in computing welfare benefits. While the intent of this is to encourage employment on the part of individuals on welfare, it may have the additional effect of making welfare more attractive, since a person can work about one day a week in some kind of part-time job without any welfare reduction. Moreover, case workers commonly ignore sporadic, non-recurring earned income, and many welfare recipients engage in baby sitting and a wide variety of other activities that are convenient for their status in life and which are difficult for welfare departments to establish as bona fide employment for purposes of reducing welfare payments.

The most generous benefits for non-work are found in AFDC, and AFDC is certainly the fastest growing form of welfare. These benefits are generally (though not exclusively) supplied to female heads of household. Thus it might be thought that the effect of this policy is to reduce the number of women in the work force. In practice, however, welfare benefits have the effect of reducing work force participation by adult male and teenage children.[1]

A recent study by the Economics Department of the First National City Bank of New York discussed changes in work force size in New York City. Figure 6 (see following page) shows a comparison of work force trends in New York City with national trends. The reduction in New York's force is accounted for by two factors, a stable level of population and a decline in labor force participation contrasted with a rising national participation rate.

The logical speculation which arises out of this bank's study is that the reduction in work force participation is in large part due to welfare alternatives. The reduction in the work force is "centered in, although not limited to, the younger segment of minority, female workers."[2] This, quite obviously, is also a reasonable description of much of the clientele of AFDC.

Where Are We?

At this point, it is clear that for many years our industries have been subject to the pressure of rising wage rates. As wage cost has increased, either productivity was increased to offset some or all of that cost by redesigning the system, using ever simpler foodservice systems as in fast food, or the price structure of the establishment was changed to pass on to the consumer the increase in the cost of the factors of production.

The rising price of the products and services of the traditional hotel and restaurant industries has provided an inducement to innovators to design still more systems which were of lower cost to operate and hence could be provided to the consumer under the umbrella of the price structure of traditional establishments.

---

1. Durbin, *op. cit.*, pp. 13-19. For an interesting and current anecdotal description of the process by which AFDC affects male and teenage withdrawal from the work force, see Gary Hoenig, "Turf," *New York Times Magazine,* Nov. 4, 1973, p. 73.
2. "Why are New Yorkers Dropping Out?," *Monthly Economic Letter*, Economics Department, First National City Bank, August, 1973, p. 13.

Fig. 6—WORK FORCE SIZE: NEW YORK CITY COMPARED TO UNITED STATES, 1960 TO 1973

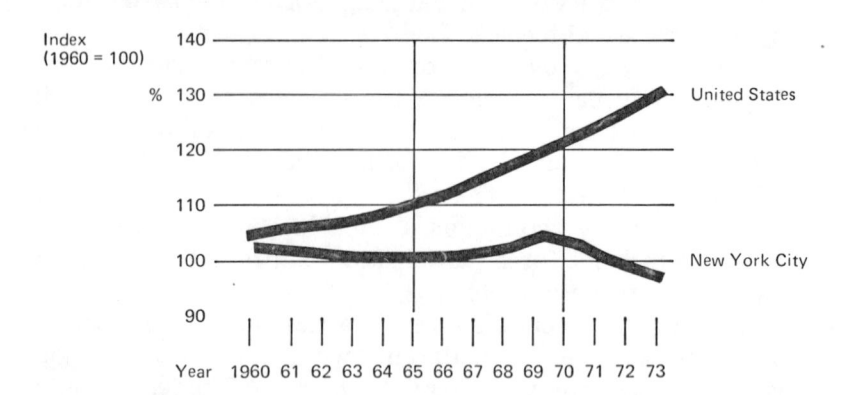

Note:
The U.S. index refers to the civilian labor force as reported by households in the Current Population Survey. The New York City index refers to the work force based on reports by business establishments to New York State Labor Dept., and on unemployment compensation data.

Source:
Economics Department, First National City Bank.

A developing trend, however, in social policy is the growth of various welfare incomes to the point where they generally approach and commonly exceed the incomes of those working at the lower end of the wage scale. It should be noted that these benefits do not apply to all workers, nor do they apply all the time. As a general rule, AFDC benefits are limited to women who are heads of households, while unemployment is available only for a period of time (an average of 26 weeks) following on some employment and thus cannot be pursued as a way of life permanently. On the other hand, the rising level of the general welfare benefit, more generous standards in the granting of food stamp benefits, and the constant pressure to raise the floor of general assistance suggest that the standards now set by AFDC may emerge as the set of standards to be applied to a broader group of welfare recipients within the foreseeable future.

At least two effects can be anticipated from an increasingly generous welfare policy. One of these is to establish an income floor for all workers that may be more significant than the minimum wage. Clearly, if an employee can make more money by not working than by working, the employee is likely to engage in a rational choice based on economic considerations and choose the more remunerative "non-work" over work.

Moreover, many observers of the foodservice and housing industries have noted that there is little in the way of intrinsic reward to be had from our industry's unskilled jobs. As Durbin has pointed out, "if working had positive value in addition to the goods and services purchaseable, the person would not have to be paid so much to give up his leisure; but, obviously, if work is actually so distasteful that it has a negative value, even more has to be paid."[1]

A second probable impact is that today's welfare benefits offer a choice between work and non-work to ever larger numbers of employees. Thus, a person who shrinks from the stigma of being a welfare recipient may nevertheless choose that role. If she is a mother for instance, she may think that stigma less important than her desire and need to be with her children. In some sub-cultures, of course, the presence of any stigma at all is open to question. Thus, we have not only the effect of a wage floor but, increasingly, of withdrawal from the work force by unskilled workers with a resulting labor "shortage" at the lower end of the skills level scale.

Where Do We Go from Here?

If we face a pattern of still steeper wage cost increases coupled with even greater scarcity of unskilled and semi-skilled labor, what kind of consequences can we expect? Perhaps the most difficult point for many operators to accept is that serious, fundamental changes in the way we do business are in the offing. This is difficult to accept because the hospitality industries are and have been anchored in our own traditions. It took a Memphis real estate developer—Kemmons Wilson—to revolutionize the post-World War II lodging

---

1. Durbin, *op. cit.*, p. 11.

industry and a handful of inventive foodservice operators to develop the fast food concept.

Faced with innovative competition, a surprising number of operators have chosen to "stand and fight" on the lines of what they have seen to be their standards of service. While there is limited quantitative support for my position, it appears that the batting average of the traditional operator faced with innovative competition has not been particularly good over the past 25 years. A few outstanding operators *have* done very well. But the number of hotel rooms in operation *declined* from 1,550,000 in 1948 to 1,265,000 in 1972,[1] the countryside is littered with closed diners and family restaurants of an old model, and many prestigious "great" restaurants have experienced difficulty as well, often closing their doors.[2]

In the lodging industry, some of the difficulty may be attributable to the separation of the operator's knowledge of what must be done from the owner's decision-making power by the ignorance of many owners, informed as they are by a view of the lodging establishment as an investment without necessarily appreciating the operating realities which govern the long run success of that investment. Still, there are enough *operators* of a traditional cast of mind that they can hardly be excepted from a general statement regarding resistance to change.

If change is coming, what kinds of change may we expect? Some obvious changes in materials used are probably at hand as are major changes in the equipment to handle whatever processes are required by the work of the establishment. More fundamentally, change in what we think of as service is almost certain to occur. What follows should not be thought of as "solutions" but rather as some preliminary speculations on the likely directions of change.

CHANGED MATERIALS. If labor becomes *both* scarcer

---

[1] *Trends in the Hotel/Motel Business,* 1973, Harris, Kerr, Forster & Co., p. 3.

[2] See, for instance, Pamela Bujarski, "The Haute Cuisine Restaurants Here Up Against The Kitchen Wall," *New York Times Magazine,* February 20, 1972, p. 10.

and much more expensive, the market for prepared foods is likely to expand. In general, it seems reasonable to assume that the large food processors' economy of scale advantages will become more pronounced as the hospitality industry's wage scale rises. As is already the case to a degree, moreover, lack of availability of unskilled labor—as well as its high cost— will force operators to move further and further toward the ready end of the raw-to-ready scale in purchasing. This larger market may increase competition in that area, hopefully resulting in improved quality and variety, and possibly—with major volume increases—reduction in prices. It is premature to predict the development of the foodservice establishment into a service-intensive retail outlet for manufactured goods, but this may serve as an approximate description of direction for some segments of the industry.

The increased use of disposable service seems virtually certain, particularly in the light of the improving quality of disposable ware. This development is, however, clearly bounded by environmental constraints, both as to scarcity of resources reflected in higher disposable ware prices and by disposal problems related to pollution. Increased concern with water quality may, however, operate to the disadvantage of permanent ware and hence to the advantage of disposables.

CHANGED EQUIPMENT. Equipment changes that were not economically feasible five years ago may well offer significant cost savings in the labor market of five years from now. If the move to manufactured foods referred to above takes place, however, the principal *on premise* foodservice equipment changes may be expected to be related to materials handling systems dealing with the way product is moved from receiving into storage, from storage to the preparation or reconstitution station, and thence to the server or guest.

Perhaps the most important development in equipment will be in the capabilities of the industry's suppliers. The computer-operated, small-scale food preparation systems,[1]

---

1. Werner Sell, "New Equipment and Systems in Mass Feeding," *Journal of the American Dietetic Association*, October, 1973, p. 413.

pioneered by European manufacturers, may make it quite possible that the structure of the prepared food manufacturing industry will change from one dominated by large companies to one in which company commissaries *and commissaries operated by institutional food wholesalers* serve a number of retail outlets in a relatively localized market.

Toward a New Concept of Service

If we are to think about service in a constructive way in an age of exponential change in costs and availability of labor, we must change the set of questions we are asking in a fundamental way. We must shift from discussing what we know to what we do not know. Discussions of service among industry people focus on alterations or reinforcements of traditional patterns of service and traditional service roles: "Bellmen carry bags and waitresses serve food. How can we change these processes to do them better or at lower cost?" These questions concentrate on what we know something about, but, from a systems analytic view, they begin at the wrong end of the process. Our question must become, "What satisfaction does the guest require in this process and how can we, without regard to traditional patterns, offer that satisfaction to the guest at a cost that is realistic? More simply, what is our objective, stated in terms of the guest's needs and wants?" This shift in orientation disposes of a lot of mental baggage but since the baggage, for most of us, is a lifetime of experience, it is hard to let go.

Jerome Vallen in his recent article, "Service: A New Definition,"[1] stated the dilemma in economic terms. To paraphrase his point, it is an economic axiom that when the marginal utility (satisfaction) per dollar is less for one good than for another, the consumer shifts his expenditures to the good with the higher economic utility per dollar. This is what has happened with service. With no real change in the absolute utility provided by personal service, the utility relative to non-service goods has dropped because of the failure of the

---

1. Jerome J. Vallen, "Service: A New Definition," *The Institute Journal*, (East Lansing: The American Hotel/Motel Educational Institute), December, 1972, p. 8.

hospitality industry to increase its productivity at the same pace as other industries.

While much of the evolution in service may be depersonalizing, it is equally possible that mechanization may make possible the "re-personalization" of some service processes by eliminating time-consuming hand labor. We may be able to move from "rooming the guest" as a physical process to "greeting the guest" in a way the guest perceives as satisfying, for instance. The key is in a shift from thinking of the traditional process to concentrating on the needs and wants of the guest as the starting point in our reasoning. It is clear that both labor cost and labor supply constraints are making impossible the delivery of traditional services in more and more operations. Rather than "whittle away" at the quality of service, it may be time to begin a basic redefinition of the process.

An Arizona eating place recently adopted an *antibreakage plan* which is working well. Whenever an employee breaks anything he contributes a War Stamp to a general fund. When $18.75 has been accumulated the manager buys a War Bond and presents it to the employee who has the *least* breakage to his credit over the period. Patriotic and practical.*

Restaurant Management, Jan. 1945, p. 9.

Scene 2
LABOR RELATIONS

The following two articles by Werne both deal with labor relations in the abstract sense. The first selection gives a clear explanation of what "collective bargaining" is all about, while the second selection deals with the advantages and disadvantages of multi-employer bargaining, such as would be entered into by a restaurant association or a state hotel-motel association. Then we return to the early twenties with the union's efforts to organize. We believe that presenting this type of material (from 50 years ago) will help us to understand better today's situation in the labor-management struggle. Finally, there is an account of how one hotel handled a six-week strike. We wonder who loses during any strike: the guests, the management, or the employees?

COLLECTIVE BARGAINING*

*BENJAMIN WERNE**

Everyone talks about the collective bargaining "system" as a way of life, but rarely does anyone step back, take a look at the "forest" instead of merely the "trees." What is collective bargaining? How did it start? What is its significance in this country's pattern of economic life?

Long before there were any labor laws, some employers decided to talk over with employees matters that directly affected their welfare. These businessmen were seeking a rational alternative to the bitterness and the struggles that marked the nation's early labor history.

Experience soon showed that when employees had a chance to discuss such things as wages, hours, benefits, lighting and sanitary conditions, and to air their gripes, there were fewer pitched battles.

We know this today as collective bargaining. When viewpoints differ, collective bargaining is a means of compromising those differences.

Nobody benefits from cracked heads, strikes, slowdowns or lockouts. Everybody suffers when work is halted. Employees lose work and wages. Employers, with nothing to sell, find their customers drifting away. Consumers face shortages, with resulting high prices. Everyone loses.

Encouraged by reports from employers and employees alike, the men in Congress decided to adopt collective bargaining as national policy. Through a series of laws, the

---

*Restaurant Business (formerly *Fast Food*), November 1973, pp. 38-41. Reprinted with permission.
**Mr. Benjamin Werne is a member of the Bar of the U.S. Supreme Court and the New York State Bar.

government tried to encourage the use of bargaining to settle disputes. The employee's right to bargain was not created by any law. Laws can only safeguard those who engage in bargaining, and lay down some ground rules for its use.

First of all, think of your business as a community. Some of these communities are small; others are large.

When there is collective bargaining, in theory at least, the spirit of democracy carries over into each and every community. We like to have our say about the rules and regulations. We may not be happy about every man in office, or like every law, but so long as they represent the choice of the majority of our fellow citizens, we accept them.

In the shop community, collective bargaining works much the same way. Before such laws as the National Labor Relations (Wagner) Act and the Labor Management Relations (Taft-Hartley) Act, a union or association was entitled to speak only for its members.

If an employee stayed on the outside, he dealt with the employer as an individual. Or, he could join another union, which also spoke for its members only.

As bargaining is practiced now, majority choice rules. Employees of a particular company in certain work classifications form a "unit." Members of the unit vote on which union, if any, they want to represent them. The union wining the highest total of votes cast becomes the bargaining representative (or agent) of all the men and women in that group. It may be AFL-CIO or an independent union such as the Teamsters. Sometimes, a union is recognized as the bargaining agent without the formality of any election.

Who Bargains?

Many factors determine who will be in the unit—the kind of union, size of the warehouse or plant, wishes of the employees, practice in the industry or in other locations of the same employer. The unit might cover all the production and maintenance workers in a plant, or all drivers and warehousemen. It might be limited to a few skilled craftsmen. Those in the foremen classification or higher are usually considered part of management and are not represented by any union.

If the company does certain dollar amounts of business

across state lines (interstate commerce) a formal election among the employees in the unit to decide which union—if any—will represent them is usually conducted by the National Labor Relations Board (NLRB), an agency of the U.S. Government. The vote is carefully supervised to make certain that every employee has a free choice. No group, union or employer, has the right to intimidate or coerce an employee to influence his vote.

The union selected by the majority of voting employees thereafter represents the members of this unit. The NLRB certifies that it is the bargaining representative.

The union then becomes the "exclusive bargaining agent." No other union may represent any members of that unit. Having been named by the majority, the favored union speaks for, acts for, and should protect the interests of all those in the unit. Member or not, voter or not, a unit employee is entitled to be treated just the same as the most active handbill passer and locker-room speaker in the group. The union must truly represent all the workers.

Those who don't like the choice are expected to go along. If, after a period of one or two years, the NLRB is convinced that some employees want to switch, another election may be ordered to make sure of the majority choice.

Skilled Bargainers

Having been selected as agent for the unit, the union now names one or two men or a committee to meet with representatives of the employer. These skilled bargainers, backed by all the necessary authority to speak for employees and management, arrange for a series of meetings.

Their function is to negotiate, with intent to reach agreement, and to put the agreed-on terms into a written, signed contract.

Negotiation is an exchange of ideas and facts, examining the views of the other side, and attempting to find some middle ground on which both can stand.

Unfortunately, negotiation sometimes becomes a tug-of-war between opposing power blocs. Bargaining must be more than an armed truce, to be successful. If the struggle for power continues, even though peacefully, permanent gains cannot be made. If the union and the employer jockey for position, waiting for the best time to start a new test of strength, the slugging will not long be delayed.

Negotiations are often long and bitter and difficult. Valid differences of opinion arise between the union and the employer. That should not be unexpected.

Few employees see eye-to-eye with their employer on many issues, great and small. The worker's viewpoint takes in the welfare of his family, and of his fellow employees. He wants higher pay, more free time, easier work, greater security, care when he is sick, ease of mind when he is old.

Your view as an employer takes in not only the men and women on the payroll, but includes supervisors and managers, your own family, possibly the company's stockholders. A business must produce, and sell goods or services at a profit, to satisfy all these people.

In addition, the employer must solve the problem of how money can be set aside to take care of the needs of the business—to buy new machinery, repair or replace the old, expand the product line, increase advertising, and maintain a reserve for emergencies.

Negotiators have to try to understand the other fellow's problems. The object should not be to squeeze the other side as much as possible, but to chart a means of working together.

Each side must be prepared to give serious consideration to the other's proposals. If the union says this is what we want and we won't budge, and the employer says the same, there is no negotiation. This intent to reach agreement is often summed up by the phrase "good faith bargaining."

Once their differences have been overcome, the parties put their agreement on paper. They have adopted a code of laws for the shop community. This contract is the evidence that your employees take part in the making of decisions affecting them as individuals and as members of a group.

The very word "agreement" points up what the parties have accomplished. Conditions are set forth under which employees and managers will work together for a stated period of time. When that time is up, they will try to get together on needed changes.

Citizen's Best Interests

The government, through our labor laws, supports collective bargaining as public policy. It is considered to be in the best interests of all citizens. Joint dealings cannot be imposed successfully from above. The relationship must be worked out freely by the parties. Laws can only set out orderly procedures for reaching the desired ends.

Certain specific abuses can be controlled. For example, the laws set out a series of unfair labor practices (ULP). These are types of conduct that unions and employers are called upon to avoid. Among the unfair practices is refusal to bargain in good faith. The law not only says that the parties should bargain, but tells what can be done if someone, on either side, refuses to go along.

Ideally, the government is more or less of a neutral referee. It should not take sides, but try to keep the scales balanced, so that no party becomes so powerful that it can trample over the other.

If, despite collective bargaining, the arguments get too big and come too often, some other way for settling disputes may have to be found. Few people want the government to play any bigger role than it now does. But we cannot stand too many periods of paralysis affecting an entire industry.

The law cannot make bargaining effective. It can only correct some abuses, spell out a few regulations, set bounds and limits, and establish machinery to smooth the process.

TO JOIN OR NOT TO JOIN MULTI-EMPLOYER BARGAINING*

BENJAMIN WERNE**

In view of the recent strike against the restaurants of New York City and the splintering off of individuals negotiating with unions separately, the problem of group bargaining is of considerable interest and concern.

Multi-employer negotiations have become an accepted way of bargaining life. Many fast food operators have sincere reservations about association bargaining, but are pressured into "going along." The Teamsters and other unions generally welcome the opportunity to deal with large groups of snack food employers, since the results are greater standardization of wage rates and benefits.

Every once in a while, however, an employer will realize that the disadvantages of tying in with a group for bargaining purposes outweigh the advantages. He then tries to break away and establish the principle of individual negotiations. Complications often ensue, and the National Labor Relations Board has been forced to set certain rules on withdrawals from multi-employer units.

The NLRB maintained that, under certain conditions, an employer could withdraw from a multi-employer group and not be bound by any agreement reached with the union. Attempting to carry out its function of "balancing" the interests and rights of both management and labor, the Board also came up with the doctrine that this same right should be accorded to the unions. Employer groups, realizing that this

---
Restaurant Business (formerly *Fast Food*), April, 1973, pp. 80-86. Reprinted with permission.
**Member of the Bar of the U.S. Supreme Court and New York State Bar.

would put them at a tremendous disadvantage in their negotiations, took the issue to the courts. The results were negative.

Unions *should* be accorded equal rights with employers to withdraw from multi-employer bargaining units, a federal court of appeals in the Midwest decided. It upheld a Labor Board finding that employers failed to bargain in good faith by refusing to bargain with the union on an individual basis. The unions gave timely notice of withdrawal and of their desire to bargain on a separate and individual basis with each company.

The court observed that the Labor Board could "with propriety" inquire into the good faith of withdrawals and whether they are harmful to either party, particularly where the unit has been in existence and has operated satisfactorily for many years. However, this is "an area which Congress has confided to the discretion and expertise" of the NLRB and in which the courts may not interfere unless the Board violates the statute or abuses its discretion.

After the union's withdrawal, the court noted, each employer would still have the right to be represented in separate bargaining by the association. The court also said that, in the face of a whipsawing strike, an unstruck employer might justifiably use the lockout "in order to prevent its business from being ruthlessly destroyed." In the court's judgment, "where the lockout is to support an employer's legitimate bargaining position, he could no more be deprived of its use than the right to strike could be taken away from the employees."

Earlier, the United States Court of Appeals in New York supported the Labor Board view that a union may withdraw from a multi-employer bargaining situation by giving timely and unequivocal notice. It added that the individual employer units must also be appropriate for bargaining. The court agreed that the companies refused to bargain by failing to negotiate except on a multi-employer basis.

A multi-employer unit is "a purely consensual device," according to the court. Since the bargaining may be initiated only upon consent of the parties, it may be terminated by timely withdrawal of consent by *either party*. The court concluded that "Congress did not intend to instruct (the NLRB) to require an unwilling union to continue in the consensual relationship, if it unequivocally withdraws its consent."

The court recognized that withdrawal of a union from certain multi-employer units "may have much more harmful effects" than withdrawal of one or more employers. But in determining the appropriateness of a bargaining unit, the Board is not called upon to "weigh and act on relative bargaining strength in the sense of the potential effectiveness of economic weapons available to each side."

Not only may a union pull out completely from a multi-employer unit, according to NLRB regulations, but it may withdraw from bargaining with respect to one or more individual employers in the unit, while continuing to bargain with the remaining employers in a multiple unit.

The remaining firms will then be free to withdraw from the multiple unit, if they believe that the other employer or employers are so vital that multi-employer bargaining is no longer desirable. Withdrawals must be "unequivocal and timely." In answer to the employer contention that this permits the union to dictate the appropriate unit, the Board noted that individual employers may also "reform" the unit by withdrawing from it. The NLRB will *not* permit a union to withdraw from bargaining with respect to a part of one employer's operations while leaving other parts in the multi-employer unit.

On another aspect of group relationships, it was held that dissatisfaction with proposed wage scales is not sufficient justification for untimely withdrawal from a multi-employer bargaining unit. The NLRB ruled, and the reviewing court agreed, that an employer was guilty of bad-faith bargaining by withdrawing from the group during a strike and refusing to execute the agreed-upon contract.

The employer argued that the wage scale being considered at the time of his withdrawal from the association was excessively high and would have been financially ruinous. The appellate court said "... to allow withdrawal from the multi-employer bargaining unit because negotiations are apprehended by one of the group members to be progressing toward an agreement, which would be economically burdensome so far as it is concerned, would be disruptive to the stability of the group bargaining process." A responsibility rests upon the company that "invokes the advantages of group bargaining" to assess and assume the limitations as well. Multi-employer bargaining does not preclude demand for specialized treatment of special problems, according to the federal appellate court in New York. The NLRB had maintained that a union could not lawfully withdraw from multi-employer bargaining by a last-minute particularized demand on one employer.

"There surely can be no general principle," the court declared "that multi-employer bargaining prevents either side from bargaining about or even from insisting on a solution of a mandatory subject peculiar to a particular plant, we should suppose that any such principle would very likely result in curtailment or abandonment of a practice deemed important to industrial peace." What is required, if an employer or union is unwilling to be bound by a general settlement, is that the particular demand be made "early, unequivocally, and persistently."

Multi-employer bargaining cannot be effective unless all employer-members are bound by the terms of the negotiated contract. One firm violated the LMRA by refusing to accept an agreement negotiated while he was still a member of the association. The company withdrew when it learned that the agreed-upon terms included a wage increase. The court said: "While it is recognized that membership in a multi-employer unit is wholly voluntary and that an employer is free to withdraw from it, the employer must clearly evince at an appropriate time its intention to do so, and the Board has ruled that withdrawal from a multi-employer unit is untimely absent union consent once negotiations on a new contract have started."

Union execution of a separate agreement with one association member does not dissolve the multi-employer unit and release other members from commitments flowing from their membership. For several years, an association bargained and executed collective contracts for its members. Failing to reach agreement on renewal terms, a strike was called against the group. Several weeks after the walkout began, one of the employers contacted the union and signed a separate contract. Another company then notified the association that it was withdrawing from membership since it appeared that the union was negotiating with individual firms. No notice was given to the union.

When the union and association finally reached an agreement, the firm refused to sign or to comply with the terms. The NLRB ruled that the employer's withdrawal was neither timely nor effective. Withdrawal occurred after the start of bargaining, but consent of the union had not been obtained. The company was not only ordered to sign the contract but to give retroactive effect to its terms and conditions, reimbursing employees for any losses suffered in wages and benefits.

Dissolution of an employer association during the certification year does not relieve the members of their obligation to bargain jointly with the certified representative. Two unions filed a petition to represent certain workers employed by members of an association. A consent election was arranged and the unions were certified as representatives of employees in the multi-employer unit. The members then voted to dissolve the association and informed the union that it no longer existed as a bargaining unit.

This was an unlawful refusal to bargain, the NLRB ruled. Through the consent election agreement, executed on behalf of the members with their apparent knowledge and acquiescence, the employer members accepted the multi-employer unit as appropriate. They were obliged to honor the statutory obligations flowing from a certification for at least one year. Withdrawal from the agreed-upon form of bargaining was untimely and ineffective, the Board said.

On the other hand, threatening an employer with a work stoppage unless he accepted an association as his bargaining representative violated the LMRA. The union also insisted that the company agree to use the joint committee established under the multi-employer agreement for handling grievances. The union thereby restrained and coerced the company in its choice of representative for purposes of collective bargaining, the NLRB ruled. These decisions have emphasized some of the negative aspects of group bargaining. Any company that enters into such an arrangement should do so with complete awareness of the extent of the obligations—and the risks—he is undertaking. The commitment to multi-employer negotiations, once assumed, cannot easily be discarded.

TO THE PUBLIC*

The striking Cooks' Union publishes as a fact that during the past two years there was no increase in wages granted Cooks serving in Minneapolis kitchens.

The facts are that during the two years immediately preceding the Strike, Cooks' wages were increased by approximately 30% in all the Kitchens in Minneapolis. The individual employe was offered an additional 20% increase before the strike.

The Union's second point is that it has in the past and will now concede the "Open Shop." Why then do they object to the "Open Shop" cards? This is a mere subterfuge. The Union has not in the past, will not now, or in the future, consent to the employers' employing their Cooks from whatever source they please, pay them according to the merits and ability of each individual Cook and arrange the hours of service as may be mutually agreed upon between the Chef and the Cook.

The Union has in the past and is now insisting that Cooks must be employed only through the Union, that the Union fixes the hours of service, the wage, and the working regulations, against which both employe and employer are powerless.

To say that it conceded the "Open Shop" is a mere play on words. So long as the Union dictates the employment of Union men only, the hours of service, the wage, the number of employes for a given job, the Union advocates the "Closed Shop."

This Association suggests the appointment of an impartial Commission to investigate the question of increase in wages during the past two years and the question whether the Unions now propose the "Closed" or the "Open" Shop. It is suggested that this commission be appointed from the middle class, that is, they shall be neither from the Union, or "Big" Employer classes. The findings of this commission to be published, that the public may know the facts.

MINNEAPOLIS HOTEL & RESTAURANT ASSOCIATION
BOONE RILEY, Secretary.

---

*The Hotel World, Sept. 4, 1920, p. 18. Reprinted with permission of *Hotel and Motel Management*.

TO THE COOK'S UNION*

You say in your public announcement that you will concede to Minneapolis hotels and restaurants the "OPEN SHOP." In order to make your position clear you are requested in next Sunday's issue of the paper to answer the following questions:

1. Will you concede to the respective Chefs in charge of the various Kitchens the right to hire such Cooks as the Chefs may select?
2. Will you revoke your rule that the Chefs must hire their Cooks through the Union Employment Agencies?
3. Will you concede to the Chefs and to the Cooks the right to fix the hours of service and the wage?
4. Will you agree to keep your Organizer, Walking Delegates and Business Agents out of the Kitchens?
5. Will you concede that the Chefs may be NON-UNION MEN?
6. Will you agree that Union Cooks shall serve waiters and waitresses alike, regardless as to whether they belong to a Union Organization?
7. Will you grant to the Chefs the right to determine the division of labor in the Kitchen?
8. Will you agree to withdraw your pickets and banners from the places where the management is not in accord with Union ideas as to control of Kitchens?
9. Will you insist on your member Cooks being economical in the use of foodstuffs and to discontinue destroying food when Union rules are disregarded?
10. Will you instruct your cooks that it is the first duty of the Cooks to attempt to please the Public?
11. Will you instruct your member Cooks to discontinue sabotage and agitation among members of other Departments, threatening violence to those who do not promptly conform to Union requirements?
12. Will you withdraw your Slogan, "The Public be Damned?"

The answer to each of these questions in the affirmative means the "OPEN SHOP." The answer to any one or all of the questions in the negative means the "CLOSED SHOP."

MINNEAPOLIS HOTEL & RESTAURANT ASSOCIATION

BOONE RILEY, Secretary.

---

*The Hotel World, Sept. 4, 1920, p. 12. Reprinted with permission of *Hotel and Motel Management.*

START THE OPEN SHOP IN ST. LOUIS*

HOTELS AND RESTAURANTS REDUCE PRICES, THE WAITERS STRIKE FOR MORE WAGES, THE OPEN SHOP IS DECLARED, AND THE HOTELS AND RESTAURANTS ARE STILL DOING BUSINESS.

An attempt on the part of officials representing the cooks' and waiters' unions in St. Louis to force a closed shop policy on all hotels, clubs and restaurants, recently resulted in a decision on the part of members of the St. Louis Hotelmen's Association and the St. Louis Restaurant Men's Association to operate their establishments on the "open shop" basis on and after October 1, 1920.

The open shop agreement was entered into by 63 members of the two associations, including the leading hotels, clubs and restaurants. Notices setting forth the future policy of the St. Louis employers concerning kitchen and dining-room staffs were posted on the evening of Sept. 30th. At midnight on September 30th, a majority of the union waiters and cooks in the establishments involved walked out.

A week before the walk-out, the principal hotels and restaurants publicly announced a decrease of from 15 to 20 percent in their retail food prices, basing their action on a desire to meet the expected postwar price readjustments.

A few days after the restaurant price reductions were made, officials of the cooks and waiters unions presented demands for wage increases. The waiters, who were receiving $15.00 a week and meals, asked for $18.00 a week and meals. Cooks demanded from $3.50 to $5.00 a week additional.

---

*The Hotel World, Oct. 23, 1920, p. 7. Reprinted with permission, *Hotel and Motel Management.*

Restaurant service was only curtailed for a few days as a result of the strike. Most of the larger hotels and clubs were able to continue the service of food without interruption. The service gradually improved and at the present time has practically returned to normal. In order to facilitate service pending the organization of permanent forces, some of the hotels and clubs are confining their menus to table d'hote meals.

The strikers refrained from the use of violence during the first few days of the strike. Recently, however, capsules containing chemicals which gave off offensive odors, were placed in some of the restaurants.

Efforts were made by the strikers to bring about "sympathetic" strikes among union teamsters and others engaged in handling hotel and restaurant supplies. These efforts proved unsuccessful. Cooperation on the part of other St. Louis union organizations has been confined to financial contributions to the cooks' and waiters' strike fund.

Unsuccessful attempts also were made to unionize hotel bellmen, maids and porters.

In a statement issued to the public the members of the association operating on the open-shop plan, declared that "acquiescence in the demands of the union officials would necessitate increasing restaurant prices at a time when restaurant prices are being reduced." This additional burden, they assert, they are unwilling to pass on to the public.

The employers further declared that "the rules the unions attempted to enforce are such as tend to create an artificial shortage of labor, thereby increasing the number of people employed and the total wages paid."

In their interpretation of the "open shop" policy the employers assert that there will be no decrease in wages paid prior to Oct. 1, 1920, and there will be no increase in hours of employment or change in general working conditions.

A similar strike was called by union officials seven years ago. The waiters and cooks, after several months, returned to their work on the open shop basis. The employers contend that through an oversight, union agents gained access to their establishments and succeeded in the course of several years in unionizing the kitchen and dining-room staffs.

Although the closed shop was never formally recognized in the past, contracts were entered into between employers and the unions. In October, 1919, the unions violated their contracts and demanded increases which were subsequently granted. The failure of the unions to abide by their contract on that occasion was instrumental in bringing about the open shop policy in St. Louis hotels, restaurants and clubs.

SQUELCHING A STRIKE*

HOW THE PHILADELPHIA HOTEL MEN FORESTALLED A STRIKE OF WAITERS.

Correspondence Hotel World.

Philadelphia, 11-26-12.

In Philadelphia there are the "International Society of Waiters and Bartenders" and a branch of the "International Geneva Association," both of which are social and fraternal organizations, whose membership is made up chiefly of waiters in local hotels and restaurants. It is said a clause in the constitution of each association prohibits a strike, wherefore these associations and the hotel and restaurant men of the city have worked in accord and without any friction whatever.

A few months ago representatives of the union, which caused the walk-out and strike of waiters in New York and other cities, established an office in Philadelphia and began a campaign of recruiting members from the ranks of the two associations above mentioned. Of course they obtained a following, although small in number. On the strength of that limited following the union leaders arranged to call out the waiters on Hallowe'en. To meet any emergency Secretary Leslie, of the Philadelphia Hotel Association, arranged for 500 colored waiters in Atlantic City and a special train to transport them on short notice to Philadelphia in ninety minutes. Meanwhile Chairman Provan, of the hotel men's strike committee, had secured 500 colored waiters in Philadelphia who were housed ready for any signs of a walk-out. At the same time Daniel Kopp, chairman of the police

---

*The Hotel World, Nov. 30, 1912, p. 19. Reprinted with permission of Hotel and Motel Management.

committee, had completed arrangements for a detail of officers at each hotel to prevent a repetition of the breakage and malicious mischief incident to the waiters' walk-out in Washington and elsewhere.

The fact of all this preparation for any crisis soon reached the ears of the union officials and no strike was ordered. In fact, waiters generally here disclaim all knowledge of strike agitation or affiliation with the union. Nevertheless, there are rumors of a walk-out on Thanksgiving or Army and Navy day. In either event the hotel men are in shape to successfully cope with the situation and the vacancies will be instantly filled by colored waiters. Furthermore, it should be said that where colored waiters are taken on they will be retained permanently as was done in Washington. A strike in Philadelphia now means the end of white crews in the dining rooms of that city.

HOW HOTEL NOVA SCOTIAN
SURVIVED THE BIG STRIKE*

"The first thing you have to do when a strike begins is carry on," says 29-year old Chris Gowers, manager of the Canadian National 325-room Hotel Nova Scotian in Halifax. And he speaks with the authority of experience and success in handling a six-week strike at his property.

Now, with the strike satisfactorily settled and with a laudatory scroll from one group of conventioners and an engraved plaque of appreciation from another, Gowers feels he has some pointers to pass on to others who may find themselves in a similar situation.

"The most important point is to plan every possible detail well before the strike, so that everyone knows exactly what to do when it begins," says Gowers.

The hotel's previous contract expired in September and efforts to work out a new two-year contract with the local Hotel, Restaurant Employees and Bartender's International Union proved fruitless. The union demanded wage increases of 20 per cent for gratuity employees, 25 per cent for nongratuity and 30 per cent for a group they identified as "tradesmen." They also wanted differentials for employees working night or split shifts, increased vacations, a limit of 14 rooms for chambermaids and a number of other items which management felt would have limited productivity and sent labor cost soaring.

The matter went before a conciliation board which split three ways. In a last-ditch effort to avert the strike, hotel

---

*Hotel and Motel Management, Aug. 1973, pp. 34-36. Reprinted with permission.

negotiators told the union at a meeting on April 8 that they were prepared to negotiate a settlement on the basis of the chairman's recommendations. This was rejected, and the union said they would go on strike at some time in the future.

Immediately Chris Gowers began to make plans. He had been executive assistant manager when the hotel had a three-day strike in 1971, so he had some experience to draw on.

The main tactic was to call on other hotels in the Canadian National chain for managerial and supervisory personnel who could be loaned to the Nova Scotian in relays. The main dining room would be closed, and all meals would be served buffet-style in the coffee shop. Guests would be encouraged to pay cash to cut down on office work. There would be no room service, and guests would be asked to bring dry-cleaning and laundry to the front desk. The "Eager Beaver" lounge would continue to operate with entertainment during every night until 1 a.m.

All management and supervisory staff—sales, accounting, secretarial and so on—would be recruited for work in hotel operations, including the laundry. A detailed list of duties was drawn up.

A letter was also prepared for placing in every guest room. It gave details of the restrictions in services and asked for understanding.

At 10 a.m. on May 4, Gowers was informed by the union that their strike would begin within an hour. As the 200 employees left their jobs, water streamed from the gravity tank on top of the property. It was one of a number of acts of alleged sabotage discovered by management immediately after the walk-off.

In addition, the thermostat controls of all ice machines on each floor had been cut, the main icemaker on the banquet floor had been put out of action, all six heavy-duty vacuum cleaners were made inoperable and the labels on the public address system had been switched. The water problem proved to be the most serious act, and until it was corrected the toilets flushed hot water and there was some danger the system would blow up.

The pickets proved to be militant. They sought to prevent trucks from making deliveries by blocking the main service entrance and by laying down broken glass and spiked "tire killers." Food and beverage manager Patrick O'Callaghan braved the pickets in a rented truck to bring in supplies. On one trip in the downtown area, he was blocked by two cars and had his tires let down. He was assaulted in the process, and charges were laid.

Two plate glass windows in the coffee shop were also smashed, and tires of cars in the parking lot—belonging to both staff and guests—were slashed or deflated.

On the basis of these acts it was decided to apply for a court injunction restraining the pickets, and this was granted on May 15. This injunction gave Canadian National and city police much greater powers in controlling pickets, since it limited them to three per entrance and expressly restrained them "from interfering or attempting to interfere with any persons or vehicles approaching or entering or leaving the premises" and "from causing a nuisance . . . in the vicinity . . . and from trespassing."

In the meantime, the Nova Scotian had handled the Canadian Pharmaceutical Association convention with 450 delegates, the Canadian Electrical Distributors with 385 and the Canadian Jewellers with 400 persons.

This meant serving banquets with more than 500 guests and handling such affairs as a champagne breakfast. But everyone pitched in to make it a success. Myles Craston, GM of Canadian National Hotels, volunteered to act as a waiter at one banquet during one of his routine visits. He handled three tables under the watchful eye of maitre d' Tommy Wolfe.

At the Canadian Jewellers' banquet, the management staff even went as far as to provide entertainment—with Chris Bowers on maracas, executive assistant manager Gordon MacKay on piano, Tommy Wolfe on drums and Patrick O'Callaghan as vocalist. The entertainment ended with a skit in which Gowers got the full custard-pie-in-the-face treatment, much to the delight of guests.

The entertainment indicated the youthful exuberance and extra effort put in by the young management staff in keeping the hotel going. The Canadian Pharmacists presented Gowers with a pestle and mortar and scroll "in recognition of the service performed by the management and management staff ... in spite of the strike. Convention guests continued to receive personal attention and consideration exemplifying the true spirit of Nova Scotian hospitality." The Canadian Jewellers awarded Gowers and staff an engraved plaque for their efforts. It said: "Canadian Jewellers Association in convention at Halifax, N.S., wish it known that in the face of considerable handicap and at great personal difficulty the supervisory staff of the Hotel Nova Scotian maintained throughout the convention the highest standards of efficiency, helpfulness and cheerful good will."

"This kind of thing makes the effort worthwhile," says Gowers. He and the other management staff were putting in as many as 18 hours a day at the beginning of the strike, but as the new arrangements began to take effect things returned more to normal.

Wherever Gowers or other key personnel went, they carried walkie-talkie radios to keep in touch and learn about any troubles as soon as they appeared.

One problem area was garbage. The hotel has a compactor which can accommodate eight days' supply, which is then taken away by a special truck. The contractor drove the truck through the picket lines himself to honor his contractual commitment.

One or two organizations—the Human Rights Association and the Musicians Union—cancelled events at the hotel because of the strike. But for the rest it was business as usual. The line-up outside the popular Eager Beaver lounge every night continued.

Throughout the strike, Gowers kept up a flow of information to the local news media on the situation, correcting erroneous reports and statements as soon as they appeared. He informed the press fully about the sabotage at the hotel. "The tendency in cases such as this is for management to clam up and say nothing," he says. "But the reporting of the damage—even though it might have had a negative effect— was necessary to show the public exactly what was going on."

Gowers also advises persons in similar situations to seek court injunctions if pickets prove to be troublesome. "The law clearly limits strikers to peaceful picketing," he states.

"However, there is a general feeling that courts will not grant injunctions because of labor pressures, and that to lose an injunction application would place management in an even worse position. We felt, however, that we had to make the application to show that we had done everything possible to protect our guests. If a guest had been injured by a picketer, the first question asked would have been, 'Did you apply for an injunction?' In order to support an application, it is important to take statements from persons relating to incidents as they happen and to have a fully-documented record of each with as many witnesses as possible."

In situations where management and supervisory staff provide services, Gowers feels it is important that they wear the appropriate uniforms, thus adding to the air of normality. "Some people commented that service in our coffee shop was better during the strike than before. This is an indication of the calibre of persons we had working there," says Gowers.

The strike has also given managers a completely new perspective on productivity and tipping. One surprised management person found himself making $80 in tips in two days working as a bellhop.

In the laundry, a staff of five management persons working from 9 a.m. to 5 p.m. handled the work load which usually takes a staff of nine from 8 a.m. to 5 p.m.

Gowers feels that, with growing militancy in labor unions, every management trainee should be given some instruction in how to deal with a strike. "The main objective is, of course, to prevent strikes by good labor-management relations," he says. "But there are occasions when even with the best of intentions you are faced with a work stoppage—and you cannot let your guests down."

Maintaining a good reputation is particularly important for the Hotel Nova Scotian at this stage. This year Canadian Pacific Hotels and Holiday Inns are opening new properties in the city of Halifax, and other new establishments are under way. The Nova Scotian, leader for more than 30 years, is determined to keep its place in the competitive race. Its Commonwealth Room has been expanded to hold 1,000 persons. All guest rooms have been refurnished and equipped with color cable TV. The redecorated coffee shop has been converted from cafeteria to waitress service. The main dining room is being enlarged and made over into a Spanish-style restaurant with menu and decor to match. A new English-style pub called the Griffin has been opened, and the kitchens completely rebuilt and re-equipped.

"This competition is one reason why it is particularly important for us to keep our labor costs in line," says Gowers. "Because we are a Canadian National hotel some people think we don't have to worry about the profit and loss position. This is completely untrue. Even the courts have recognized that we are governed by provincial and not federal wage minimums. If our wage costs go too high, we will be priced out of the market."

Says Gowers, "I hope our striking people realize that our efforts were made to protect their jobs, too. We would all have lost had the Nova Scotian closed down."

Scene 3
HUMAN ENGINEERING

Statler, the former president of the Hotel Statler Company, presents an insight into his thinking about hotels and employees in hotels. He believes that a hotel is a triumph of engineering but that it takes concerned employees to make it a place where guests want to stay.

Productivity in our industry is on the minds of many. David's article on "Techniques of Industrial Engineering Can Improve Effectiveness of Food Service Operations" presents an overview of certain techniques which are considered today in food service, specifically in hospital food service.

Matthews describes a procedure which allows the establishment of standard times for production items in food service operations. The significance of the establishment of standard times should not be overlooked; it could significantly influence the menu price.[1]

---

1. L. A. Kreck, *Menus: Analysis and Planning*, (Chicago: Cahners Publishing Co., 1975) pp. 143-150.

Both of Kotschevar's articles are concerned with conserving human energy. In "The Human Body, How to Increase Its Efficiency," the author suggests proper body motions. In "Help Workers Work Easier," he suggests methods other than proper body motions, such as breaks between jobs, quiet atmosphere, proper work heights of tables and sinks, and compares the calories required to do the same job at varying work heights.

OPERATING A HOTEL IS A FEAT OF HUMAN ENGINEERING*

*E. M. STATLER***

I come to acknowledge my great debt to engineering, for without science and engineers there would be no hotels.

Not only has engineering made great buildings possible, but within the space of a few years there have been so many improvements in methods of construction and in equipment and this, more than anything else, has revealed to me what too few people realize: that science and engineering are constantly progressing; that the search for new knowledge and efforts to apply it for the good of mankind is without end. We live in a matter-of-fact age and take so much for granted that many of the wonders of modern civilization are given but superficial attention.

I want to say that in watching the structures of my company grow from their foundations and finally take their places on the sky lines of cities, I have come to realize and appreciate what engineering is doing. I think I can understand some of the problems, and I do appreciate the manner and spirit in which men of the engineering professions have overcome them and gone on building.

There is something of engineering in the hotel business, for after all, operating a great public institution is a work in human engineering which has never lost its fascination for

―――――
*The Hotel World, Nov. 20, 1926, pp. 11-27. Reprinted by permission of Hotel and Motel Management.
**Ellsworth Milton Statler is considered the dean of hotelmen in the U. S. He brought more changes and innovations into hotels than anyone before. A concise account of his life can be found in D. E. Lundberg, The Hotel and Restaurant Business, (Boston: Cahners Books, 1974, rev. ed.), pp. 251-256.

me. You design in steel and stone and in your calculations can be reasonably sure that what you plan, whether it be a bridge or a building, will bear a given load and withstand certain strains and stresses.

There you have the best of it!

In our work we are dealing with human loads and strains and stresses. We must calculate not only for known conditions, but must be ready to meet some we never heard of before.

No one has yet been able to devise a slide rule to solve all human problems. Dr. Samuel Johnson said, "There is nothing which has been contrived by man by which so much happiness is produced as by a good tavern or inn."

He loved city people, the art of conversation, good food. Of course he made his statement before anyone had thought of prohibition, for he no doubt also had in mind a tankard of the good ale of his day. But the modern god, economics, slew the inn of Dr. Johnson's day, and now hundreds seek the shelter and comforts of our modern hotels to the dozens of patrons of the old inns. But our great American hotels with hundreds of rooms and thousands of daily visitors, offer a variety of life and a richness of contact which the tavern of the eighteenth century never gave.

The hotel of today is a self-contained community and a good hotel meets almost all the daily needs of man. It offers food from every corner of the earth and the comforts of a luxurious home, with the magic of electric light and heat that is automatically controlled.

If you are in need of clothing it usually can be obtained without leaving the building; there are druggists' shops and ticket offices where one may purchase transportation to any country in the world. And close at hand are telegraph lines and cable facilities. The large modern hotel has its own laundry, post office, hospital, dental office, transportation system and lines of communication.

In the hotels operated by my company there are libraries and, in The Hotel Pennsylvania, there is edited and printed within the hotel a daily newspaper devoted to the news of the world without, as well as our world of 10,000 souls within the building.

I am saying these things to picture for you, if I may, what operating a hotel means. We have many of the varied problems that arise in community government and some peculiar to our business.

A hotel has just one thing to sell. That is service. And service, intangible as it often may seem, can be made as real as a piece of machinery, a pound of sugar, or a favorite hat that feels just right. In our hotels we strive to give the best service it is possible to find anywhere.

I said a few minutes ago that there is constant progress in engineering with improvements and refinements, new methods, greater efficiency. Our organization is constantly striving along similar lines, working always to progress in service, doing what is, in fact, research in human relations. We, too, are trying to improve and refine, to gain greater efficiency, to do old things better and to find new ways of raising service to a higher standard.

Although we have made great strides in our modern civilization there is much more to be done. And it will be done. Some of this we can see ahead of us. There will be other developments, no doubt, of which we now have no conception.

It would not surprise me to hear that in the future the traveler will step into an airship in an air station on top of his hotel in Europe and land on top of another in New York within the compass of a day or so.

However, I have not made any plans for altering the roofs of my hotels to meet such progress.

Meantime there is enough to do to keep us all busy. There is still room for improvement in heating, greater efficiency in the use of fuel, a problem on which I am told much attention is now being given. We can do something more in improving ventilation systems, and in getting more from our light, not alone from the source, but in the placing of it and in utilizing reflecting surfaces to the best advantage. We use a lot of light. And I think the day is not far distant when we will have glass that will allow all the beneficial rays of the sun to penetrate into our rooms.

I believe that with the increased demand for concentration of facilities there will come buildings in which will be combined living quarters, offices, stores, theatres and even churches, and we hope that our own experiment in building an office building and a hotel under the same roof in Boston will go far toward proving the worth of the idea.

In the early days of hotels that part of the building in which were located the kitchen, the storerooms and workshops was called the "back of the house." The idea then was to make these departments as unobtrusive as possible.

We still call it "the back of the house" and the tradition that the visible part of the hotel shall be dedicated to the use of the guest still persists.

But there have been changes. The kitchen of yesterday is an engineering work today, a veritable laboratory. It must be a place of rapid production and that can be done only with an organization of great efficiency.

The hotel chef of today is a scientist and artist combined. He is paid a high salary and his work demands the utmost in executive ability in supervising and directing the efforts of a large force.

And the storerooms of yesterday have been developed today to high efficiency in the preservation of foods. The refrigerating plant in the average hotel would take care of a fairly large town, and the supply of food on hand would feed a multitude.

The workshop of the old inn has become a machine shop and power department in this age. Nothing can be left to chance in hotel operation and the mechanical department is prepared always to meet almost any emergency. The boiler rooms and the power plants are models of engineering efficiency.

The lines of communications in the modern hotels are as numerous as in the large community. In The Hotel Pennsylvania, for instance, there are 3,340 telephone instruments operating a service of more than 210,000 calls a month, which is comparable with the business in a town of 10,000 population.

My life is bound up in hotels and I find my greatest pleasure in seeking to constantly improve our service to the public. If you will bear with me, I will speak for a few moments of the methods developed in our own organization.

In the first place we guarantee courteous, interested and helpful service from every Statler employee to every guest, and should the guest at any time fail to get such service and should the local management fail to satisfy him, I myself will undertake to do so.

That guarantee, which has been published to the public, is the foundation upon which our organization is built. A business, like a building, cannot stand and last indefinitely unless it is built of good material on a solid foundation.

Our employees are human beings, not automatons or gods. They do and will make mistakes. But I can promise that each and every one of them will have some inkling of the ideal of the golden rule as applied to their work. Otherwise they do not long remain in our service.

Our company has provided for the employees a savings plan under which they may become stockholders with additional pay as an incentive for thrift. Under this plan the company pays to the subscriber's account $3 for each share subscribed at the end of the first year, the amount increasing to $7 for each share subscribed at the end of the fifth full year of membership.

All employees are automatically insured under the group system after a full year of service without expense to them. The amounts range from $300 to not more than $3,000.

Employees are also provided with free medical attention without cost, and have vacations with pay.

Our service codes provide for a definite and constant training in the principles of service as developed by our company. Every employee is required to study the service codes and abide by them. We want in every department employees who have pleasant dispositions—who know how to serve willingly with a smile; people whose desire to serve is evident in their attitude toward the guest.

Department heads not only are expected to be competent for their particular positions, but they must be able to teach, train and supervise. Management is their work and good management is all there is to business.

It is good management to be the first to discover an elevator signal out of order; that salt is damp in the shakers on our tables; that a guest's mail or telegrams have been delayed.

Service in a hotel is not a thing supplied by a single individual. It is not a special attention to any one guest. In our organization we strive to make service mean the limit of courteous, efficient attention from each particular employee to each particular guest.

A doorman may swing a door in such a way as to make the guest feel that he is in a hotel where he will be promptly served. Or the doorman may sling the door in a way that irritates and makes the guest expect to find a sputtery pen sticking in a potato at the desk.

When our clerks say, "Please show Mr. Roberts to his room," instead of "Show the gentleman to his room," the guest has a warm feeling that he is being welcomed. There is personal service in addressing a man by his name.

A waiter who can say, "Pell Mell," when the guest says "Pell Mell," or "Pall Maul" when the guest says "Pall Maul," makes us feel the waiter is ALL RIGHT.

There always has been a great deal of interest in the subject of tipping in hotels. Our company can operate a tipless hotel, but a good hotel cannot be operated on that basis because a certain percentage of guests will tip in spite of all rules. But our company can and does do this: It guarantees to the guest who does not wish to tip EVERYTHING in the way of service and courtesy that the tipper gets. In simple we say: "Do not tip unless you feel like it. But if you do tip let it be from genuine desire, not because of custom."

We are continually conducting a campaign of education for our employees. It will last as long as our company. Courteous service is not enough. It must also be helpful service, and helpful service can be rendered only by those who have intelligence and the right training and experience in how to be helpful. But people may be of the right material. They can have intelligence and experience, and yet fail miserably. No matter how much a man may know, he will not give good service in operating a hotel until he puts himself in the other fellow's place. That is what the Golden Rule has to do with the hotel operation.

TECHNIQUES OF INDUSTRIAL ENGINEERING CAN IMPROVE EFFECTIVENESS OF FOOD SERVICE OPERATIONS*

BEATRICE DONALDSON DAVID, Ph. D.**

The value of applying industrial engineering to management in hospitals is receiving increasing attention.[1] The underlying principles of this discipline certainly are applicable in hospital food service operations. However, some are directly applicable and some must be adapted for use in this complex field. In most commercial food service operations, improvement of the management system is directed toward economic growth, increased profits, and survival in competition. The goal of hospital food service management is wiser utilization of resources in the realization of the objective of providing high-quality food and service to patients and personnel. There is increasing pressure to do this through more effective use of space, equipment, food, supplies, and personnel; however, both quantitative and qualitative aspects of

---

*Reprinted, with permission, from *Hospitals, Journal of the American Hospital Association*, June 16, 1973, pp. 80-88.
**Beatrice Donaldson David, Ph. D., is Professor of Food Science specializing in Food Administration at the University of Wisconsin, Madison. She received a bachelor's degree from the University of Nebraska, Lincoln; a master's degree from Columbia University, New York City; and a Ph. D. from Iowa State University, Ames. Dr. David served her dietetic internship at Michael Reese Hospital and Medical Center, Chicago, and has been an Administrative Dietitian at the University of Iowa, Iowa City, and at the Columbia-Presbyterian Medical Center, New York City. Dr. David currently is adviser to the board of directors of the American Society for Hospital Food Service Administrators. She has served as a board member of the American Dietetic Association and the Society for the Advancement of Food Service Research.
1. Smalley, H. E. and Freeman, J. R., *Hospital Industrial Engineering*, (New York, N. Y.: Reinhold, 1966), p. IX.

measurement should be considered with emphasis on the quality of food and service.

Systems Approach

Although industrial engineering techniques are being applied in a number of hospital food service operations, in many cases attempts are still being made to solve problems using only one aspect of the new technology and within the concept of the traditional food production and service system. There is definitely a need for the total systems approach. According to Neibert, as long as the new technology is used simply for convenient methods to accommodate current and isolated problems, the growth of traditional problems will be perpetuated.[1] Many innovations in hospital food services have been attempts to solve some of these problems. These include more central preparation, with satellite service; use of prepared foods; the initiation of chilled food systems; shared services, such as purchasing; the four- or five-meal-a-day plan; and automated tray assembly and cart distribution.

Industrial engineering concepts and techniques can be used to foster optimal use of available resources. This requires total systems analysis and the development of innovative methods of operation, which include the design, improvement, and installation of an integrated system of men, materials and equipment. Engineering analysis and design is needed to specify, predict, and evaluate the results to be obtained from such systems.[2] Quantitative formulation and analysis can help identify sources of instability in a food service system and offer clues for correction. Without this approach, "tampering with the system" on a piecemeal basis can prevent achievement of the department's objectives.

Gilbreth said that when the similarity between food service operations and other industrial production and distribution operations is recognized, a good start has been made toward applying the industrial engineering approach. Smalley refers

---

1. Neibert, W. O. "Obsolete Food Service; Six Causes and Eight Cures," *Modern Hospital,* 110:97 June 1968, p. 97.
2. Smalley, H. E. and Freeman, J. R. *Hospital Industrial Engineering* (New York, N. Y.: Reinhold, 1968).

to some of these similarities.[1] The hospital food service department is involved in a considerable amount of preparation, processing, fabricating, storing, assembling, and distributing. These operations, however, traditionally have been diversified and largely nonstandardized. In fact, there is a tendency to adapt the processes and methods of preparation and service in the home kitchen but on a magnified scale. Yet there are many routine and repetitive procedures in food service operations that have characteristics more nearly like the production and assembly lines in industrial production than in many job-type manufacturing plants.

There are many examples of applications of industrial engineering techniques to hospital food service operations. There has been progress in systems design and analysis; improvement of work systems, work centers, and work methods; and the development of job descriptions, job analyses, and employment motivation plans.[2] There also are advances in work measurement, work sampling, standard data development, materials handling, engineering economy studies, information systems design, and quality control.[3] Systems analysis and design using computer simulation and decision theory are proving feasible.

System Specification and Design

The application of industrial engineering concepts and techniques to the development of managerial planning and controls for hospital food systems includes the formulation of specifications and design.[4] Basic to systems design and analysis is the development of objectives and methods of forecasting demand for services. For example, before making any changes, a hospital may set up a series of short-range (one to five years) objectives, involving specification and design,

---

1. Smalley, H. E. "Hospital Industrial Engineering." *J. of Ind. Eng.* 27:511 October 1966.
2. David, B. D. "A Model for Decision Making." *Hospitals, J.A.H.A.* 46:50 August 1, 1972.
3. Kazarian, E. A. *Work Analysis and Design for Hotels, Restaurants, and Institutions* (Westport, Conn: AVI Publishing Co., Inc., 1969).
4. Rathe, A. W. and Gryna, F. M. *Applying Industrial Engineering to Management Problems* (New York, N. Y.: Amer. Manage. Assn., 1969).

as well as long-range (five to 20 years) objectives, including analysis and evaluation for determining future needs.[1]

After systems analysis of a hospital food service operation, forecasting of production demand can help control food cost and production scheduling.[2] A history of daily demand for general and modified diets can provide the information necessary for developing a model to predict demand for diets and meal items.[3] Figure 1, below, is a profile of such a demand. A long-term history will show a general trend; the peaks indicate the middle of the week, when patient census

FIG. 1—PROFILES OF TRAY COUNT, GENERAL AND MODIFIED DIETS, JANUARY THROUGH MARCH

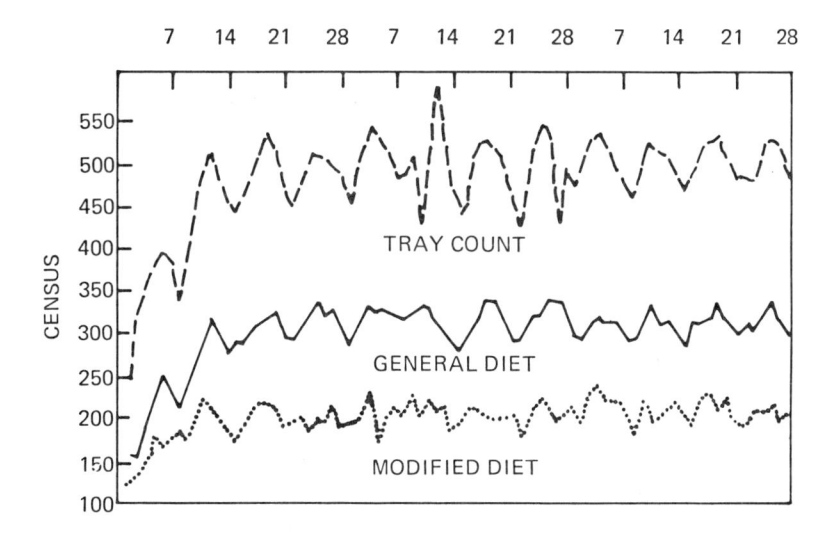

1. Husk, J. M. "Staggered Cooking Schedule Keeps Food Hot Patients Cool." *Mod. Hosp.* 116.98 June 1971.
2. Blaker, G. and Donaldson, B. "System Analysis - A Tool for Management." *J. Amer. Diet Assn.* 55:121 August 1969.
3. Uhrich, R. V. and Noort, A. J. "Production Demand Forecasting." *Hospitals, J.A.H.A.* 45:106 February 1, 1971.

in this hospital is highest. Periodic events, such as holidays, will affect the demand. This profile shows the effect of New Year's Day. Using this type of forecast, a model can be developed as a basis for a formula to forecast menu item requirements for a week as well as food purchases for longer periods.

Daily operations too, can be streamlined.[1] To avoid daily peak periods of activity, the time between food preparation and service can be prolonged and the product stored for later use. The many pre-prepared foods have helped separate functions within the food service operation that have often caused problems. New technology is making it possible to avoid the problems of spread-of-service periods by allowing for a five-day-a-week production schedule. Scheduling long production runs and stockpiling menu items have made it possible to economically produce a large quantity of one product and then concentrate on production of another item.

Standards for control should be developed based on a continual recording of data to show the use of resources in relation to time and money. Costs per unit of productivity (food, labor, and supply costs per meal), number of meals produced per man-hour, and percentage distribution of labor time among the various activities can give a measure of system effectiveness. Comparing such information before and after a system change can show whether or not the objectives for change have been achieved.[2] Overtime controls can be set for establishing acceptable deviations from standards.

Information and Materials Flow

The percentage distribution of labor time among work activities to indicate the need for further system specification and design, can be obtained through work sampling.[3] Such studies have shown that changes in the flow of information and materials would improve system effectiveness.

1. Rodenborn, B. "Industrial Engineer Streamlines Dietary Operation." *Hospitals, J.A.H.A.* 46:97 Aug. 1, 1972.
2. Kaud, F. A. "Implementing the Chilled Food Concept." *Hospitals, J.A.H.A.* 46:97 Aug. 1, 1972.
3. *Methodology Manual for Work Sampling: Productivity of Dietary Personnel* (Madison, Wis.: Dept. of Food and Nutrition, Univ. of Wis., 1967).

FIG. 2—FLOW DIAGRAM OF PATIENT'S DIET PRESCRIPTION

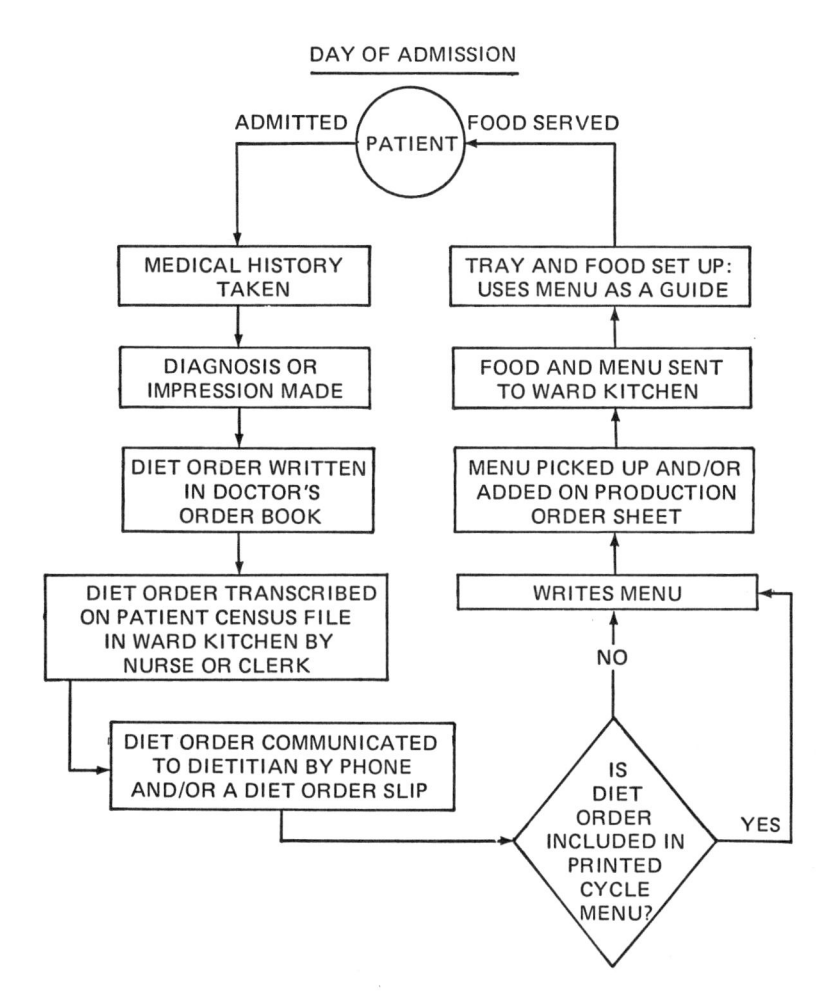

DAY OF ADMISSION

```
                    ADMITTED  ┌─────────┐  FOOD SERVED
                    ────────► │ PATIENT │ ◄────────
                              └─────────┘
                    │                              ▲
                    ▼                              │
        ┌───────────────────┐         ┌──────────────────────┐
        │  MEDICAL HISTORY  │         │  TRAY AND FOOD SET UP:│
        │      TAKEN        │         │  USES MENU AS A GUIDE │
        └───────────────────┘         └──────────────────────┘
                    │                              ▲
                    ▼                              │
        ┌───────────────────┐         ┌──────────────────────┐
        │   DIAGNOSIS OR    │         │  FOOD AND MENU SENT  │
        │ IMPRESSION MADE   │         │   TO WARD KITCHEN    │
        └───────────────────┘         └──────────────────────┘
                    │                              ▲
                    ▼                              │
        ┌───────────────────┐         ┌──────────────────────┐
        │ DIET ORDER WRITTEN│         │ MENU PICKED UP AND/OR│
        │   IN DOCTOR'S     │         │ ADDED ON PRODUCTION  │
        │   ORDER BOOK      │         │     ORDER SHEET      │
        └───────────────────┘         └──────────────────────┘
                    │                              ▲
                    ▼                              │
        ┌──────────────────────┐      ┌──────────────────────┐
        │ DIET ORDER TRANSCRIBED│     │     WRITES MENU      │◄──┐
        │ ON PATIENT CENSUS FILE│     └──────────────────────┘   │
        │  IN WARD KITCHEN BY   │                ▲               │
        │    NURSE OR CLERK     │                │ NO            │
        └──────────────────────┘                 │               │
                    │                            ◇               │
        ┌──────────────────────┐              ╱ IS  ╲            │
        │ DIET ORDER COMMUNICATED│           ╱  DIET ╲            │
        │ TO DIETITIAN BY PHONE │──────────►  ORDER   ────YES─────┘
        │ AND/OR A DIET ORDER SLIP│        ╲ INCLUDED ╱
        └──────────────────────┘            ╲PRINTED╱
                                             ╲CYCLE╱
                                              ╲MENU?╱
```

A flow chart is a simple and effective technique for analyzing and improving various parts of the management information system. Figure 2 shows a typical flow of information for a patient's diet prescription. The flow diagram can help an industrial engineer and food service director visualize the information flow and needs of each component of the hospital's dietary service to the patient.

With this chart as a guide, a computerized system of information transfer, storage, and retrieval—capable of delivering, as needed, accurate and timely information to each element in the diagram—can be developed.[1]

Work sampling in hospital food systems shows that the major factor increasing total direct labor time is the time spent in transportation and service—materials handling. In the manufacturing industry, the cost of moving materials and equipment during processing and distribution is often more than the processing costs; this appears to be true for some food service operations. A list of danger signs indicating problems of materials handling looks quite familiar to anyone who has been involved in food service. It includes idle machine time, production bottlenecks, rehandling of material, backtracking in work and product flow, large inventories, poor space utilization, lack of storage space, excessive maintenance costs, inefficient use of labor, damaged materials, demurrage, and inefficient use of equipment.

Attempts are being made to combat these problems in hospital food service operations. An entire issue of this Journal was devoted to a discussion of materials handling systems and included an article on the importance of including the food service operation in the planning of the total hospital system.[2] Four innovative systems—the monorail, the automatic food supply, the automatic car, and the automated tray assembly—have one basic goal: to effect economies in food service by automating both the transport of materials and the assembly and distribution of meals. Although these systems are expensive, they present an alternative to the antiquated methods of materials handling that now contribute to the high cost of labor.[3,4]

Tray assembly systems are somewhat similar to industrial production lines. Interruption in the flow of materials

1. DeMarco, M. R. and Lovell, J. O. "Centralized Food Service: Computer Increases Efficiency." *Hospitals, J.A.H.A.* 47: 109 June 1, 1973.
2. Devine, H. "Impact of Convenience Foods in Food Handling Facilities." *Hospitals, J.A.H.A.* 43:63 Feb. 1, 1969.
3. Doyon, P. R. "Automated Food Delivery Systems." *Hospitals, J.A.H.A.* 44:109 Feb. 1, 1970.
4. Gagilano, A. "Automated Tray Assembly." *Hospitals, J.A.H.A.* 46:87 Aug. 1, 1972.

through the assembly system and unequal division of work among the work stations causes performance ratings to fall below standard expectancy.[1] Industrial engineering techniques can be applied to streamline the systems and increase the number of trays assembled per minute, reduce the number of work stations, improve the design to facilitate menu identification, and provide quantitative data useful in the determination of whether the tray assembly system could service the hospital adequately for a proposed increase in the number of patient meals.[2]

A precedence graph is used to visualize the relationships that exist among the work units on a tray assembly line.[3] Figure 3 (on the following page), shows that the tray must precede all other work units and that the cold food items have precedence over hot food items. Precedence graphs can be used to design or analyze layout of other work units for optimal flow of materials, just as the flow chart can be used in the flow of information.

Analysis and Evaluation

After changes in operations have had sufficient time to function, a planned program of analysis and evaluation is essential. The objective data should be used to determine what effects the changes have on the product and service quality, the organization and personnel involved, and the consumer. The degree to which departmental and hospital objectives have been achieved can then be determined.[4] Such a review includes work measurement, feasibility studies, value engineering and analysis, quality and reliability analyses, and management audits.[5] In the dietary department of a

---

1. Stockdale, L., Matthews, M. E. and Mateicka, B. A. "Streamlining Central Tray Assembly." *Hospitals, J.A.H.A.* 46:75 Nov. 16, 1972.
2. Stewart, J. T. "Tray Assembly Procedures." *Hospitals, J.A.H.A.* 44:112 Oct. 1, 1970.
3. McGary, V. E. and Donaldson, B. "A Model of a Centralized Tray Assembly Conveyor System for a Hospital. II. Station Work Content." *J. Amer. Diet. Assn.* 55:480 Nov. 1969.
4. Donaldson, B. "Managing Change in Food Service Operations." *J. Amer. Diet. Assn.* 57:335 Oct. 1970.
5. Rathe, A. W. and Gryna, F. M. *Applying Industrial Engineering to Management Problems*, (New York, N. Y.: Amer. Manage. Assn., 1969).

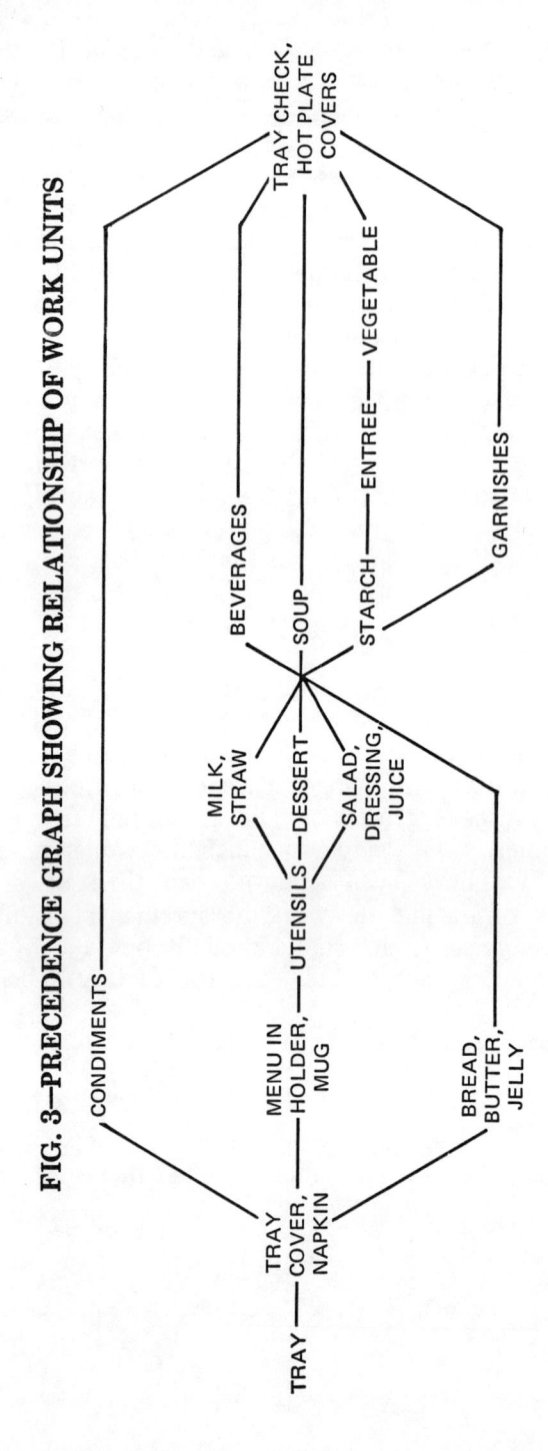

FIG. 3—PRECEDENCE GRAPH SHOWING RELATIONSHIP OF WORK UNITS

Madison, Wis., hospital, a management evaluation program was adapted and used to correlate findings from work sampling and performance rating with other control indexes, such as food and labor cost per meal, nutritional content of meals served, and patient satisfaction.[1] This analysis of operations took place prior to a change from three to four meals a day. After the change, the study was repeated to evaluate the effect on cost of operations and quality of the food. The degree of achievement of objectives of the hospital and the food service department was quantitatively analyzed and evaluated using the industrial engineering approach. The analysis and evaluation are again being conducted while major changes in facilities and operational methods are taking place.

Quality control, another important aspect of analysis and evaluation in industry, is changing from a function of inspection of the final product to a quality program that reviews the product from the initial design concept of menu planning to consumer use. Although product life of food items for the menu has been extended by means of the new technology, the associated problems of maintaining and improving food quality are a real challenge. A program of food and service quality control would provide management with a way to evaluate the success of a specific operation in achieving its quality objective.

Industry uses quality control as a management tool to establish standards during product development according to quality and economic objectives and to evaluate conformance with these standards throughout the production and distribution process. There has been minimal application in the food service industry of such procedures because of the difficulties encountered in sensory measurement of food quality and the lack of standards for measuring total food and service quality.[2] Research on the application of quality control to the food service industry should be increased.

1. Williams, J. E. and Donaldson, B. "SCORE: A Management Evaluation Program for Dietary Departments." *J. Amer. Diet. Assn.* 54:289 April 1969.
2. Christensen, S. W. "Quality Control: A Food Service Management Evaluation Tool." Unpublished research paper. Department of Food Science, Univ. of Wisc., Madison, 1967.

Summary

Those involved in research related to hospital food production and service could make major contributions to the development of more effective operations through application of some of the more sophisticated industrial engineering techniques used for analysis and evaluation. Reliable historical data from operating departments are needed by researchers for developing models and simulating operations. More emphasis should be placed on quantitative methods of quality control and on development of models for forecasting meal demand to improve information systems that can be easily adapted to computer-assisted systems. When applied to food formulas, the Critical Path Method, a technique for planning and control can help in staffing, production scheduling, optimal equipment use, and optimizing the make or buy decision. Research has shown the feasibility of using predetermined motion time to predict labor time in food production.[1, 2] The development of coded standard data elements with universal application in the food service industry has been recommended as a means to establish labor time for food production.[3]

Using the industrial engineering approach to cope with current changes in hospital food service operations requires significant deviations from past practices; yet the traditional approach will not be sufficient to attain hospital and departmental objectives and relieve the stress imposed by the changing environment, economy, and technology. The creative, problem-solving, forecasting, and planning abilities of analysts, systems engineers, and food administrators will be needed to convert the qualitative concepts of health services into real

---

1. Montag, G. M., McKinley, M. and Klinschmidt, A. "Predetermined Motion Times—A Tool in Food Production Management." *J. Amer. Diet. Assn.* 45:206 Sept. 1964.
2. Waldvogel, C. F. "Quantity Food Production Master Standard Data Code for Synthesis of Entree Production Time." Unpublished thesis. Department of Foods and Nutrition. Univ. of Wis., Madison, 1967.
3. Ruf, K. and Matthews, M. E. "Production Time Standards Cut Time and Costs in Food Service Operations." *Hospitals, J.A.H.A.* 47:82 May 1, 1973.

working systems.[1] The methods that have been useful in developing production operations in industry should be used in organizations devoted to human welfare.[2] Surely this can be done through cooperative effort among food administrators, associated administrators, specialists, researchers, and educators concerned about the future of food service operations in hospitals.

1. Flagle, C. D. and Young, J. P. "Application of Operations Research and Industrial Engineering to Problems of Health Services, Hospitals and Public Health." *J. of Ind. Eng.* 27:609 Nov. 1966.
2. Emma, C. K. "Engineering Technics Can Improve Food Service." *Mod. Hosp.* 11:128 July 1968.

PRODUCTION TIME STANDARDS*

KATHLEEN RUF and M. EILEEN MATTHEWS, Ph.D.**

The importance of standard formulas within a food service operation has long been acknowledged. The need for standard operation times in food service establishments has become more apparent as rising labor costs force a closer look at productivity.

Time standards can provide management with specific labor information that can be utilized in menu planning, work scheduling, job definition, price setting, and new facility design. Several methods for establishing time standards have been developed by industry, but few have been applied to food service operations.

In an effort to develop a method for establishing time standards that would be economical, easy to use with a minimum of training, adaptable to variations in layout and

---

*Reprinted, with permission, from *Hospitals, Journal of the American Hospital Association*, June 16, 1973, pp. 83-91.

**Kathleen Ruf, R.D.*, is Vice President, Hospital Division, P.D. Food Services, Inc., Riverside, Calif. She received her bachelor's degree from Union College, Lincoln, Nebr., and her master's degree from Loma Linda (Calif.) University, and is currently enrolled as a doctoral candidate in Food Administration at the University of Wisconsin, Madison. She is a member of the American Dietetic Association and the Seventh-Day Adventist Dietetic Association. *M. Eileen Matthews*, Ph.D., is an Assistant Professor of Food Administration in the Department of Food Science at the University of Wisconsin, Madison. She is a member of the American Dietetic Association, the American Society for Hospital Food Service Administrators, the Institute of Food Technologists, and the Society for the Advancement of Food Service Research. Dr. Matthews earned a bachelor's degree from Drexel Institute of Technology, Philadelphia, Pa., a master's degree from Oklahoma State University, Stillwater, and a doctoral degree from the University of Wisconsin, Madison.

storage, and accurate, a student project for a food administration course at the University of Wisconsin was initiated. The project utilized the Predetermined Motion Time System, Master Standard Data (MSD), developed by Crossan and Nance in 1962.[1]

MSD is a consistent, economical technique with a built-in performance rating factor suitable for usage on long-cycle, nonrepetitive work. According to Niebel, MSD unquestionably represents a significant contribution to the area of synthetic basic motion times.[2]

Master Standard Data contains seven basic elements; obtain, place, rotate, use, finger shift, exert force, and body motions. The procedure for using MSD involves recording the motions of the operator and assigning symbols and time to each motion.

Crossan and Nance recommended that these basic MSD elements be condensed into larger elements for economic application. This is possible through the construction of an alphamnemonic code consisting of special code systems to indicate a series of motion patterns that always occur when a certain task is performed. This code derives its symbols from the alphabet so that identification is easy for the user.

Application to Food Service

Montag, McKinley, and Klinschmidt applied MSD to production activities in a bakeshop.[3] They developed 68 coded standard data elements and applied these to the preparation of baked pudding and yeast rolls. The authors concluded that MSD was more accurate than time study and recommended the development of a universal code applicable in all production areas.

Waldvogel developed a structural framework for a quantity food production standard time data code based on the ele-

---

1. Crossan R. M. and Nance, H. W. *Master Standard Data* (New York: McGraw-Hill Book Co., Inc., 1972).
2. Niebel, B. J. *Motion and Time Study*, 5th ed. (Homewood, Ill.: Richard D. Irwin, Inc., 1972).
3. Montag, G. M., McKinley, M. M. and Klinschmidt, A. C. "Predetermined Motion Times—a Tool in Food Production Management." *J. Amer. Diet Assn.* 45:206 Sept. 1964.

ments utilized in the production of three single-item entrees.[1] The relationship of production volume to time was estimated for the entrees through the standard data established. Using MSD, Waldvogel developed a universal alphamnemonic code for quantity food entree production. Production activities were divided into general categories, each of which was assigned one letter of the alphabet to describe and identify the basic elements. These categories were:

A—Get and aside	M—Measure
B—Bread	O—Obtain
C—Combine	P—Pan
D—Dip	Q—Open
F—Flour	S—Shape
G—Grease	V—Weigh
I—Inspect	W—Wash
L—Load	

A second and third letter were added to the code. The second letter identified the tool or ingredients used. Generally, the third letter indicated the place from which the item was obtained. For example, MDC indicates the motions involved in Measuring Dry ingredients into a Cup. Similarly OIC is Obtaining Ingredients from a Can.

For this study, additional standard coded elements were developed as needed from the several basic elements. First, the beginning and end points of the coded element were determined. The motions within a coded element were limited to a maximum of 15. MSD times were applied to each basic element and the total time for the coded element computed.

Four formulas—egg cutlets, lasagna, nutmeat a la king on rice, and hot soya-beef sandwich—were selected to test the application of the coded data and to develop additional quantity food production standard time data based on elements utilized in multiple-item entrees. Each formula was analyzed for 100, 300, and 500 servings to determine the relationship of volume to time. Three basic steps, identified and described

---

1. Waldvogel, C. F. "Quantity Food Production Master Standard Data Code for Synthesis of Entree Production Times Relationship of Production Time to Volume." Unpublished thesis. Department of Foods and Nutrition, University of Wisconsin, Madison, 1967.

in this article for hot soya-beef sandwich, were followed for each of the four formulas.

Standardize Formula and Methods

The first step in the procedure was to standardize production formulas and methods. Ingredients were already standardized. Previous experience with the production personnel working with these formulas was utilized to standardize methods.

The layout of the White Memorial Medical Center, Los Angeles, was simulated to establish standardized parameters of distance.

Layouts for production routes with traffic patterns and the work areas were defined and standardized for each of the four formulas. Equipment in the work places included mobile carts and bins, laundry and waste containers, storage racks for pans, and worktables. Large utensils were available on the rack above the worktable and small utensils were stored inside the drawers. Spices and measures were located on a shelf above the worktable.

Food ingredients were stored in the cooks' storeroom or on freezer shelves. Transportation of food and equipment was via mobile carts fitted with adjustable shelves to facilitate movement of varied quantities. Prepared food items were placed on carts and transferred to the food warmer and/or tray line.

Divide Work into Basic Elements

The next step in the procedure was to subdivide the production method for hot soya-beef sandwich into eight basic elements for analysis: (1) assemble ingredients, (2) assemble equipment, (3) prepare gravy, (4) pan and cook soya-beef slices, (5) unload soya-beef slices, (6) pan gravy, (7) deliver to serving area, and (8) cleanup. The activities required for each element were identified and each basic activity was assigned a symbol and time.

Tables 1 to 8 show the coded activities with their associated Time Measurement Unit (one TMU = .0006 minute) value, the frequency of occurrence, and the total element time for 100 portions, resulting from the application of the basic MSD

322 DIMENSIONS OF HOSPITALITY MANAGEMENT

elements to the alphamnemonic code. The identical procedure was followed to estimate production times for 100, 300, and 500 portions of egg cutlets, lasagna, and nutmeat a la king on rice.

TABLE 1—APPLICATION OF CODED STANDARD DATA TO ELEMENT 1: ASSEMBLE INGREDIENTS

Activity	Code	TMU	Frequency for 100 servings	Element time in TMU
Walk to cart storage area	BW	17	8	136
Obtain cart	OK	53	1	53
Push cart to freezer	BW	17	20	340
Open refrigerator and freezer doors and return	QR	90	4	360
Close refrigerator and freezer doors and return	QRC	54	4	216
Obtain cart	OK	53	1	53
Push cart to storage shelf	BW	17	2	34
Obtain soya beef from shelf	OIR	30	3	90
Place on cart	P12C1	31	1	31
Obtain cart	OK	53	1	53
Push cart to large refrigerator	BW	17	13	221
Open refrigerator door	QR	90	2	180
Close refrigerator door	QRC	54	2	108
Obtain cart	OK	53	1	53
Push cart to margarine storage	BW	17	3	51
Obtain margarine from rack	OIR	30	1	30
Place on cart	P12C1	31	1	31
Obtain cart	OK	53	1	53
Push cart to worktable	BW	17	8	136
Obtain measure from rack	OCR	83	1	83
Measure flour from bin	OB	280	1	280
Obtain salt from rack	OIR	30	1	30
Obtain measuring spoon from drawer	OUD	104	1	104
Measure dry ingredient (salt) into spoon	MDS	143	1	143
Obtain measure from rack	OCR	83	1	83
Obtain beef-like seasoning from rack	OIR	30	1	30
Measure beef-like seasoning into container	MDC	143	1	143
Obtain coloring from rack	OIR	30	1	30
Place on cart	P12C1	31	1	31
Total element time				3186
Total minutes (TMU x .0006)				1.9116

The last step in the procedure was to synthesize total production time for the eight basic elements of hot soya-beef sandwich. Table 9, which gives the synthesized times, shows that labor time per portion decreased as production volume increased. However, this decrease in time per portion was not directly proportional to the increase in volume. Time differences within the eight elements were due to the increased frequency of coded activities such as measuring amounts of food or handling equipment. For example, in Table 9, the increase in time in relation to volume in element 2, assemble equipment, resulted from handling the number of pans required for the various volumes of hot soya-beef sandwich, thus causing a greater frequency of these specific coded activities.

TABLE 2—APPLICATION OF CODED STANDARD DATA TO ELEMENT 2: ASSEMBLE EQUIPMENT

Activity	Code	TMU	Frequency for 100 servings	Element time in TMU
Obtain cart	OK	53	1	53
Push cart to pot and pan storage area and return to worktable	BW	17	15	255
Obtain pans from rack to cart	OPR	79	2	158
Place 12- by 20- by 2-in. pans on table from cart	APT	87	1	87
Place containers of flour, beef-like seasoning and coloring from table to cart	ACC	87	3	261
Obtain mixing spoon from drawer	OUD	104	1	104
Obtain gallon measure from rack	OCR	83	1	83
Obtain whip and measuring spoon from table	OUT	38	2	76
Place above (3) on cart	AUC	61	3	183
Total element time				1260
Total minutes (TMU x .0006)				.7560

TABLE 3—APPLICATION OF CODED STANDARD DATA TO ELEMENT 3: PREPARE GRAVY

Activity	Code	TMU	Frequency for 100 servings	Element time in TMU
Obtain cart	OK	53	1	53
Push to steam-jacketed kettle	BW	17	8	136
Turn on steam-jacketed kettle	CKB	79	1	79
Unwrap margarine	QBW	104	2	208
Measure margarine	MSK	129	1	129
Place in steam-jacketed kettle	P12C2	57	1	57
Obtain whip from cart	OUT	38	1	38
Pour flour and seasonings from measure into steam-jacketed kettle	OMP	128	1	128
Mix with whip while cooking	CHW	202	2	404
Obtain measure from cart	ACC	121	1	121
Measure water from overhead faucet	MFB	155	2	310
Pour into steam-jacketed kettle	OPP	151	2	302
Mix with whip	CHW	202	2	404
Obtain coloring and measuring spoon from cart	ACC	121	1	121
Measure coloring	MQS	67	1	67
Add to gravy	RHW	15	1	15
Mix	CHW	202	1	202
Turn steam kettle to simmer	CKB	79	1	79
Obtain cart	OK	53	1	53
Push to worktable	BW	17	8	136
Total element time				3042
Total minutes (TMU x .0006)				1.8252

TABLE 4—APPLICATION OF CODED STANDARD DATA TO ELEMENT 4: PAN AND COOK SOYA-BEEF SLICES

Activity	Code	TMU	Frequency for 100 servings	Element time in TMU
Open packages of soya-beef	QPE	395	2	790
Obtain tongs from drawer	OUD	104	1	104
Pan slices	PTS	60	100	6000
Load pans on cart	LC	74	2	148
Obtain cart	OK	53	1	53
Push to compartment steamer	BW	17	6	102
Open unlatched steamer door	QO	66	1	66
Load steamer	LS	128	2	256
Close steamer door	QS	295	1	295
Set timer	ITS	154	1	154
Total element time				7968
Total minutes (TMU x .0006)				4.7808

TABLE 5—APPLICATION OF CODED STANDARD DATA TO ELEMENT 5: UNLOAD SOYA-BEEF SLICES

Activity	Code	TMU	Frequency for 100 servings	Element time in TMU
Obtain cart	OK	53	1	53
Push to steamer	BW	17	6	102
Open latched steamer door	QS	295	1	295
Unload pans to cart	LU	296	2	592
Push steamer door shut	QO	66	1	66
Obtain a cart	OK	53	1	53
Total element time				1161
Total minutes (TMU x .0006)				.6966

TABLE 6—APPLICATION OF CODED STANDARD DATA TO ELEMENT 6: PAN GRAVY

Activity	Code	TMU	Frequency for 100 servings	Element time in TMU
Push cart to steam-jacketed kettle	BW	17	10	170
Empty gravy from kettle to pan	OIK	674	1	674
Load pan into cart	LC	74	1	74
Fill steam kettle with water	MFB	155	1	155
Total element time				1073
Total minutes (TMU x .0006)				.6438

TABLE 7—APPLICATION OF CODED STANDARD DATA TO ELEMENT 7: DELIVER TO SERVING AREA

Activity	Code	TMU	Frequency for 100 servings	Element time in TMU
Obtain cart	OK	53	1	53
Push to warmer	BW	17	12	204
Open warmer door	QO	66	1	66
Place pan of soya slices in warmer	LO	128	1	128
Close warmer door	QO	66	1	66
Obtain cart	OK	53	1	53
Push cart to tray line	BW	17	5	85
Load gravy and soya slices into steam table	LS	134	2	268
Obtain cart	OK	53	1	53
Push cart to storage area, leave, return to worktable	BW	17	13	221
Total element time				1197
Total minutes (TMU x .0006)				.7182

TABLE 8—APPLICATION OF CODED STANDARD DATA TO ELEMENT 8: CLEANUP

Activity	Code	TMU	Frequency for 100 servings	Element time in TMU
Obtain cart	OK	53	1	53
Push to worktable	BW	17	8	136
Pick up empty packages	O12H2	38	2	76
Place in waste container beneath table	P12C2	54	2	108
Pick up used utensils and place on cart	AUT	61	2	122
Place in table sink and return	BW	17	4	68
Wash table	WT	399	1	399
Remove pans and measures from table, place on cart	ACT	121	1	121
Return seasoning and coloring containers to rack	OIR	30	1	30
Obtain cart	OK	53	1	53
Take to pot and pan sink and return	BW	17	28	476
Place pots and pans on pot and pan drainboard	ACT	121	1	121
Walk to steam-jacketed kettle and return	BW	17	16	272
Wash steam-jacketed kettle	WK	540	1	540
Walk to range and return	BW	17	4	68
Obtain extra margarine	O12S1	17	1	17
Place in grease container	P12C1	31	1	31
Place hands by side	P126	13	1	13
Total element time				2704
Total minutes (TMU x .0006)				1.6224

TABLE 9—SYNTHESIZED PRODUCTION TIMES BY VOLUME: HOT SOYA-BEEF SANDWICH

Elements	Time in minutes		
	100 portions	300 portions	500 portions
1. Assemble ingredients	1.9116	2.1720	2.3118
2. Assemble equipment	.7560	1.1400	1.5954
3. Prepare gravy	1.8252	3.4572	4.9338
4. Pan and cook soya-beef slices	4.7808	13.0554	21.9048
5. Unload soya-beef slices	.6966	1.2294	2.1384
6. Pan gravy	.6438	1.5414	2.4570
7. Deliver to serving area	.7182	1.1022	1.5630
8. Cleanup	1.6224	1.7400	1.8540
Total time	12.9546	25.4376	38.7582
Time per portion	.1295	.0847	.0775

Figure 1 indicates no linear relationship between the 100, 300, and 500 volumes of the four formulas. Production time per portion decreased more for the production of the first 300 portions, than for the additional 200 portions. These data emphasize the error in determining the labor time for all volumes of production by multiplying the labor time for an individual portion by the number of portions produced. The figure indicates that labor time per portion decreased as production volume increased for all formulas except egg cutlets. This increase in production time per portion for 500 servings of egg cutlets was due to the additional oven and steamer space required. Similar curves were observed by Waldvogel,[1] implying that as facility capacity is reached, the decrease in time per portion becomes relatively stable and the optimum volume is approached.

Utilization of these predetermined production times, adding process time and a 10 to 15 per cent standard allowance for delay and personal time, provides management with quantitative data to make production decisions.

---

1. Waldvogel, C. F. "Quantity Food Production Master Standard Data Code for Synthesis of Entree Production Times Relationship of Production Time to Volume." Unpublished thesis, Department of Foods and Nutrition, University of Wisconsin, Madison, 1967.

FIG. 1—SYNTHESIS OF ENTREE PRODUCTION TIME: RELATIONSHIP OF TIME PER PORTION TO PRODUCTION VOLUME

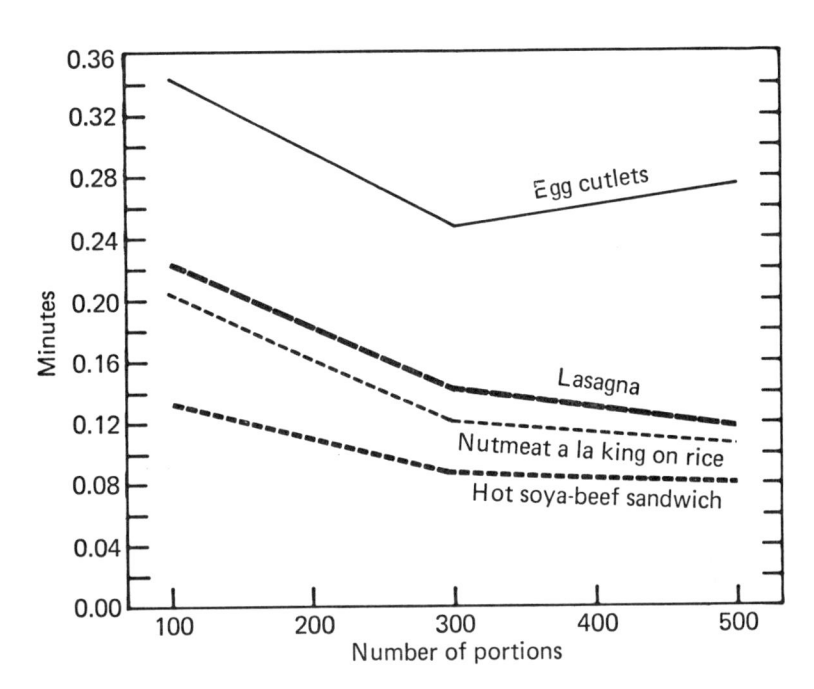

Because these four formulas appear on the same day of the cycle menu, the data were evaluated in relation to skill level required of production employees. Inspection of the elemental breakdown may lead to changes in work loads, job procedures, and/or layout. Four to 12 per cent of the total production time for preparation of these four formulas was spent walking; between two and three per cent delivering finished products to the serving area; and four to 12 per cent cleaning. Translated into working hours, this is approximately three-quarters to two and one-quarter hours per working day spent on what is normally considered nonproductive work. By studying the elemental breakdowns, management should be able to shift some of these tasks to less skilled employees.

Proposed changes in layout or equipment arrangement may be evaluated by applying MSD to the simulations and comparing the findings with present data before making expensive physical changes.

Production models can be developed from this elemental data to further the best usage of materials, methods, machines and employees. For hospitals considering a change to the incentive method of payment, MSD provides a quick, accurate, and fair way to determine time standards for incentive levels.

Many management tools, such as computer simulation models, linear programming, PERT network scheduling, make-or-buy-decision techniques and cost-effectiveness analysis, require labor data that can be obtained from the application of MSD to formulas or task analysis. Initial development is time-consuming; however, the resulting universal standard time data may ultimately be computerized for rapid retrieval in optimizing the work loads within food service operations and in designing future facilities.

Master Standard Data has potential for establishing time standards for all production items. Adjustments of time values in relation to distance, number, and amount of ingredients and utensils assembled and total number of portions are allowed for in MSD. Time data thus obtained are of value to management as a quantitative basis for making production decisions.

A Frenchman went into a West street restaurant and seated himself before a mound of butter, a bottle of catsup, and a soiled table-cloth.

"What'll yez have?" demanded the waiter.

"*Parlez-vous—*"

"Barley-soup!" shouted the Irish waiter. "D'ye want tay or coffy?"*

---

*The Hotel World, Nov. 30, 1889, p. 9. Reprinted by permission of Hotel and Motel Management.

HOW TO INCREASE THE EFFICIENCY
OF THE HUMAN BODY*

L. H. KOTSCHEVAR, Ph.D.

Work simplification requires, among other things, a knowledge of body mechanics. Just as engineers are always trying to develop machines with more reliable operation, those engaged in work simplification are always seeking methods of making the human machine operate more efficiently. For whether the machine is mechanical or human, the same principle applies, i.e., production is very closely related to efficiency.

Consider first of all the structure of the human machine. The weight of the body rests on the spine and the hips. In other words, the body is supported by an inverted "T." When the body is held erect, the weight is evenly distributed over this "T," and very little energy is required to support the body. However, when the body bends out of line, then the weight is unevenly distributed over this "T" and the muscles affected by additional weight must perform extra work to support it. Thus, as in the case of the worker who must bend too far over a work table or a sink, the carrying of extra weight adds tremendously to the energy required. (See illustration on following page.)

The more the body is kept in alignment, the less energy is required for performance of the task. Studies have shown that an employee who sits and works with poor posture will use more energy and become more quickly fatigued than one who stands and works with good posture.

Body fatigue due to the lifting, lowering and carrying of heavy objects also can be lessened. In lifting heavy loads it

---

**Institutions Magazine*, 1958. Reprinted with permission.

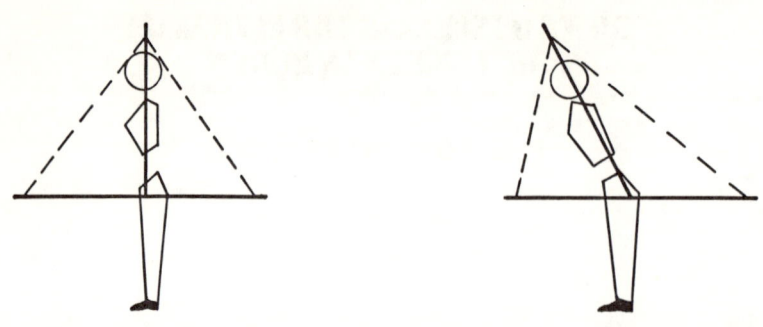

The head, chest and trunk of the body rest on an inverted "T" formed by the hips and spine. Correct posture insures that the weight will be evenly distributed over this "T." Poor posture will impose a heavier work load on some muscles, causing strain and fatigue.

should be remembered that the leg muscles are stronger than those of the back. Therefore, the problem of lifting or lowering a load can be simplified if (1) the feet are firmly placed about 10 in. apart, (2) the bending is performed by the leg muscles while the back is kept straight, and (3) the object is firmly grasped and lifted slowly. The leg muscles also should do the bending while the load is slowly being lowered.

It is recommended that if the lifting is performed repetitively, weights be limited to 50 lbs. for men and 35 lbs. for women. This limitation actually makes it possible to lift more over an extended period of time than if heavier loads are lifted. One of the early experiments in work simplification showed that when men were given a smaller shovel with which to move coal, they shoveled greater quantities than when they used the larger tool provided by management.

When carrying a load, it should be remembered that a weight held away from the body exerts a greater force than the same weight held close to the body. Therefore, when carrying a heavy load, it should be kept close to the body's center of gravity.

The weight of the body lifting a 50-lb. object is only of relative significance; the weight of the human being involved is important only from the viewpoint of the total amount of

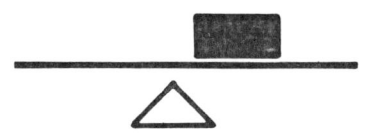

The closer an object is to the fulcrum (triangle) of a lever, the better the balance. This is a good rule to remember when carrying loads—keep them close to the body.

force available. The weight has nothing to do with the efficiency of that force.

The body acts as a lever, and the center of gravity of the body is like the fulcrum point of a lever. If a 50-lb. object is held 3 in. from the body, the units of energy necessary to move that force would be 12.5 ft-lb. If that same object is held 1 in. from the body, then the necessary force would be about 4.16 ft-lb; a distance of 6 in. would require 25 ft-lb.

It is wise to have heavy loads lifted by two or more people. As in any operation which requires teamwork, one person should be appointed to give the signals so that all lift together. If the object to be carried is long, then the workers should be of about equal size and build and should walk out-of-step. This will prevent the weight from bouncing or shifting.

Heavy items should never be stacked more than 7 ft. high since even this height imposes a severe strain on workers as they lift weights over their heads. When lifting to shoulder height or above the head, body fatigue can be lessened if the load first is raised to waist level and then rested on a support. The grip can be changed at this point, and the knees bent to give added power for the final lift.

Momentum, when properly used, can assist greatly in making work easier. Watch a pair of professional piano movers and note what little effort they expend to move a heavy piano. Similarly, if a man uses a heavy mop to wash a floor, his work will be much easier if he will release the pressure on each swing as soon as the mop passes the center of his body. The momentum will carry the mop to the end of the swing, which is more efficient than if full pressure is applied on the

Position I (left) shows the worker's left hand on the top left back of chair, ready to grip left rung (base). Position II shows chair properly inverted.

mop until the end of the stroke. In the latter case, pressure must be used to stop the mop.

Workers who lift chairs and stack them on tables prior to a floor washing operation can perform this task much more easily if they take advantage of the momentum generated in the original lift. Also, swinging a chair with an arc-like movement makes this task less fatiguing. The employee should stand directly behind the chair and place his left hand at the top left back of the chair. With counterclockwise motion, he swings the chair to the right and immediately places his right hand on the left rung or base. He then takes one step forward and places the now upside down chair on the table.

In this case, the lifting should be done from the waist and abdominal areas rather than the shoulders. This, in combination with a rhythmic swinging motion, will enable an average employee to set up 20 to 25 chairs a minute.

Generally it can be said that rocking a barrel, swinging a sack—getting things in motion before lifting—are tricks of the trade for a professional mover who knows how to utilize momentum to make work easier.

Frequently it is easier to pull or push loads than it is to lift and carry them into place. Placing a very heavy object on a broom and pulling it is much easier than carrying the load. If a load is to be pushed, the worker should stand away from the item so that body weight can be used to assist in this job. If the worker stands close to the object to be pushed, the muscles alone will have to do all the work.

The tired worker is the accident-prone worker. As important as working properly is permitting the worker to take a rest period. This also increases the efficiency of the human body and will lessen the chances of accidents. Statistics show that the maximum period of accident occurrence is three hours after starting and three hours after the noonday meal. The harder the work the earlier this period occurs. Statistics also show that one injury out of every four occurs from the handling of material.

For the easiest, most efficient way to handle and move heavy loads, it would be well to keep this principle in mind—using headwork before footwork frequently saves time, energy and tempers.

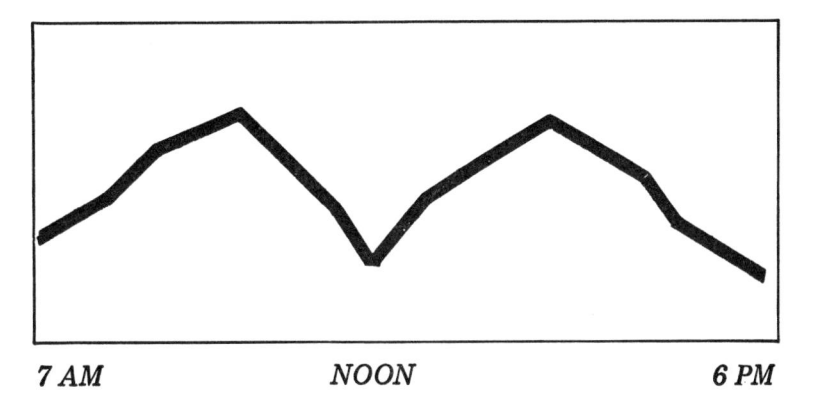

7 AM   *NOON*   *6 PM*

Data compiled by the National Safety Council indicates that there is a sharp rise in accident probability 3 hours after starting time and 3 hours after the noonday break. This substantiates the author's statement that tired workers are accident-prone workers. Monotony and fatigue can be alleviated by work breaks.

HELP WORKERS WORK EASIER*

L. H. KOTSCHEVAR, Ph. D.

Knowing what makes workers tired—and doing something about it—can cut labor costs substantially.

When a worker grows tired, his production drops. For this reason, it is essential to prevent fatigue if employees are to maintain a good rate of production during a shift. To prevent fatigue in a worker we need to know what makes him tired. We also want to know how being tired affects a worker's production.

Our bodies are machines. They consume fuel to create energy to do work just as an engine burns fuel to do work. In the human body the fuel used is a sugar called glucose; when this sugar burns in our bodies we develop heat and energy plus certain waste products such as carbonic acid, pyruvic acid, lactic acid, and others. When the body turns portions of fats or proteins into glucose, then waste products other than these from glucose also accumulate in the body.

The problem is to work just hard enough to allow the body to get rid of the waste products as they accumulate. If these burnt-out particles pile up in the body, that is, if we burn foods faster than we eliminate the waste products, we get tired. Some say the piled-up acids and other waste products cause a tired or an aching feeling in the muscles. Certainly, we know our muscles get sore after heavy exercise and they stiffen up, especially if we are not used to the exercise.

But, the human body also differs from a machine. When an engine is stopped, it ceases to use fuel, but not the human body. It has to keep running even though it is doing no work.

Institutions Magazine. Reprinted with permission, 1958.

ENERGY COST OF DOING WORK*

Activity	Calories required per hour by average man
Sleeping	65
Sitting at rest	100
Standing relaxed	105
Standing at attention	115
Singing	122
Dishwashing	144
Sweeping bare floor (38 strokes per minutes)	169
Walking slowly (2.6 miles per hour)	200
Walking moderately	300
Walking down stairs	364
Severe exercise	450
Walking very fast (5.3 miles per hour)	650
Walking up stairs	1100

The basic energy required to keep the body going when it is at complete rest is called the *basal* requirement. It is said to take about 1700 calories per day to keep the body of a man functioning when he is at complete rest.

When we work, energy over and above this basal requirement must be obtained to do the work. The harder we work the more fuel it takes. (See table above.)

For instance, a man whose basal requirement is 70 calories per hour will use about 100 calories per hour while sitting still. If he works at a moderate rate, he will require about three times this amount and if he carries a load up stairs, it will take over 11 times his basal rate.

How to Conserve Energy

Frequently work which should require only a small amount of energy actually requires lots more and this is because a worker is wasteful of the energy he has or does the work improperly. A smart employee gets to know Mr. Less Effort for he is the fellow who can keep him from wasting "gas" and from making needless demands upon his fuel reserves.

---

*C. Sherman, *Chemistry of Food and Nutrition* (New York: MacMillan Company, 1941), p. 185.

There is a maxim in work simplification which when followed cuts down consistently on the use of energy; it states:
> Never walk when you can stand.
> Never stand when you can sit.
> Never sit when you can lie.
> And be surprised how work hours fly.

Working with tense muscles rather than relaxed muscles increases the amount of energy required to do work. Workers should learn to use their muscles properly. Rhythmic, smooth motions take less energy than jerky motions or motions which stop and start suddenly. In the first article of this series *How to Increase the Efficiency of the Human Body*, the proper way to make motions in work was summarized under the principles of motion economy.

Hard work at a fast pace is wasteful of energy and causes rapid tiring of the worker. Over a period of time doing less at a steady rate produces more work than trying to do a lot with erratic bursts of speed. There is a saying which goes: "Life by the yard is apt to be hard, but life by the inch is more of a cinch." The turtle knew this when he won his well-known race with the hare.

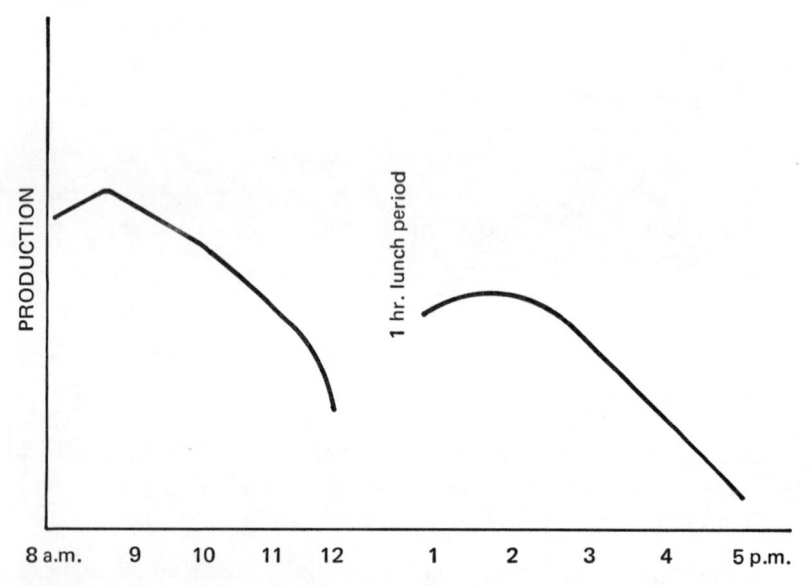

Production curve of a worker doing heavy work at a fairly rapid pace.

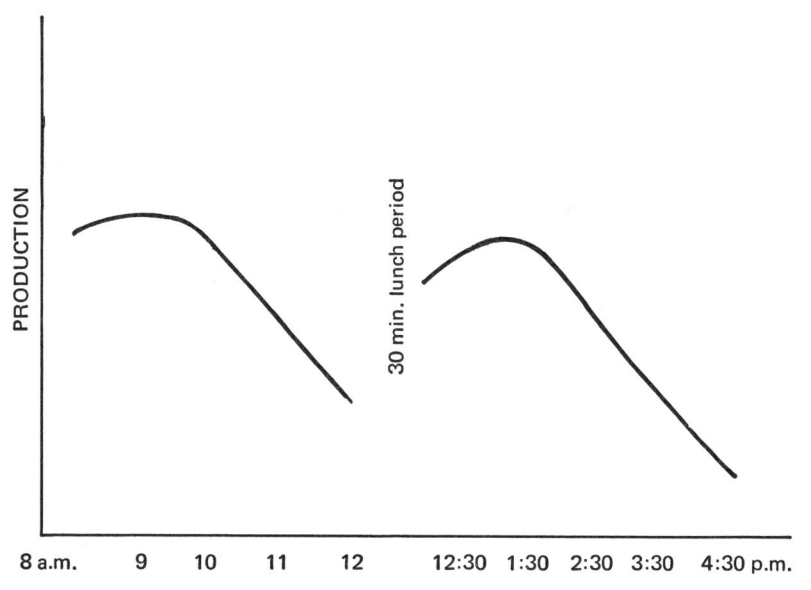

Production curve of a worker doing heavy work but not at a fast pace drops toward end of shift when worker is tired.

Variations in Production

Studies also show that workers at the end of a shift use more energy in doing their work than they do earlier in the day. Perhaps the muscles grow more tense and the worker has to exert more force upon his muscles to accomplish the work. Whatever it is, as the worker tires, his production drops. Under normal working conditions a worker should feel tired during about one-fifth of his shift and most of this tired feeling should occur at the end of the shift.

Some workers vary in their ability to produce according to the time of the day. This may be because their blood sugar level is low at a particular time and they are, therefore, tired. Because of this some workers cannot get going in the morning but later in the day reach their peak and really accomplish something. Others start out like a house-afire but are burnt out by evening. These variations in production among workers are called diurnal variations. Most workers would prefer not to work at times when their ability to produce is low. This is important to remember in scheduling employees.

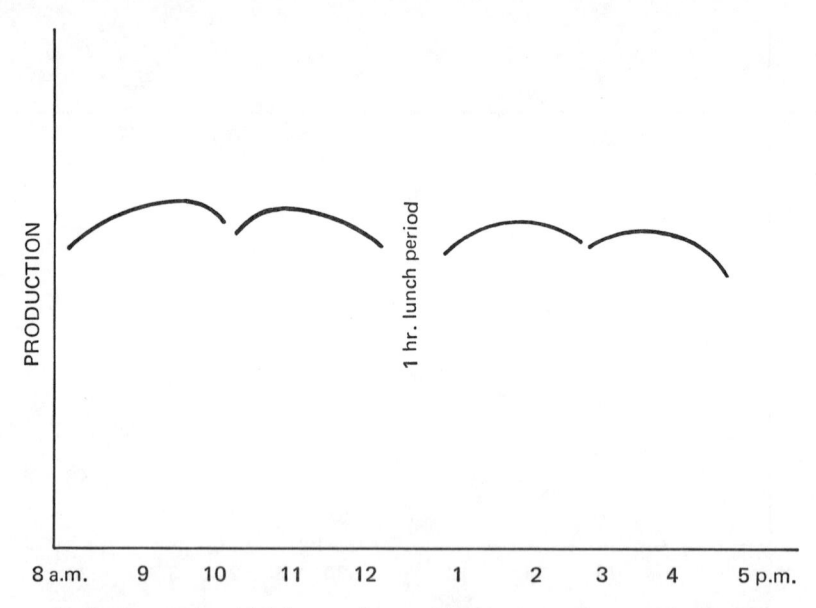

Production curve of kitchen worker working at a normal rate with two 10-min. coffee breaks during a shift.

Value of Coffee Breaks

When a worker burns energy too quickly or gets tired at the end of a shift, a part of this tiredness may arise because he is running out of fuel. When this occurs the blood sugar level drops—the gas tank runs dry—and he lacks fuel to create energy to do work. Rest allows the blood sugar level to rise and the fatigue goes away. We can raise the blood sugar level quickly by eating something sweet. That is why candy bar manufacturers talk about a "quick lift" from their product. Sugars are absorbed quickly into the blood stream thus raising the blood sugar level.

An interesting thing about the coffee break is that, besides providing rest which restores blood sugar, the caffeine in the coffee stimulates the liver to release stored glucose thus providing a quick shot of sugar that gives a "lift" and erases the feeling of tiredness. However, when the liver is stimulated by too much coffee, it becomes fatigued and then we have what is known as the "coffee jitters," produced because the liver has completely exhausted its reserve supply of glucose.

All this is vital information to employers who wish to help their employees maintain good production rates. It points out the value of a short rest period in the shift just as the worker begins to tire. Furthermore, we realize, when we know these facts, how planning work ahead and developing smooth, flowing work habits can reduce fatigue and maintain production.

We can be of assistance to workers in maintaining production by scheduling their easiest work near the end of a shift or at a time when their energy level is low. It is wise, for instance, to schedule cooks' preparation work, which can be done seated, toward the end of a shift and not at the beginning. It is wise also to schedule the filling of salt shakers, folding of napkins, and other work requiring less effort toward the end of a waitress' shift rather than at the beginning of it.

Some investigators think that fatigue is not as much a result of accumulated waste products in the body as it is a nervous reaction to work. Fatigue of this kind is thought to arise at the nerve endings, the synapses, or the place where one nerve ends and the other begins. It is thought that a worker gets tired because nerve impulses at this juncture have difficulty in being passed along to the next and so blocks occur. These blocks cause a loss of coordination and efficiency and thus work becomes difficult to do and production drops.

Boredom, monotony, dislike of a job, frustration, poorly planned work, and similar conditions can cause a worker to become tired on the job. Perhaps nerve blocks occur and that is why some easy jobs become very tiring to some people.

The production of workers will be higher where good working conditions exist. Good air—an air change about every 5 minutes—good light—about 20 to 40 foot candles—comfortable clothes, good floors, good colors, all relieve strain at work and assist in keeping up the productive rates of employees.

A quiet atmosphere and freedom from noise is important. Recently an air hammer had to be used to break out a cement wall in some kitchen construction. The work had to be done while the kitchen was in operation. It was noted that this constant hammering increased tension among the kitchen employees, a tension which increased as the days of hammering continued, and that production dropped among many of the employees as the tension increased. Production rose again when the hammering ceased.

Proper work heights are necessary if fatigue is to be minimized. For years work heights in kitchens have been 34 inches. Somehow or other this became a standard to which most equipment manufacturers adhered. However, it should never have been a standard. The work height should vary according to the work done and the body dimensions of the worker.

Poor work heights demand more energy from the worker. When one worker worked on a 31-in. table rather than a 34-in. table, the energy requirement rose over basal from 14 percent to 32 percent; the heartbeat increased over basal from 28 percent to 30 percent; breathing increased from 10 percent to 51 percent over basal, and the blood pressure

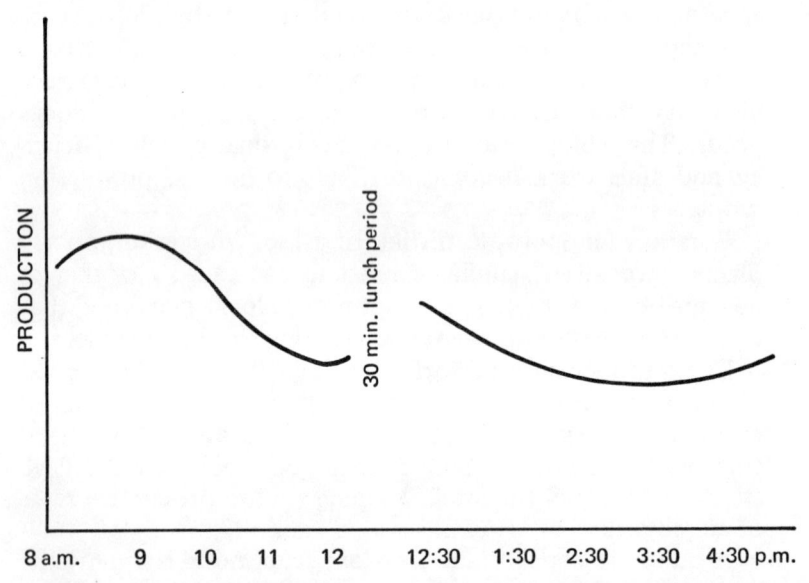

Production curve of a bored worker. Note how when worker sees end of shift approaching, work production increases.

increased from 2 percent to 21 percent over basal. This is startling evidence of the extra work or energy required by an improper work height.

In another study a dishwasher washed dishes in a sink with a bottom 25.6 in. high, then in a sink with a bottom 29.4 in. high and finally in a sink with a bottom 33.5 in. high. The calories required per hour over basal were respectively 30, 24.4, and 20.3. Again, concrete evidence of the work required when work heights are not proper.

A work table on which beating or mixing occurs should be lower than one where hand work occurs. In certain sections of the country, where workers in food services are larger and taller, it has been found that hand work table heights are better at 37 in. In college dormitories the beds for men are now 80 in. long instead of 72 in. long. Our boys are growing bigger and where these men work in the kitchens we have found a work height of 37 in. is a better height than the old 34 in. However, in the New York area, and other areas where short, foreign-born workers predominate, it has been found that work heights should be lower than 34 in.

For years sink manufacturers have been manufacturing sink bottoms too low for easy work by our workers. For the average woman lap boards about 26 in. off the floor make for easy work with the feet resting comfortably on the floor. At higher tables adjustable chairs should be used and the seat of the chair should be adjusted so that the forearm of the worker is on a level with the counter rim or table top. A foot rest should be provided about 16 in. below the seat and the width of the seat should be between 14 and 16 in. A back rest should be provided which supports the back fully. A full back rest is preferred by most workers.

Test for Height

In order to determine if a work table on which mixing, beating, or other such work will occur is correct for a worker, have the worker stand up next to the table and press his hands down flat on the table top. If this can be done with the arm fully extended but not stretched to the table, then the height of the work surface is proper for that person.

Where a worker stands and works with small tools, pares

vegetables for instance, the height of the work table should be about 4 in. below the worker's elbow. This allows the worker to stand and hold the arms naturally without having to lift the arms up higher or lower than necessary to do easy and accurate work.

> Customer: "Is it customary to fee the waiter here?"
> Waiter: "Yes, sir."
> Customer: "Then hand over your fee. I've waited for you nearly an hour."—*The Jury.**

---

*The Hotel World, Nov. 30, 1889, p. 9. Reprinted by permission of *Hotel and Motel Management.*

QUERIES

1. Describe the justification of management as well as employees for accepting or rejecting the ideas of "working overtime without pay" and "informing management about a rule breaker."
2. Define the needs and wants of the guests of the Brown Palace Hotel, Denver, Colorado, and of the Holiday Inn, Star City, N. W.*
3. Provide a plan of action showing how the above needs and wants of the Brown Palace Hotel's guests can be supplied with today's labor market and labor cost.
4. Find a hotel or restaurant employee union which was involved in a strike and report on the strategy to make their strike at the operation effective.
5. Investigate the working of the Critical Path Method (mentioned in David's "Techniques of Industrial Engineering Can Improve Effectiveness of Food Service Operations").
6. Kotschevar suggests that the weight of goods to be lifted should be limited to 50 pounds for men and 35 pounds for women. Is this not discrimination? Which federal act deals with this issue? What does the act say?
7. How would you organize your work station to prepare two dozen ham and cheese sandwiches?

---

*N.W. = No Where

SUBJECT INDEX

A&W International	126
Abhorrence of Dissent	156-57
Abouliacs (decision-avoidance)	
Methods of overcoming	176-77
Tactics of	180
Ad Hocism	155-56
Administration	64-65
Alliances	
Establishment of	116-18
Alternatives of Replacement	161-62
Analysis	
Quality and reliability	313
Authority	
Acceptance	72
Formal theory	58
Impacts	59-61
Source	58
vs. autocracy	72
Automation	18-23
"Back of the House"	303
Background "Mix"	199-200, 205-07
Bargaining Representative	276-77
Baskin-Robbins	125, 127
Behavior	244-46
At-work	244-45
Away-from-work	246
Body	224-26, 332-36
As lever	333
"Brown Bagging"	32-33
Business	
Interests	52
Proper conduct	52
Reality	55
Social role	52
Camara Inns	33
Candlewyck	45
Captain Service	20-21
Chalet Suzanne	49
Climate	
Motivational	15
Collective Bargaining	275-79
Communications	
Definition	198, 216
Failures	200-02, 205-06
Upward distortions	214, 216, 218, 221
Communications *(continued)*	
Verbal	200
Constraint	11
Control	308-10
Food cost	309-10
Production scheduling	309-10
Cooperatives	
Congress Hotels	26
E Hotels (Finland)	29
Inter Hotels	25
Interchange	25
Swedish S Hotels	25
US Friendship Inns	25
Corporate Administration	10
Producer	10
Corporate	
Constitutionalism	152-53
Alternatives to	165-66
Cost	315
Food	315
Labor	315
Deceitful Practice	53
Decentralization	63
Delegation	
Degrees of	171-72
Effects of	173-74
How to	172
Delphi Technique	66
Dibble's Inn	44
Diets	309
General	309
Model to predict	309
Modified	309
Dunfey Family Corp.	131
Earnings	260-62
Rise	260-62
Ecology	53-54
Economic Expediency	52
Short term	52
Employee	114
Criticizing of	193
Disadvantaged	187
Fair treatment	154
Loyalty	115
Relations	12-15
Responsibility index	249-50
Turnover rates	187

Energy	337-43	Labor-Management	
Human	337-43	Communication	198-209
Engineering		Labor Management Relations	
Economy studies	310	Act	276
Hotel	300-05	Negotiations	209
Industrial	306-17	Layout	321
Executive as Politician	119-21	Leadership Development	160
Executive "Perquisites"	140-49	Leavitt, H.	66
Feasibility Studies	313	Line Management	235
Flow	310-13	Linear Charts	124
Information	310-13	Lodging Industry	269-73
Materials	310-13	Difficulty	270
Food Service		Management	
Contract feeding	42	Accountability	128
Standard formulas	318-21	Audits	313
Standard operation		Managerial Decision Making	37
times	318-19	Maple Shade Farm	36
Food Systems	312-13	Marketing	12
Hospital	312	Marriott	130, 132, 136
Fringe Benefits	189	Maslow, A.	60, 202
Geisha Gardens	34	Master Standard Data	319-20
Gilbreth, F. B.	238	McGregor, D.	202
Golden Rule	305	Melia, F.	19
Grievances	253	Michigan State University	138
Hardee's	134	Minorities Right	53
Hawthorne Studies	184	Modular Construction	33
Hierarchical Levels	15	Monmouth Community	
Hollys Inc.	137	Memorial Hospital	40-41
Hospitality	18	Motion Study	238
Hotels	7-8	Motivation, Employee	
"Dives"	8	Atmosphere for	195-96
Human Asset Accounting	160-61	Barriers to	193
Human Engineering	237-38	Methods of	192
Human Motivation	60	*See also Human Motivation*	
See also Motivation, Employee		National Labor Relations Act	276
Human Resource Management	159	National Labor Relations	
Hyatt Corp.	130	Board	276
Information Technology	63	Need Fulfillment	13
Innkeepers		*See also Needs*	
Liability	7	Needs	60
Intermountain Boarding School	43	Hierarchy	60
Intourist	74	*See also Maslow*	
See also Soviet Union		Negotiations	280-86
Job Image		Unions-multi-employer	281-84
Effect on performance	190	"New Morality"	57-58
Jumer's Castle Lodge	47-48	"Open Shop"	287-89
Koontz, H. and O'Donnell, C.	65	Open Systems	16
Management functions		Optimal Use	307
Labor		Resources	307
Cost	262-63	Organization	
Minimum wage	257	Dynamic	244
Unskilled	263, 265	Goals	15

Organization *(continued)*		Social	
Needs	13	Environment	199
Profitability	249-50	Interaction	54
Responsibility	243-44	Near-Sightedness	52
Organizational Dissent	11	Society	
Organizational Structure	59	Changing values	52
Peoria's Heritage House	44	Impingements	52
Perceived Discrimination	218-20	Soviet Union	
Personnel Administration	232	Hotels	74
Functions	232-38	Ministry of Trade	87
Personnel Department	232-33	Restaurants	74
History	232-33	"The Plan"	90-91
Personnel Role of Manager	249-50	Span of Control	58
Philosophy in Business	10-15	Standards	
Pick Congress Hotel	133	Formulas	318, 321
Power (Executive)	111-21	Methods	321
"Power of the Purse"	118	Time	318-29
Pratt's Barn	34	Statler, E. M.	300
Prepared Foods	307, 321	Stouffers	133
Price Controls	53	Strikes	287-89, 290-97
Private Property	55	Subordinates	252-56
Production	10	Typology of	214-16
Productivity		Supervisor	
Costs per unit	262, 310	Job	251-56
Public		Responsibilities	251
Nuisance	53	Systems	
Safety	53	Analysis	308-10
Purchasing	27-28	Design	308-10
Bulk	27-28	Specifications	308-10
Red Circle Inn	37	Tray assembly	312-13
Redrat Saloon	48	Tahoe Forest Hospital	38
Relationships		Taylor, F. W.	59
Intragroup	201-02	Thayer, L. O.	199
Reprimands	253-56	U.S.S.R., Ministry of Trade	75
Risk-Taking Propensity	216, 218	*See also Soviet Union*	
Robbins, I.	122	U.S.S.R., *see Soviet Union*	
St. Martin's College	41	"Under Casting"	160
Satellite Service	307	Unions	275, 280-99
Sayles, L.	151-52	Agreement	284
Scale Value		Negotiations	282
Difference Ratios	187	University of Georgia	42
Sears, Roebuck and Co.	15	Weber, E. S.	126
Security	218	Wee Willie's	46
Gap	154	Welfare Benefit	265-67
Insecurity index	218	Policy	268-69
Self-Service Units	20	Western Pancake House	131
Service	19-23	Work	
Shambarger's	47	Environment	15
Simon, H. A.	69	Height	342-43
Skoby's World	32	Measurement	313
Sky Chefs	134	Simplification	331

INDUSTRY SECTOR INDEX

The following index has been developed to aid the readers who are interested in one specific sector of the hospitality industry. It will permit them to quickly locate the articles that deal directly with their chosen interest. The sectors are presented alphabetically and each one has a primary listing of the most direct articles and a secondary one containing the readings that are somewhat less directly related ("See Also"). For articles covering a specific topic or phase of the management process, the Table of Contents and/or Subject Index should be consulted.

CLUB MANAGEMENT
    Do You Really Know Your Employees?   182-91
    Labor Supply, Payroll Costs and Changes   257-73
    Techniques of Industrial Engineering Can Improve
        Effectiveness of Food Service Operations   306-17
    See Also:
        Collective Bargaining   275-79
        Help Workers Work Easier   336-44
        How to Increase the Efficiency of the Human Body   331-35
        The New Psychology of Success   129-39
        Production Time Standards   318-30
        To Join or Not to Join Multi-Employer Bargaining   280-89

COLLEGE AND SCHOOL FOOD SERVICE MANAGEMENT
    Help Workers Work Easier   336-44
    How a Supervisor Wins Employees   251-56
    How to Increase the Efficiency of the Human Body   331-35
    The New Psychology of Success   129-39
    Production Time Standards   318-30
    Techniques of Industrial Engineering Can Improve
        Effectiveness of Food Service Operations   306-17
    See Also:
        Do You Really Know Your Employees?   182-91
        Grass Roots—Where the Good Times Are!   32-50
        Labor Supply, Payroll Costs and Changes   257-73

FAST FOOD RESTAURANT MANAGEMENT
    Collective Bargaining   275-79
    Help Workers Work Easier   336-44
    How to Increase the Efficiency of the Human Body   331-35
    Labor Supply, Payroll Costs and Changes   257-73
    The New Psychology of Success   129-39
    Production Time Standards   318-30
    To Join or Not to Join Multi-Employer Bargaining   280-89
    See Also:
        Do You Really Know Your Employees?   182-91
        Techniques of Industrial Engineering Can Improve
            Effectiveness of Food Service Operations   306-17

FULL-SERVICE RESTAURANT MANAGEMENT

Do You Really Know Your Employees?	182-91
Grass Roots—Where the Good Times Are!	32-50
Help Workers Work Easier	336-44
Hotel and Restaurant Management in the Soviet Union	74-91
How to Increase the Efficiency of the Human Body	331-35
Labor Supply, Payroll Costs and Changes	257-73
The New Psychology of Success	129-39
Production Time Standards	318-30
Start the Open Shop in St. Louis	287-89

See Also:

Collective Bargaining	275-79
Techniques of Industrial Engineering Can Improve Effectiveness of Food Service Operations	306-17
To Join or Not to Join Multi-Employer Bargaining	280-89

HOSPITAL FOOD SERVICE MANAGEMENT

Help Workers Work Easier	336-44
How to Increase the Efficiency of the Human Body	331-35
Labor Supply, Payroll Costs and Changes	257-73
The New Psychology of Success	129-39
Production Time Standards	318-30
Techniques of Industrial Engineering Can Improve Effectiveness of Food Service Operations	306-17

See Also:

Collective Bargaining	275-79
Do You Really Know Your Employees?	182-91
How a Supervisor Wins Employees	251-56
To Join or Not to Join Multi-Employer Bargaining	280-89

HOTEL MANAGEMENT

Automation and the Guest	18-23
Hotel and Restaurant Management in the Soviet Union	74-91
Hotel Cooperatives—Can Voluntary Hotel Groupings Save the Independents?	24-31
Hotel Management	104-10
How Hotel Nova Scotian Survived the Big Strike	292-97
Labor Supply, Payroll Costs and Changes	257-73
The New Psychology of Success	129-39
Operating a Hotel Is a Feat of Human Engineering	300-05
Start the Open Shop in St. Louis	287-89
What Is a Hotel?	7-8
Why Hotel Employees Fail to Rise	241-42

See Also:

Collective Bargaining	275-79
Do You Really Know Your Employees?	182-91
Grass Roots—Where the Good Times Are!	32-50
Slightly Sarcastic	92-94
To Join or Not to Join Multi-Employer Bargaining	280-89

Index   351

INDUSTRIAL FEEDING MANAGEMENT
    Help Workers Work Easier   336-44
    How to Increase the Efficiency of the Human Body   331-35
    Labor Supply, Payroll Costs and Changes   257-73
    The New Psychology of Success   129-39
    Production Time Standards   318-30
    Techniques of Industrial Engineering Can Improve
        Effectiveness of Food Service Operations   306-17
    See Also:
        Collective Bargaining   275-79
        Do You Really Know Your Employees?   182-91
        How a Supervisor Wins Employees   251-56
        To Join or Not to Join Multi-Employer Bargaining   280-89
MOTOR-HOTEL/MOTEL MANAGEMENT
    Do You Really Know Your Employees?   182-91
    Hotel and Restaurant Management in the Soviet Union   74-91
    Hotel Management   104-10
    Labor Supply, Payroll Costs and Changes   257-73
    The New Psychology of Success   129-39
    Why Hotel Employees Fail to Rise   241-42
    See Also:
        Automation and the Guest   18-23
        Collective Bargaining   275-79
        Grass Roots—Where the Good Times Are!   32-50
        Hotel Cooperatives—Can Voluntary Hotel Groupings
            Save the Independents?   24-31
        Operating a Hotel Is a Feat of Human Engineering   300-05
        To Join or Not to Join Multi-Employer Bargaining   280-89
RESORT MANAGEMENT
    Do You Really Know Your Employees?   182-91
    Labor Supply, Payroll Costs and Changes   257-73
    Why Hotel Employees Fail to Rise   241-42
    See Also:
        Automation and the Guest   18-23
        Collective Bargaining   275-79
        Grass Roots—Where the Good Times Are!   32-50
        Hotel and Restaurant Management in the Soviet Union   74-91
        Hotel Cooperatives—Can Voluntary Hotel Groupings
            Save the Independents?   24-31
        Hotel Management   104-10
        The New Psychology of Success   129-39
        To Join or Not to Join Multi-Employer Bargaining   280-89
TRAVEL INDUSTRY MANAGEMENT
    Grass Roots—Where the Good Times Are!   32-50
    Hotel and Restaurant Management in the Soviet Union   74-91

ABOUT THE AUTHORS

LOTHAR A. KRECK is presently Director of the Department of Hotel and Restaurant Administration, Washington State University, Pullman. Over the past twenty years he has held a variety of positions in the hotel and restaurant industry in Germany, Spain, Switzerland, the United Kingdom, Sweden, Canada, and Pakistan, as well as the United States. Dr. Kreck's teaching experience includes positions at Paul Smith College, the University of Nevada at Las Vegas, and the University of Denver. He spent two years as Director of Training with Intercontinental Hotels in Pakistan and has served as a consultant to airlines, clubs, hotels, restaurants, and resorts.

JOHN W. McCRACKEN serves on the faculty of Washington State University, Pullman, where he is a Lecturer in Hotel Administration. Formerly, Mr. McCracken was Assistant Professor of Hotel Administration at Luzerne County College, Wilkes-Barre, Pa. He has also had considerable operating experience in a number of hotels, clubs, and restaurants. Mr. McCracken received the B.A. and M.B.A. degrees from Michigan State University and the M.A. degree in Economics from the State University of New York. He is currently completing the Ph. D. program in Economics at Washington State University, Pullman.